Max R. Hyman

Hyman's Handbook of Indianapolis

An outline history and description of the capital of Indiana, with over three hundred illustrations from photographs made expressly for this work.

Max R. Hyman

Hyman's Handbook of Indianapolis
An outline history and description of the capital of Indiana, with over three hundred illustrations from photographs made expressly for this work.

ISBN/EAN: 9783337288709

Printed in Europe, USA, Canada, Australia, Japan

Cover: Foto ©ninafisch / pixelio.de

More available books at **www.hansebooks.com**

HYMAN'S

HAND BOOK OF

INDIANAPOLIS

AN OUTLINE HISTORY AND DESCRIPTION OF THE CAPITAL OF INDIANA

WITH OVER THREE HUNDRED ILLUSTRATIONS FROM PHOTOGRAPHS MADE EXPRESSLY FOR THIS WORK

MAX R. HYMAN, Editor

INDIANAPOLIS
M. R. HYMAN COMPANY
1897

PREFACE

It has been the editor's aim in preparing this work to make it the most complete illustrated history of Indianapolis ever published. The text gives a comprehensive but condensed history and description of the city; also of every notable public institution and feature of especial interest. The illustrations cover a longer period and are far more numerous than have ever before been published on this subject and they furnish many interesting reminders of the earlier history of the city as well as of the present.

In the preparation of this volume, I have consulted all known available sources of relevant information. I make particular acknowledgment of my obligations to the local histories, published years ago, by Col. W. R. Holloway and Ignatius Brown, and to the files of the newspapers of this city for their rich stores of material; also to Mr. W. H. Smith for valuable assistance.

The engravings were nearly all made by the H. C. Bauer Engraving Co., expressly for this work from photographs taken by Joseph Van Trees. The book is issued from the press of Carlon & Hollenbeck.

This edition is now submitted to the public with the hope that it will be found to be useful as well as interesting, and that its support will necessitate many editions.

MAX R. HYMAN, *Editor.*

Indianapolis, February, 1897.

HISTORICAL.

INDIANAPOLIS FROM THE EARLIEST PERIOD TO THE PRESENT.

WHEN Indiana was admitted as a state into the Union it contained fewer inhabitants than now live in Marion county. The settlers had not strayed very far away from the Ohio river, but there were a few settlements along Whitewater, and a few along the Wabash; but most of them were along the southern border of the state. The state stretched from the Ohio to the lake, but the central and northern sections were an unknown wilderness given over to the Indians. Dense forests covered the central section, while to the north stretched away the trackless prairies. It was not an inviting field for the hardy pioneer. South was Kentucky with its richness of soil and its admirable climate; to the east was Ohio already beginning to teem with a hardy and industrious population, while all the best portions of Indiana still claimed the savages as masters. Even in that early day the word had gone out that Indiana was the land of chills and fevers, and seekers for new homes came, saw, and passed on, or returned to the places from whence they came.

It was a struggle for existence. The soil was rich enough, but it was the work of years to clear a farm and get it ready to produce, and when its productions were ready for the harvest there was no market, and the malaria arising from the decaying of vegetation, with no antidote except whisky and wild cherry bark, made the outlook anything but favorable. It was under such circumstances Indiana became a member of the great Federal Union. Indian wars had about ceased east of the Mississippi river, but Indian massacres had not come to an end. It was not safe to stray very far away from the confines of the few settlements, and if human life was spared stock was stolen and driven away, thus depriving the settler of all means of cultivating his homestead. The capital was a little village on the southern border, some miles back from the river, and hidden among the hills; hard to get at in the best of seasons, in the winter it was almost inaccessible. Around it there was nothing that gave promise of future growth; there was no future for it even if the capital remained there. There was absolutely no foundation on which to build a city.

When the state was admitted into the Union congress donated to the infant commonwealth four sections of land on which to build a capital city, the land to be selected by the state from any that remained unsold. So, in 1820 the legislature determined to go out into the wilderness and hunt for a site for its future capital city. It followed in this the example of the national government. When the jealousies between the colonies were about to destroy the new made Union, congress went out in search of a home, and found it on the banks of the Potomac. The members of the Indiana legislature in 1820 may have hoped that their state would grow, and afterwhile become fairly prosperous, but their wildest dreams never reached the reality, that within two score years the state would be so populous that it could send to the field of battle 200,000 armed men, and yet not exhaust its capacity. Yet such was the case.

In 1820 the legislature sent out its commissioners to seek for the site of its future city, and make selection of the land donated by congress. It might have been a prescience of what was to come that led the commissioners to seek a spot as near the geographical center of the state as possible. It may be they naturally concluded that in time the geographical center of the state would be also the center of population, but it is more probable they thought only of finding a spot to reach which would take about the same number of miles travel from the four corners. Whatever may have been their motive, they did determine on the geographical center. Water furnished then the only, or rather the best and surest means of communication with

THE OLD GOVERNOR WRIGHT MANSION.

the outside world, and as they did not want to get too far away from some stream supposed to be navigable, they clung to the banks of White river. Three sites were offered, one a few miles south of the present city, and one a few miles northeast. They came here through the wilderness, and after much debating and considerable disputing, decided on accepting four sections of land around the mouth of Fall creek. It was a most unpromising site. White river itself was not very inviting, while deep bayous and ravines cut up the land in a way to make it look anything but attractive to one seeking for town lots. But here were the four sections with only half a dozen or so settlers. It was in the wilderness, it was near the geographical center.

With the exception of a lonely cabin here and there, it was sixty miles away from the nearest settlements. All around were dense forests; to the south were the hills reaching to the Ohio river, and to the north the woods and prairies stretching out to the lake. Only a few miles away was the boundary which divided the "New Purchase" from the lands still claimed by the Indians. There was no town, no people, not a road leading anywhere. A town had to be built, people induced to come, roads to be opened. But when the people should come, how were they to be fed? No farms had been opened up, and supplies of every kind would have to be wagoned many miles over roads often almost impassable, but at that time pack-horses were the only means of conveyance. But here, in this unpromising locality, the commissioners staked off a city that in less than three-quarters of a century was to become the largest inland city on the continent. They fondly believed that White river would prove to be navigable for the only boats then known on the western waters, and by it the people of the new city could be fed and clothed.

The legislature approved the report of the commissioners and proceeded to hunt for a name for the new city. It was a difficult thing to find. Every member of the legislature had a name to propose. Some were of Indian origin, and some compounded from Latin words, and others from Greek. Finally "Indianapolis" was determined upon, and the city in embryo had a name. It had little else. As said there were no roads, and the supplies for the settlers had to be carried on horseback from the settlements on Whitewater. Going sixty miles to mill or to store in those days was no small journey. It took longer

WASHINGTON STREET, 1854, NORTH SIDE

WASHINGTON STREET, 1854, SOUTH SIDE.

than it does now to go to New York. Then, too, it was a more hazardous journey.

There has been much dispute as to who was actually the first settler of this section of the state and the honor has been contested between the friends of George Pogue and those of two brothers named McCormick. The dispute never will be satisfactorily settled, and it is not a very important historical event. Neither Pogue nor the McCormicks dreamed of emulating Romulus and Remus, and building a city. The one sought only to live by hunting and trapping, and the others by cultivating the soil. It was only after the location of the capital city they

"OLD SEMINARY."

dreamed of achieving fame by being called the first to discern the future possibilities. Both Pogue and the McCormicks were here when the commissioners of the legislature came, as were a few other families, all of whom would have liked to get away to some healthier spot, if they could. They must have laughed in their sleeves at the commissioners thinking to build a city on such an unlikely spot.

In April, 1821, the work of "laying off" the city actively began. Christopher Harrison, representing the state, appointed as surveyors, Elias P. Fordham and Alexander Ralston. Some years before, Ralston had been employed in some of the work of mapping out Washington, the national capital, and had great ideas of what a city in the woods ought to be, and at his suggestion the city was to be one mile square, with streets crossing each other at right angles, and with four wide avenues pointing toward a circle that was to be the center of the new city. The ground was uniformly level, but a slight knoll was found, and it was determined the city should start from that point, or rather that the knoll should be in the center, and that it should be crowned by a residence for the chief magistrate of the commonwealth. It was a pretty idea; as he was to be the center of influence and power, it was right and proper that his home should be the center of the city, and as he was the highest in power and honor, his home should be on the highest ground; but, alas, the idea was all that was fully developed. The circle was there, the knoll was there, but the governor's residence was never there.

Streets were marked off, lots laid out and the new city was ready for business, that is, the sale of lots. It is true the streets ran through the woods and the lots were all heavily timbered, but they were there, and could be determined by the stakes set by the surveyors. Certain plots of ground were reserved for public purposes. One was to be the site of the expected statehouse. One was for the court-house, and one was reserved on which to build a great state educational institution, which already had been designated as a university. Like the governor's residence, the university never materialized. It having gone abroad through the settlements that the new capital city had been located, and information given as to where it could be found, immigrants began to arrive, and among them was the first lawyer, eager as ever for strife. A store had been opened up and a saw-mill started.

Most of the settlers had located along the bank of the river, taking it for granted that the choice corner lots would be in that section. The land outside of the mile square was to be laid off into out lots and farms. Mr. Ralston and the commissioners evidently thought that the mile square would contain all the inhabitants the city was ever likely to have, and had provided no division of the city lots from the out lots but the imaginary line, but some one suggested that it would be the proper thing to bound the city by streets, and name them East, West, North and South streets, and it was done accordingly.

In October, 1821, the sale of lots began. The money arising from the sale was to be used in erecting the necessary buildings

PENNSYLVANIA STREET IN 1856. NORTH OF WASHINGTON STREET.

for the use of the state, and it was expected that there would be a great demand. After continuing the sale for several days, and disposing of three hundred and fourteen lots, the real estate business was stopped for awhile. Something more than $7,000 was realized in cash, the rest of the purchase price of the lots being evidenced by promissory notes running over a period of four years. But few of the lots were eventually paid for, the purchasers forfeiting the advance payments and abandoning their purchases. Ten years afterward the state still owned three-fourths of the lots in the city limits, and nearly all of the out lots. They were not finally disposed of until 1842, and for its mile square of town lots, and the three outlying sections, the state realized less than $150,000.

If the commissioners and the early settlers had become discouraged at the outlook it would not have been a matter of surprise. This thing of building a city in the wilderness was a new enterprise in those days. Now, such things are of almost daily occurrence, but then we have railroads now, and gas and oil fields, and coal, silver and gold mines. Seventy years have wrought great changes. This first year of the life of the city witnessed the birth of the first child, and the marriage of the first couple, the happy bridegroom having been compelled to go to Connersville, sixty miles away, for his license.

Here was the new city duly staked off and the few settlers who had come in and purchased lots began to prepare for the winter. Rude log cabins were hastily erected. They were put up here and there, with some sort of regard to street lines, but as the lots purchased were not in regular order, great stretches of vacant ground were found between the new homes, and paths from one house to another were made through the deep woods on the shortest lines without regard to streets or private property. Winter was coming and it was a desolate outlook. The nearest post-office was sixty miles away; the only store was a little affair where iron, salt and dye stuffs furnished about all the stock. In those early days the winters began about the middle of November and lasted until the last of March. The snow fall was generally abundant. often being a foot or two deep, and lying on the ground for weeks. The people were "neighborly" and the winter was spent in some kind of comfort, but still many of those who had thus built homes for themselves longed for the coming of the spring when they could go out and hunt more desirable spots on which to dwell. In the spring of the year, about the time the commissioners were busy laying out the new town, George Pogue, the traditional first settler,

VIEW OF INDIANAPOLIS FROM BLIND INSTITUTE LOOKING SOUTH-WEST, 1854.

was killed by the Indians, and this tragedy kept up the excited fears of the people for some months, but it was the last of the Indian killings in this section.

The spring of 1822 came, and brought with it more new settlers to take the places of those who were dissatisfied and desired to move away, and the town began to show some signs of improving. It had been rumored around that notwithstanding

KEARSARGE ON STATE-HOUSE GROUNDS DURING G. A. R. NATIONAL ENCAMPMENT, SEPTEMBER, 1893.

the town had been laid out for the capital of the state, the capital would not be removed here on account of the unhealthy location, and this deterred a number from coming who had designed doing so. The town thus received a "black eye" at the very start, and then, too, the seasons were not favorable for crops for a year or two, and this gave Indianapolis a bad name. A few hardy souls stuck to it, however, and began to clamor for recognition. They were tired of being the capital of the state and having the county-seat sixty miles away. They were also anxious for mail facilities.

In the beginning of 1822 the little town boasted of about five hundred inhabitants, and they thought it was time they were being served with a mail. They had a tavern, and sundry other town luxuries, but no post-office. When the American people want anything the first thing they do is to have a public meeting, with a president and secretary, and a committee on resolutions. So a meeting of the citizens of Indianapolis was called at Hawkins' tavern. Mr. Aaron Drake was appointed postmaster, and he made regular trips to Connersville, received the mail for the new settlement and transported it through the woods to its destination. This was all done by private enterprise, thus proving in that early day that a spirit of enterprise pervaded the residents on the "donation." He returned from his first trip, reaching the settlement some time after the pall of darkness had fallen over the woods, but the loud blowing of his horn called the people together and he was given a royal welcome. A few weeks later the government assumed the duty of conveying the mails and distributing them and appointed Samuel Henderson as postmaster.

The settlers also began asking that the streets be cleared, so that they could see the houses, and at least look a little like a town, and the commissioners undertook to have the streets opened by cutting down the timber. The trees were cut down, rolled into huge piles and burned, but the stumps remained for many a long day. Roads were needed, and the legislature, in the winter of 1821-2 appropriated $100,000 to open up and construct a number of roads to its new capital. One led from the Ohio river near Lawrenceburg to Indianapolis, and another came up from Madison, while Noblesville, Crawfordsville and other settlements were to be connected in the same way with Indianapolis. The trees were cut out, leaving the stumps still standing, and in rainy seasons, when the mud was deep, those stumps were terrible annoyances to wagoners. The wheels would sink so deep in the mud that the axle-tree of the wagon would strike on the stump, and thus the wagon would be stranded sometimes for hours. The wants of the new settlement began to be numerous, and all supplies had to be hauled over these roads, that in the winter were sometimes impassable for weeks. They were just as bad in the rainy seasons of the spring and fall.

The same legislature also organized Marion county, making Indianapolis the county-seat, appropriating a square of ground

EX-PRESIDENT HARRISON'S RESIDENCE.

and $8,000 to build a court-house. Attached to the new county, for judicial purposes, was the territory now comprising the counties of Johnson, Hamilton, Hancock, Madison and Boone. A new county demanded a new judge and a new sheriff. Hon. William W. Wick was made judge, and Hervey Bates, sheriff. The new city might now be said to be fairly launched on the road to greatness. It had a judge of its own, a lawyer, Calvin Fletcher, to look after the legal wants of all the people, a store, a tavern, a saw-mill or two, a post-office, and was soon to have its first paper.

Among the enterprising citizens of Indianapolis were George Smith and Nathaniel Bolton, and they became the editors and proprietors of the *Gazette*, Indianapolis' first newspaper. It made its appearance on the twenty-eighth day of January, 1822. It was not a great paper, as papers are now, but it was a beginning, and like all beginners had its ups and downs. At that time nearly all the houses were built along the line of Washington street, which presented a remarkable sight, with its stumps so thick that it was almost impossible for a vehicle to wind in and out among them. The rest of the city was a dense woods, in many parts covered with an almost impenetrable growth of underbrush. Along this uninviting street were strung the cabins of the five hundred people who formed the population of the town.

The legislature could name a judge for the new county but could not choose the other officers, so in February, 1822, Sheriff Bates issued forth his proclamation calling on the people of the new county to meet together at certain named polling places and choose for themselves two associate justices, a clerk, a recorder and three county commissioners. Two of the voting places were in Indianapolis, one near Noblesville, one at Strawtown, one at Anderson and the other near Pendleton. A list of those who presented themselves for the various positions discloses the fact that the people were as hungry for offices in those good old days as they are in these degenerate times. Only 336 votes were cast in the entire county. The vote of Indianapolis was about 100. James M. Ray was elected clerk, James C. Reed, recorder; John T. Osborne, John McCormack and William McCartney, commissioners; Eliakim Harding and James McIlvain, associate judges. In the August following, the election for governor took place, when 317 votes were cast, 315 of them being thrown for William Hendricks.

On the twenty-sixth of September the court began its first session. There being no court-house its sessions were held in the cabin of Jonathan Carr, it being the most pretentious struct-

VIEW OF INDIANAPOLIS FROM BLIND INSTITUTE LOO KING SOUTH-EAST, 1854.

ure in the town. The grand jury returned twenty-two indictments for sundry and various offenses against the peace and dignity of the commonwealth. A candidate for naturalization appeared, in the person of Richard Goode, late of Ireland, and a subject of George IV. No jail had been provided, and as the laws then made imprisonment for debt permissible, certain streets were named as the boundaries within which imprisoned debtors should confine themselves.

The county commissioners, as soon as they had been inducted

SCENE ON WHITE RIVER.

into office, set industriously about the work of erecting a court-house and jail. The state had appropriated $8,000 to assist in this work, and in September the plan for the proposed structure submitted by John E. Baker and James Paxton was accepted and the contract for the building awarded them. They did not begin the work of construction until the next summer, and it was not until 1824 the building was completed. The square of ground selected for a court-house and jail was covered with heavy timber. A jail made of hewed logs was erected and remained as the bastile of Marion county until 1833, when it was destroyed by fire, the fire being started by a negro prisoner. A brick jail was then constructed, and in 1845 it was enlarged by an addition made of logs a foot thick.

In the midst of the turmoil of starting a new city on its upward way patriotism was not forgotten, and the fourth of July, 1822, was duly celebrated by an oration, the reading of the Declaration of Independence, and a barbecue. The first camp-meeting was also held that fall, under the auspices of Rev. James Scott, the first Methodist preacher of the town. This year was also signalized by the organization of a militia regiment, the fortieth, with James Paxton as colonel; Samuel Morrow, lieutenant-colonel, and Alexander W. Russell, major. Those days all the able-bodied citizens had to attend regular musters of the militia.

The year was not one of prosperity to the new settlement, but was marked by several important events, among them being the establishment of a ferry across White river; the opening of a brick-yard; the erection of the first brick and the first two-story frame house. The first brick house was erected by John Johnson on Market street opposite the present post-office. The frame house was on Washington street, a little east of the present site of the Park Theater. It was long used for the storage of documents belonging to the state, and afterward became a tavern.

At that time the capital of the state had no member of the legislature to represent its interest, and so the actual capital remained at Corydon. Again the rumors began to circulate that after all Indianapolis would never be the capital, and holders of real estate began to get a little shaky over their purchases. There was a leaven of faith, however, and the citizens began to petition the legislature for representation, and at its session in 1823 the people of the new county were authorized to elect a representative in the following August. In the early days of the spring a new newspaper was started with a rather startling name—*Western Censor and Emigrant's Guide*. Harvey Gregg and Douglass Maguire were the two adventurous citizens who undertook the work of guiding so important an enterprise. This was now the third year of the town, and the second since it had been given its high sounding name, but the election in August disclosed the fact that its growth during the last year had been very limited. In August, 1822, at the election for governor the county had polled 317 votes, and at the election in 1823 only 270. It was an "off" year, and that may account for the falling off of the vote.

WHITE RIVER NEAR BROAD RIPPLE.

Having a representative in the legislature, the town began to prepare for the advent of the capital, and a new tavern was built by Thomas Carter. It was now a rival of Hawkins' tavern that had first opened out its doors for the "entertainment of man and beast." It became celebrated as being the place of the exhibition of the first show ever given in Indianapolis. It was given on the last night of the year 1823, the bill being "The Doctor's Courtship, or the Indulgent Father," and the farce of the "Jealous Lovers." The admission was thirty-seven and a half cents. One lone fiddle made up the orchestra, and by the orders of Mr. Carter, owner of the tavern, only hymn tunes were played during the performance.

The town had not recovered from the blow it had received by the sickness among the settlers in 1821. The fame of that hard year had gone abroad throughout the state, and it looked as if nobody wanted to come to a town where at one time everybody was sick. The first one of the settlers to die was Daniel Shaffer, the first merchant of the town, and twenty or twenty-five deaths in a single season in a settlement of only four or five hundred was rather appalling, and the rival towns in the state made the most they could in spreading abroad this evil name, but the settlers generally stuck to their new town, only moving further away from the river. The "old graveyard," however, had got a pretty good start.

In those early days the prices of what are now called the necessaries of life were very high. Coffee sold at fifty cents a pound, tea at two dollars, corn one dollar a bushel, flour five dollars per hundred, and coarse muslin at forty-five cents a yard. The nearest grist-mill was on Whitewater, sixty miles distant. This was not to remain so always, and a run or two of stone was soon added to the saw-mill and the farmers around could get their corn and wheat ground nearer home, and a keel boat or two were forced up the river bringing supplies, mostly whisky and salt, and by thus cutting freight rates over the pack-horse line reduced prices somewhat. A school had also been started in 1821, but its teacher was shortly afterward elected recorder of the county and the school suspended temporarily.

The morals of the community were not neglected. In the first settlement of this country by the French the missionaries were in advance of the white immigrants, and when the adventurous pioneer would reach a point he almost invariably found the missionary there preaching to the Indians. When the country was wrested from the French the order was changed somewhat, but it was never very long after the hardy pioneer had

EAST WASHINGTON STREET, 1862.

erected his cabin, until the "itinerant circuit rider" was knocking at his door with his bible and hymn-book in hand. It has never been definitely settled who preached the first sermon in Indianapolis, the honor lying between John McClung, a preacher of the New Light school, and Rezin Hammond, a Methodist. They both preached here in the fall of 1821, and it is not particularly important as to which came first. They were both very devout men and earnest preachers of the word. They were soon followed by Rev. Ludlow G. Haines, a Presbyterian. The

VIEW IN WOODRUFF PLACE.

Presbyterians organized the first church, and in 1823 began the erection of a house for worship on Pennsylvania street opposite where the Denison hotel now stands. It was completed the following year at the cost of $1,200.

The Indianapolis circuit of the Methodist denomination was organized in 1822, under the charge of Rev. William Cravens, but Rev. James Scott had preached here before that and held one or two camp-meetings. The Methodists did not begin the erection of a church building right away, but in 1823 purchased a hewed log house on Maryland street near Meridian, to be used for religious meetings. The Baptists organized a society in 1822, and held meetings at different places until 1829 when they erected a church. By this it will be seen that before the town had grown very large, or had the time to get very wicked, four denominations were here to look after its morals.

Not long after the school of Joseph C. Reed suspended on his being elevated to the office of recorder of the county, a meeting of the citizens was called to make arrangements for a permanent school. Mr. Reed's school-house had been at the intersection of Kentucky avenue and Illinois street. Arrangements were made with a Mr. and Mrs. Lawrence to open out a school and keep it going. There were no free schools then maintained by public tax, but thus, soon after its first settlement, Indianapolis laid the foundation of an educational system that has since made it the envy of many a larger city.

From churches and schools to courts is not a very long step, especially as marriages are usually solemnized by preachers, and divorces granted by the courts. Soon after the introduction of preachers the court was called upon to divorce a couple who had been unhappily mated. Elias Stallcup and his wife Ruth Stallcup were the first to be divorced by the courts of Marion county. This was before the county had a court-house of its own. The divorce was granted in 1823. In those days litigation was not very abundant, and crime, except the unlicensed selling of liquor, or an occasional assault and battery, was unheard of, so the courts did not have a great deal of work to do.

As said before, the board of county commissioners, as soon it was organized, set about the work of contracting for the erection of a court-house, and after it was completed it was for many years used for about everything. Concerts, shows, meetings of the citizens, lectures, political speakings, conventions, religious meetings and the legislature all took their turn, and, so far as the record shows, nobody paid any rent. The commissioners also interested themselves in paternally administering the affairs of the new community. They regulated the prices to be charged for toll on the only ferry, and then made a schedule for tavern charges. The price of whisky was fixed at twelve and a half cents per half pint; and of imported rum, brandy, gin or wine twenty-five cents were allowed to be charged for each half pint; peach and apple brandies were rated at eighteen and a half cents per half pint. Taverns were allowed to charge twenty-five cents for each meal and twelve and a half cents for lodging. There have been some changes in the prices since those pioneer days.

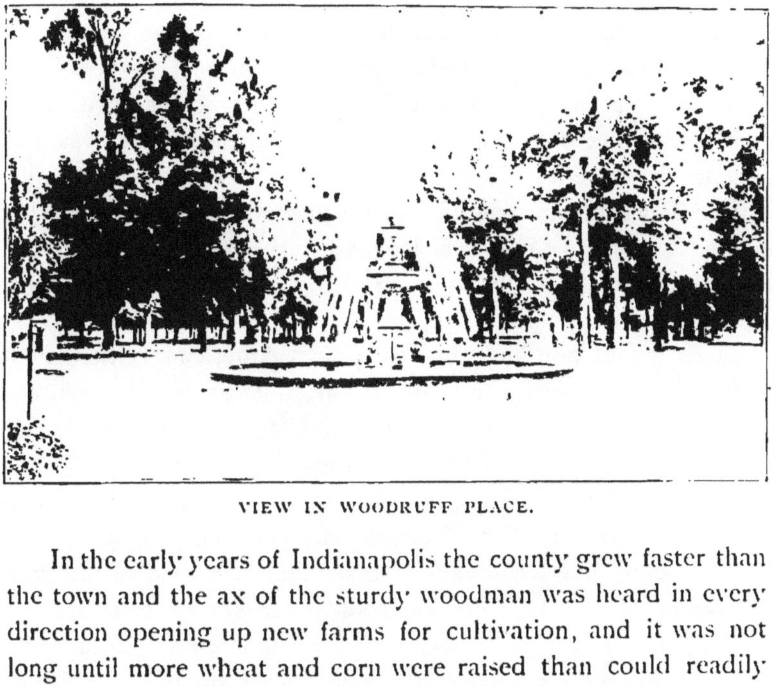

VIEW IN WOODRUFF PLACE.

In the early years of Indianapolis the county grew faster than the town and the ax of the sturdy woodman was heard in every direction opening up new farms for cultivation, and it was not long until more wheat and corn were raised than could readily be disposed of, as there was no place to market the surplus. The farmers began to turn their attention to raising hogs as they could be made to move themselves to market, and for some years hogs were the chief product of the farmers in all this section of the state.

At the meeting of the legislature in January, 1824, the final order was made for the removal of the capital to Indianapolis, and this gave an impetus to the town and more emigrants began to flock in. In the meantime the scare arising from the bad health reports of 1821 had measurably died out, and were forgotten. The removal was to be made by the tenth of January, 1825, and the next legislature was to assemble in the courthouse of Marion county. When Marion county's representatives to the legislature returned home from the session of 1824, they were given a grand reception at Washington Hall, which was then the great tavern of the city, and many speeches were made much after the order of those now indulged in on similar occasions. In November of that year, State Treasurer Samuel Merrill set out on his journey to the new capital with the archives of the state, in a large two-horse wagon. It was a slow journey over the hills and through the woods, a dozen miles a day being all that could be accomplished, and that by the hardest effort. By the end of November the state was settled in its new quarters, and the meeting of the first legislature was impatiently waited for.

It would not have been a typical American settlement had not politics played a prominent part. 1824 was the year of the great presidential contest between Clay, Adams and Jackson. Party names were not known in those days, but the people were divided off into "Clay men," "Jackson men," and "Adams men." At that time Indiana was very largely settled from Kentucky, and Kentuckians, as a rule, were loyal to the gallant Harry. When the vote was counted in November it was found that Clay had received 217 votes, Jackson 99 and Adams 16.

When the members of the legislature came to the new capital in 1825 they found it a straggling village with only one street "cleared," and that was still full of stumps. It was a town in the mud, hard to get to, and almost impossible to move around in after once reached. But it was the capital, the state officers were here, and the "donation" of the general government had been accepted, and they had to make the best of it. It was a

PACKET GOVERNOR MORTON ON WHITE RIVER, 1865.

dreary winter, though, here in the deep woods, with the houses scattered around over a mile square, with only cow tracks through the woods from one to the other. The three taverns were the center of interest in the evenings, and around the huge fires in their "bar rooms" the legislators and the citizens gathered to discuss matters of state. During the session one of the taverns, Carter's, was destroyed by fire. Some efforts were made by the legislature to improve the town, and fifty dollars were appropriated to clean out Pogue's run, so as to cut off some of its malaria-breeding powers. The outlying portions of the dona-

HENDRICKS MONUMENT.

tion were also ordered sold or leased in four-acre tracts to encourage farming.

The coming of the legislature did not add greatly to the permanent growth of the town, for in February, 1826, the population consisted of seven hundred and sixty-two souls, of whom two hundred and nine were children. But the town did begin to show signs of permanency and several societies were organized, among them being the Indianapolis Bible Society, which is still in existence. An agricultural society was also organized, but it did not last long. The United States land office was removed to Indianapolis from Brookville, and thus the future great city was recognized by the federal government. Indian depredations had ceased, but the military spirit was strong, and an artillery company was formed with James Blake as captain. The government furnished the company with one cannon of small caliber, but it was big enough to make a noise on the fourth of July, and that was all the use it was ever put to. The burning of Carter's tavern demonstrated the necessity of a fire company, and as the town was too poor to buy an engine a bucket and ladder company was organized, which did service for ten years until the first fire engine was purchased. In August of that year the news reached Indianapolis that on the fourth of July previous John Adams and Thomas Jefferson, two of the fathers of American independence, had died, and a public meeting was held in the court-house, to give due utterance to the feelings of the community. B. F. Morris and Douglass Maguire pronounced eulogies on the deceased.

The spirit of enterprise that had been slowly festering among the people began to show some headway early in 1827, and demonstrated that there were three men, at least, who had faith in the new capital. They were James M. Ray, James Blake and Nicholas McCarty. Through their efforts the legislature ordered the sale of seven acres of land fronting on the river, for milling purposes, and a company was organized to carry on the enterprise. It took two years, however, to get the stock subscriptions, and in 1831 the work of building was begun. It was to comprise a steam saw, grist and woolen mill, and a very pretentious structure was erected. The boilers and machinery were hauled overland from Cincinnati, taking some weeks in their transportation. This was the introduction of steam as a power into the city, but the speculation did not pay, as there was little demand for lumber, and it cost too much to transport the flour to market. In 1835 the speculation was abandoned and the machinery offered for sale, but it found no buyers, and was left to rust itself away. In 1847 the Geisendorffs undertook to use the machinery and building for carding and spinning wool, but after trying it for five years, they in turn abandoned it, and the next year it was destroyed by fire. It had long been a rendezvous for thieves, prostitutes and other vicious characters.

The same year the legislature attempted to build a residence for the governor. In the original laying off of the town the circle in the center of the plat was intended for such a structure, and so designated, but up to this time no provision had been made for its building. The governors had been living around

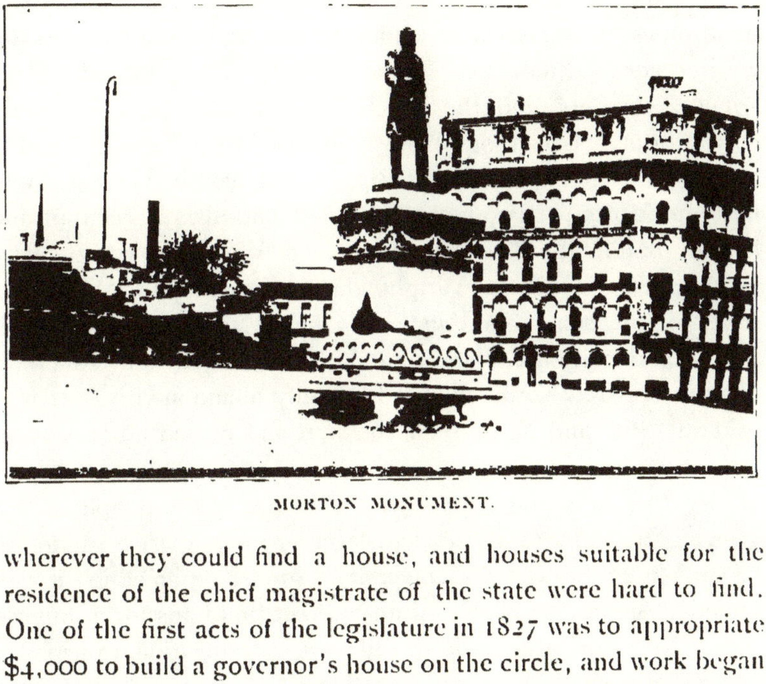

MORTON MONUMENT.

wherever they could find a house, and houses suitable for the residence of the chief magistrate of the state were hard to find. One of the first acts of the legislature in 1827 was to appropriate $4,000 to build a governor's house on the circle, and work began by enclosing the circle with a rail fence. Under this appropriation a building was begun, but it was never finished. It was rather elaborate in design, square in form, two stories high and a large attic. It had a semi-basement. The building was completed far enough to be used for public offices, and was turned over for that purpose. It 1859 it was sold at auction and torn down. Since then the circle has had a varied experience. It was made a park, but was used as a cow pasture until the trees and grass were ruined. It was then enclosed by a fence and again set out in trees, and about the time it was once more beginning to look like a park, the trees were cleared off, and the grand monument to the soldiers and sailors now occupies the space.

The governors were still left to hunt homes for themselves, until 1839, when the legislature ordered the state officers to purchase a suitable building for such a residence. At that time the handsomest and largest dwelling in the city was on the northwest corner of Illinois and Market streets. It was owned by Dr. John H. Sanders, and the state officers decided upon it, and it was bought. Governor Wallace moved into it, and it was occupied in turn by Governors Bigger, Whitcomb, Wright, Willard and Morton. From some cause it had always been an unhealthy building. The wife of Governor Whitcomb was the first to die there. Governor Wright, during his occupancy, lost two wives in the same building. The family of Governor Willard was sick during the whole time he occupied it, and Governor Morton suffered so much that he finally abandoned it. It was sold in 1865, and since then the state has owned no executive mansion.

By this time the educational demands of the people of the growing town induced the legislature to set apart a square of ground to be known as "University" square, upon which it was intended sometime in the future to erect buildings for a university. No effort was made to utilize it for educational purposes until 1832, when a part of it was leased for a county seminary. It was afterward used by the city for a high-school for a number of years.

The growth of the town was very slow for some years. The building of the National road gave it a slight impetus and brought here the first and only steamboat that ever succeeded in navigating White river to this point. It rejoiced in the name

OLD STATE-HOUSE, 1865. FROM PHOTOGRAPH TAKEN THE DAY LINCOLN'S BODY LAY IN STATE.

of "Robert Hanna," and was owned by General Hanna, one of the contractors building the new road for the government. It was brought here to tow barges loaded with stone and timber for use in constructing the road and its bridges. It arrived here on the eleventh of April, 1831. All the people turned out to welcome this wonder, and Captain Blythe, with his artillery company, saluted it with several rounds from his one cannon. The next day a free excursion was given to the citizens, but the overhanging boughs of the trees lining the banks knocked down her chimneys and pilot-house and smashed a wheel-house. The

COLUMBIA CLUB.

next day she ran aground and remained fast several weeks. When the high water came in the fall she took her way down the river and was never seen in this latitude again. Many years afterward a little steamer named after Governor Morton was built here to ply up and down for the amusement and entertainment of the people, but it had bad luck, and was soon destroyed. Even keel-boats and flat-boats early abandoned all efforts to navigate the stream which Mr. Ralston had declared to be navigable for at least four months in the year.

Governor Noble, however, would not give up his hopes that

the river would prove navigable, and offered a reward of $200 for the first boat that would land at the town. Two efforts were made, and one steamer reached Spencer and another came a few miles further. A plan for slack water navigation was submitted to the legislature and pressed for several years, and in 1851 the White River Navigation Company was chartered, but it accomplished nothing.

About this time the town thought it was old enough to have a historical society, so one was formed, with Benjamin Parke for president, and B. F. Morris for secretary. It did not have many active members, but elected about all the distinguished men of the nation as honorary members. The organization of the society was preceded by the arrival of the first menagerie that ever exhibited its wild animals to the people of the Hoosier capital.

The craze for internal improvements, that had been sweeping over other parts of the country, struck Indianapolis early in 1831, and the legislature spent most of its session in granting charters to railroads. Six such roads were projected, to center in Indianapolis. The country was new and sparsely settled, but the wise men of the legislature thought it would be a profitable thing to build roads paralleling each other, and only a few miles apart. The roads were all to run to the south as there was no population to the north. Some of the projected roads were partly surveyed and then the work was dropped. A few years later, however, the state entered upon a wholesale system of internal improvement, including railroads, canals and turnpikes. None of the projected works were ever fully completed by the state, but the state debt was increased enormously, and the state had to practically go into bankruptcy. This was a great blow to Indianapolis, and retarded its growth very materially. The state sold out its interest in all the works, together with 2,000,000 acres of land, in discharge of half of the debt that had been contracted.

The state had been occupying the court-house for the use of

the legislature, and in making its appropriation to erect that building had reserved the right to so occupy it for fifty years, but it was deemed the time had come to erect a building for the use of the state. It still owned a considerable portion of the original donation by congress, and it was estimated that the lots would sell for $58,000, and this was deemed sufficient to erect a suitable building. Ithiel Town was the architect and contracted to build the house for $58,000, and actually did complete it for $60,000. It was begun in 1832 and finished in time

COUNTRY CLUB.

for the meeting of the legislature in 1836, or two years ahead of time. For those days it was an elegant public building, though the style of architecture was a little mixed; but it served the state for forty years.

The year 1832 brought with it the news of the Black Hawk war, and three hundred of the state militia were called out, and rendezvoused in a grove on West Washington street. Alexander W. Russell was the colonel, and J. P. Drake, J. W. Redding, and Henry Brenton, captains. John L. Kinnard, the adjutant, was afterward elected to congress, but on his way to

Washington to attend the second session was killed in a steamboat explosion on the Ohio river. The war ended before they got further toward the scene of conflict than Chicago. On their departure they were surrounded by the whole population, and in firing a salute, William Warren, one of the cannoneers, had both arms blown off.

The town had grown enough to need a new market house and several meetings of the citizens were held to devise ways and means to secure one, which finally culminated in the building of one the following year. A foundry was also started by R. A. McPherson, it being the first effort toward the introduction of manufacturing industries, and was the forerunner of what Indianapolis is to-day. In 1838 John Wood established a steam foundry on Pennsylvania street, north of University square. It was operated for many years.

In 1832 Indianapolis had about 1,000 inhabitants, and as it was the capital of the state it was deemed right and proper that it should have some municipal government of its own. Up to that time it had been acting under state laws, and as an unruly element was beginning to find a lodgment it was conceived that town ordinances and town officers would be more efficient in keeping the peace and dignity of the community than the 'squires and constables. The general laws of the state provided for the incorporation of towns, and on the 3d of September, 1832, the citizens took the first step toward incorporation. Five trustees were elected, and Samuel Henderson, who had been the first regularly appointed postmaster of the town, was appointed president of the board, with J. P. Griffith clerk, and Samuel Jennison marshal and collector. This municipal government lasted until 1836, when the legislature granted a special charter. About the only notable thing the old municipality did was to purchase the first fire engine for the town, the state giving one-half of the price. The organization had lasted four years, and the entire income of the fourth year was only $1,510. The new organization went zealously to work to enact ordi-

THE INDIANAPOLIS NATIONAL BANK

nances for the suppression of vice and disorder, and there was urgent demand for this action.

The building of the National road and the other improvements carried on by the state had brought into the town a large number of wild, reckless and dangerous men. Not all of them were wholly vicious, but when filled with whisky they were reckless and oftentimes dangerous. So the new municipality found its hands full. The roughs were organized into a band and were commonly known as the "chain gang." A year or two after

POST-OFFICE BUILDING.

the new municipality went into power the "chain gang" was at its height as a disturber of the peace. They were loafers and generally idle, doing odd jobs occasionally of digging cellars and wells and moving houses, receiving therefor money enough to keep themselves well supplied with whisky. At that time there were but very few colored people in the town Against these the "chain gang" entertained a most intense hatred. The leader of the negroes was an old man by the name of Overall. Several collisions had taken place between the "chain gang" and the negroes. At last the white toughs resolved on cleaning out the negro settlement. Old man Overall was notified of this intention and of the night on which the attack was to take place. He called in his colored friends, barricaded the doors and windows of his cabin and loaded his guns. When the attack came the "chain gang" encountered a defeat that taught them a much needed lesson.

The leader of the "chain gang" was one Dave Buckhart. Tradition reports him as having been a square built man of great physical strength, and very courageous. He was of a naturally jealous temper and fond of a fight, and when filled with whisky was disposed to be very ugly. Soon after his contest with the negroes he received his quietus at the hands of a Methodist preacher. The Methodists were holding a camp-meeting under the direction of Rev. James Havens, a man fully as courageous as Buckhart, and of greater physical strength. The worshipers had been much annoyed by the conduct of the rougher element of the community. One afternoon while the services were progressing Buckhart began marching around the seats singing an obscene song at the top of his voice. Mr. Havens several times requested him to be quiet, but he paid no attention. Finally, when Mr. Havens saw that nothing else would do, he left the pulpit and walked directly up in front of the rowdy and ordered him off the grounds. The bully with an oath declared that he would not go, when quick as lightning the fist of the preacher shot out and Buckhart fell like an ox. Before he could recover himself the preacher had him by the throat and gave him a thrashing such as he had never had before. The next day he was arrested and heavily fined. While on trial before the justice he boasted so much that Samuel Merrill, who was present, told him that he was the better man of the two, and on a trial of strength threw him violently on the floor of the court room. These two defeats broke his power with the gang and he soon left the town.

The first murder committed within the bounds of Indianapolis was on the eighth of May, 1833. William McPherson was the victim, and the murder was committed by Michael Van Blaricum. Van Blaricum was the ferryman across White river. McPherson took passage in the ferry boat, and when it reached the middle of the river Van Blaricum purposely upset the boat, throwing McPherson into the river, where he was drowned. This took place in the presence of a number of persons who were standing on the bank of the river. The murder created the most intense excitement, but by the time the trial came off the

PENNSYLVANIA STREET.

excitement had died away to such an extent that Van Blaricum was let off with a sentence of three years in the penitentiary, but served only one-half of his term when he was pardoned out. The second murder occurred in the spring of 1836, when Arnold Lashley killed Zachariah Collins. There was some talk of lynching the murderer, but finally quiet was restored and after a preliminary trial Lashley was admitted to bail. He forfeited his bail, running away and never returning.

Murders were not of very frequent occurrence, but still a

number have occurred in the history of the city. For many years the murderers were either acquitted or escaped with prison sentences. The first man to be condemned to death was William Chuck, for the murder of his wife. The gallows had been erected for his hanging, when, the night before it was to take place, he poisoned himself in the jail. The next notable criminal trial was that of Nancy E. Clem, Silas W. Hartman, her brother, and William J. Abrams for the killing of Jacob Young and his wife in 1868. Jacob Young and his wife were found one morning on the bank of White river near Cold Springs, both dead from gunshot wounds. It developed that there had been some very mysterious money transactions between Young and Mrs. Clem, and the detectives soon arrested her and the two men. No other trial had ever caused so much excitement in Indiana. Mrs. Clem was tried first and sentenced for life. The next night her brother committed suicide in jail. Mrs. Clem succeeded in securing a new trial and was again convicted, and again obtained a new trial, until finally she wore out the prosecution and the matter was dropped. Abrams served a term in the penitentiary.

The first hanging took place in 1879. A number of murders had been committed and the escapes from punishment had been so numerous that public sentiment became intensely aroused, and when John Achey, in November, 1878, killed George Leggett, his gambling partner, there was a disposition to enforce the extreme penalty of the law. Soon after the arrest of Achey the community was startled by the discovery of a crime combining many most atrocious features. William Merrick had seduced a young school teacher and finally married her. One day he took her out riding and compelled her to drink liquor in which poison had been mixed. She died in the buggy in the most intense agony. He drove with the dead body several miles into the country and buried his victim with her new born babe under a pile of logs. His arrest and trial soon followed and he was also sentenced to hang. In the same year Louis Guetig shot and

BIRD'S-EYE VIEW OF INDIANAPOLIS, 1871.

killed a young lady by the name of McGlue, in the presence of a number of witnesses. He was sentenced to hang with Achey and Merrick but secured a new trial. Achey and Merrick were hanged upon the same scaffold. Guetig was again convicted and on September 19, 1879, was also hanged.

In 1834 the legislature chartered the State Bank of Indiana, with a capital of $1,600,000. Up to that time Indianapolis had contained nothing but a small private bank. The charter of the

SOUTH MERIDIAN STREET, WHOLESALE DISTRICT.

state bank was to run twenty-five years. The state was to take one-half of the capital stock, and raised the money by the sale of bonds. Her share of the dividends after paying the bonds was to go to the establishment of a general school fund. This was the starting point of Indiana's splendid endowment of her public schools. The state's share of the proceeds was loaned out from time to time on real estate security. The final yield of this investment by the state was $3,700,000, after paying off the bank bonds. The main bank and one of its branches were located in Indianapolis. The bank began business on the 26th day of November, 1834, in the building on the Governor's Circle which had been intended as a residence for the governor. It was afterwards removed to Washington street. Samuel Merrill was the first president, and Calvin Fletcher, Seaton W. Norris, Robert Morrison and Thomas R. Scott were the directors. In 1840 the bank removed to its new building at the corner of Kentucky avenue and Illinois street. The Indianapolis branch was organized by the appointment of Hervey Bates, president, and B. F. Morris, cashier. At the expiration of the charter the Bank of the State of Indiana was started, with Hugh McCullough as president. In this bank the state had no interest. It remained in business, with its seventeen branches, until wiped out by the institution of the national banks.

The great financial panic of 1837 proved very disastrous to Indianapolis. It stopped all work on the great enterprises undertaken by the state, leaving contractors and laborers without their pay. The banks were compelled to suspend specie payments and private business was overwhelmed with the credit of the state. Large stocks of goods had been purchased by the merchants and remained unsold on their shelves, or had been disposed of on credit, and collections were impossible. Nobody had any money. Eastern creditors were disposed to be very liberal and extend time of payments, trusting to a revival of business to relieve their debtors from their embarrassment. The legislature came to the help of the debtor by providing that property sold on execution should not be sold for less than two-thirds of its appraised value. It also exempted a certain amount of household property from execution. These two measures proved of great benefit, but did not relieve the distress altogether. There was a lack of currency, and the legislature issued bills secured by the credit of the state, and bearing six per cent. interest. This "scrip" was made receivable for taxes, but from the want of credit by the state abroad the scrip passed only at a heavy discount. After awhile, when confidence was restored again, the "scrip" commanded a large premium, and before it was all finally redeemed it was worth about two dollars for one. It was not until 1843, when the Madison railroad was approaching completion, that an upward tendency in business occurred.

The city has suffered from several panics since, the worst in the earlier years being in 1840, '41 and '42. The State Bank resumed specie payment in June, 1842, but it was a year or more before business generally revived. These were the famous "hard times" following the election of William Henry Harrison. So grievous were the times that an effort was made in 1842 to

DEAF AND DUMB INSTITUTE.

abolish the town government on account of its expense, although the entire cost of operating the municipal government was a little less than $3,000. It might be well to note at this point the salaries paid to the municipal officers in those early days. Members of the council received $12 each a year, the secretary $200, the treasurer and marshal each $100, and the assessors $75. The other salaries were in a like proportion.

For some years after the organization of the state, a militia was maintained by requiring all the able-bodied men between certain ages to be enrolled and report at stated periods for muster. When the danger from Indian wars ceased these musters ended. The military spirit of the people, however, did not die out, and in February, 1837, the first company of militia was organized with Colonel Russell as captain. It was called the "Marion Guards." Their uniform was of gray cloth with patent leather shakoes. They were armed with the old fashioned flint-lock muskets, and drilled according to the Prussian tactics. Thomas A. Morris, recently a graduate of West Point, succeeded Captain Russell. In 1838 Captain Thomas McBaker organized the "Marion Rifles." The uniform of the Rifles was a blue fringed hunting shirt, blue pantaloons and caps. In 1842 the two companies organized into a battalion under the command of Lieutenant-Colonel Harvey Brown, and Major George Drum.

In 1837 was opened the first female school of the city. It was called the "Indianapolis Female Institute," and was chartered by the legislature. It was opened by two sisters, Mary J. and Harriett Axtell. It flourished for several years, and its reputation was so high that quite a number of pupils from other towns and states attended it. The same year a neat frame school-house was erected on Circle street, adjoining what was so long known as Henry Ward Beecher's church. The school was opened by Mr. Gilman Marston, afterwards a member of congress from New Hampshire and a distinguished general during the late war. It was called the "Franklin Institute."

In 1842 Indianapolis entertained its first ex-president. Prior to that time several distinguished men had visited the city among them having been Vice-President Richard Johnson and Henry Clay, but in 1842 Martin Van Buren, who had but recently vacated the executive mansion at Washington, made a tour through the west. He traveled in a stage coach over the old National road. He was received by a procession composed of four military companies, the fire companies and citizens generally, who escorted him to the Palmer house where he made a speech, and in the evening he held a reception at the state-

G. A. R. PARADE, NATIONAL ENCAMPMENT, SEPT. 4, 1893.

house. The next day being Sunday, he attended church twice, once to hear Lucien W. Berry at Wesley Chapel, and once to hear Henry Ward Beecher. On Monday he left for St. Louis. In October following Henry Clay paid the town a visit. He was accompanied by Governor Thomas Metcalfe, and Hon. John J. Crittenden. It was a semi-political occasion, in which Mr. Clay was laying the foundation for a future presidential nomination. It was a great demonstration, winding up with a barbecue.

The next distinguished visitor to Indianapolis was Kossuth,

INSTITUTION FOR THE BLIND.

the great Hungarian patriot, who came in response to an invitation of the governor and the legislature. He arrived here on the 27th of February, 1852, coming from Cincinnati by the way of Madison. He was met by a large concourse of people, and escorted to the state-house square, where he made one of those remarkable speeches for which he was justly so famous. He was entertained at the Capital house, at the expense of the city. At night he was given a reception by the governor, and the next day was presented to the legislature. On Sunday he attended church at Robert's chapel and visited several of the Sunday-schools of the city. On Monday night he delivered a lecture on Hungary at Masonic hall.

On February 11, 1861, Abraham Lincoln visited the city on his way to Washington to be inaugurated President. The demonstration made in his honor surpassed all others ever witnessed in the city to that time. He came from Lafayette and left the train at the intersection of the railroad and Washington street. A magnificent carriage drawn by four white horses was waiting him, and escorted by the military, the fire department, the legislature, the city council, hundreds of carriages and several thousand citizens on horseback, he went through some of the principal streets. At the Bates house he addressed an immense throng. The streets along the line of parade were profusely decorated, and all classes united to pay him honor. At night a reception was given at the Bates house, attended by several thousands of the citizens. He left the next morning for Cincinnati.

On September 10, 1866, President Andrew Johnson, accompanied by several members of his cabinet, and by General Grant and Admiral Farragut, visited the city. It was soon after the close of the war, before the animosities of that great struggle had passed away. At that time the president and congress were in a struggle over measures of reconstructing the south and the Union men felt very bitter toward him. His reception was disgraced by a riot deplored by all good citizens. Mr. Johnson attempted to speak, but the crowd made so much noise he could not be heard. In the confusion several fights occurred and five or six persons were wounded by pistol shots. A few minutes after the rioting had been stopped an old man by the name of Andrew Stewart was shot and killed by Howard Stretcher. The president was so alarmed that he sent for a guard of soldiers, who guarded his room all night. He attempted to speak again the next morning before his departure, and a little better order was observed, but still the unruly element was predominant.

The greatest demonstration ever made in honor of any man, however, was that to General Grant on December 9, 1879. It was after he had completed his tour around the world. A cold rain was falling but more than forty thousand citizens took part in the grand parade, either in the line of march or lining the streets through which the procession passed. Never before had Indianapolis been so elaborately or profusely decorated. The cheers that went up from the crowds on the streets as the nation's hero passed along resembled the roar of a great battle

INDIANAPOLIS ORPHAN ASYLUM.

more than anything else. It was a non-partisan affair in which all parties united. Both Hayes and Cleveland, during their terms, visited the city and were warmly greeted, but nothing equaled the demonstration for Grant.

The nearest approach to the Grant demonstration was that made when General Harrison left the city to be inaugurated president. For many years he had been a prominent citizen of Indianapolis, and the esteem in which he was held by all prompted the citizens to unite in doing him honor on his departure to accept the highest office to which any Indianian had ever been exalted. Great crowds came from other parts of the state and filled the streets.

Indianapolis has witnessed many notable political gatherings in its time. Indiana has always been famous for being able to turn out immense crowds on political occasions. In 1860 a short time previous to the October election the Republicans got up a monster day and night parade. The city was so thronged with people that the parade could hardly move along the streets. In the day parade were many unique features. One was an immense flatboat drawn by forty yoke of cattle; and filled with young ladies bearing streamers and banners. Another was one hundred yoke of oxen drawing an immense log wagon, on which a number of sturdy men were splitting rails. The night scene was one of peculiar beauty, the procession numbering thousands carrying torches, and along the line of march were placed hundreds of other torches. During the same year the Democrats got up a meeting in honor of Stephen A. Douglas, their candidate for president, who was present on the occasion. The meeting was not so large as that of the Republicans, but was fully as enthusiastic.

In 1872, Horace Greeley, candidate for the presidency on the ticket of the liberal Republicans and the Democrats, visited the city, and was greeted with a turn-out that put all previous political demonstrations in the shade. Both a day and night parade were given and the crowd was estimated at forty thousand. The torchlight procession was more than two miles long. It was only a few days before the October election, and it was hoped by the adherents of Mr. Greeley that the demonstration would make the state sure for the Democratic ticket, but in that they were disappointed.

Two great political demonstrations were gotten up by the Republicans in honor of Mr. Blaine. The first was in October, 1884, when he was himself a candidate for the presidency. His party did its utmost to pour into the capital city an immense throng, to impress the people with Mr. Blaine's popularity, and

SCENE NEAR BROAD RIPPLE.

so far as the crowd was concerned they succeeded. In point of numbers it surpassed the great Greeley meeting of twelve years before. The second demonstration in honor of Mr. Blaine was in 1888 when he came to assist the candidacy of General Harrison. It was a great affair but did not equal the one in 1884. The last big political demonstration occurred on October 6, 1896, when William J. Bryan, democratic candidate for president, visited the city. It was a very great meeting, but in point

LAKE IN MILITARY PARK.

of numbers fell below that of Greeley in 1872 and that of Blaine in 1884.

To go back now to the history of events as they occurred. The session of the legislature of 1842–3 was a very busy one, and did much to advance the future interests of the state. In 1839 the subject of erecting a hospital for the insane of the state had been broached, but nothing definite was done, owing to the financial embarrassment of the state and people, but as soon as business began to exhibit signs of recovery the matter was again taken up. Dr. John Evans, of Chicago, who had made a study of mental diseases, delivered a lecture before the members of the legislature, and the governor was directed to obtain plans for the erection of suitable buildings. At the next session of the legislature the plans were approved and a tax of one cent on each one hundred dollars' worth of property was levied to provide the means for erecting the buildings. All this was but carrying out a direction in the constitution adopted at the organization of the state, one of the cares of the framers of that document being to provide for the unfortunate. Dr. John Evans, Dr. L. Dunlap and James Blake were appointed a commission to obtain a site for the proposed buildings. They selected Mount Jackson, where the hospital now stands. In 1846 the legislature ordered the sale of "hospital" square, a plat of ground that had been reserved for hospital purposes, the proceeds to be applied to the work, and an additional sum of $15,000 was appropriated.

The work of construction was begun at once, and the main building was completed the next year at a cost of $75,000. Since then several additions have been made to the building, and others erected, until now Indianapolis can boast of one of the most substantial, convenient and imposing structures of the kind in the United States. The grounds are handsomely laid out, and every convenience and comfort for this class of unfortunates have been provided. The legislature of 1843 also began the work of caring for the deaf mutes, by levying a tax of one-fifth of a cent on each one hundred dollars of property. The first work of this kind in the state, however, was done by William Willard, a mute who had been a teacher of mutes in Ohio. He came to Indianapolis in the spring of 1843 and opened a school on his own account. In 1844 the state adopted his school, and appointed a board of trustees, consisting of the governor, treasurer of state, Henry Ward Beecher, Phineas D. Gurley, L. H. Jameson, Dr. Dunlap, James Morrison and Matthew Simpson, afterwards a distinguished bishop of the Methodist church. They rented a building at the corner of Maryland and Illinois streets, and opened the first asylum in October, 1844.

In January, 1846, a site for a permanent building was selected just east of the town. The permanent building was completed in 1850, at a cost of $30,000.

During the winter of 1844-5, through the efforts of James M. Ray, William H. Churchman, of the Kentucky Blind Asylum, was brought here with some of his pupils and gave an exhibition or two in Mr. Beecher's church. This had a decidedly good effect on the legislature which was then in session, and a tax of one-fifth of a cent was levied to provide support for the

STONE BRIDGE IN GARFIELD PARK.

blind. James M. Ray, George W. Mears and the secretary, auditor and treasurer of state were appointed a commission to carry out the work, either by the establishment of an asylum or by providing for the care and education of the blind at the institution in Ohio or that in Kentucky. In 1847 James M. Ray, George W. Mears and Seton W. Norris were appointed to erect a suitable building, and $5,000 appropriated to purchase a site. They purchased the ground now occupied, and while waiting for the erection of a building opened a school in the building that had been used for the first deaf and dumb asylum. The present building was completed in 1851 at the cost of $50,000.

The town but slowly recovered from the effects of the hard times which followed on the collapse of the state's internal improvement schemes. Population did not come, and there was not much here to attract immigrants. A few attempts at manufacturing were made, among them being the establishment in 1843 by Robert Parmlee of a factory for the manufacture of pianos. It was not a successful undertaking as the town was too young, and the people too poor to indulge in the luxury of such musical instruments.

The year 1846 brought some excitement, and for a while made things a little more lively. The war with Mexico was on, and troops called for. Indianapolis raised one company for the first regiment. It was officered by James P. Drake as captain, and John A. McDougal and Lewis Wallace as lieutenants. Captain Drake was afterward made colonel of the regiment. The next year Indianapolis furnished two additional companies, one each for the fourth and fifth regiments. Those two companies were with General Scott on his march to the capital of Mexico, and participated in some of the battles of that campaign. They were commanded by James McDougal and Edward Lander.

While the Mexican war was going on the railroad that was building to connect Indianapolis and the Ohio river at Madison was slowly creeping along. It was finally completed to the city in 1847 amid great rejoicing. This and the Mexican war, and other circumstances, had brought to the little city a large number of gamblers and vicious persons, and crime was rampant. The citizens held several meetings to devise means of ridding the town of this undesirable element, and finally a committee of fifteen was organized. The committee proceeded in a vigorous but orderly manner, and soon the town was as quiet and peaceable as any in the country.

Up to 1847 it had been a struggle for existence in the capi-

VIEW ON WHITE RIVER.

tal of the state. Its business was purely local. Farmers had no way of getting any surplus they might have to a market, and hence confined themselves to producing only enough to supply the local demand. Of manufacturing there was none. Several attempts in this line had been made in a small way, but as they had nothing but the local demand to depend upon they soon died. The only ambitious attempt that had been made was the steam mill heretofore referred to, and it had been a lamentable failure. With the opening of the Madison railroad a change came, and the town put on a bustling air of activity.

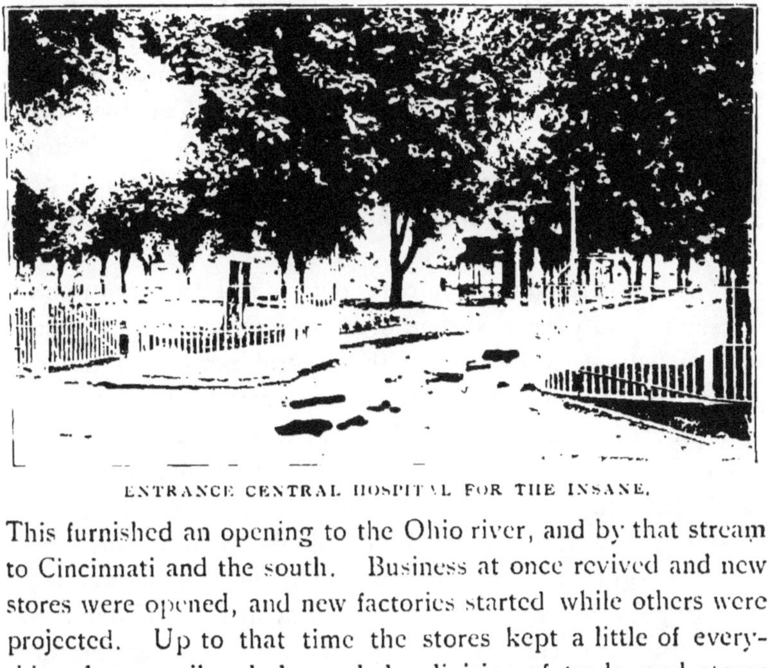

ENTRANCE CENTRAL HOSPITAL FOR THE INSANE.

This furnished an opening to the Ohio river, and by that stream to Cincinnati and the south. Business at once revived and new stores were opened, and new factories started while others were projected. Up to that time the stores kept a little of everything, but a railroad demanded a division of trade, and stores for dry goods and stores for groceries were opened. The price of property advanced, and a new city government organized. At the first settlement of the town, lots along or near the river front were the favorites in the market. The sickly seasons soon drove business and the settlements further east, and the opening of the railroad attracted everything toward the south, so as to be near the depot.

In February, 1847, the legislature granted a city charter to Indianapolis, and on the 27th of March an election was held to determine whether the people would accept or not. It was approved by a vote of 449 to 19. An election for municipal officers was held on the 24th of April, and Samuel Henderson was elected the first mayor of the city. The population of the city was estimated at that time at 6,000. Practically there were no streets, except Washington, and it was still full of stumps. Some of the other streets had been partly cleared, but no attempt had been made to improve any of them. Here and there on Washington street were patches of sidewalks, some of brick and some of plank. Dog fennel covered the streets and all the vacant ground, and there was a good deal of ground vacant. When it rained mud predominated on the only streets that had been opened and used, while in the summer the dust was thick enough to be almost stifling.

The new city council at once determined to enter upon a systematic and general system of street improvements. Stumps were pulled out, the streets in the central portion of the city graded and graveled and sidewalks were made. This first effort at improvement caused a good deal of friction and litigation, the property owners objecting to the expense entailed upon them. Bowldering for streets was not introduced until 1850, when Washington was so paved from Illinois to Meridian. Free schools also made their appearance soon after the formation of the city government. The state had provided a small fund, but it was only large enough to keep the schools going for three or four months of the year. It was decided to levy a small tax on the citizens to provide funds for the erection of houses and to pay teachers, and by 1853 this tax furnished enough to make a more permanent organization of the schools necessary.

The year 1847 brought also the first hall erected for the use of the public. The Grand Lodge of Free Masons determined to erect a building that would contain rooms for lodge purposes and a large hall that could be used for entertainments, public meetings, etc. The location decided upon was the southeast corner of Washington and Tennessee streets, now known as Capital avenue. The corner-stone was laid on the 25th of October, but the building was not finally completed until 1850. The convention to revise the constitution of the state held its sessions in the public hall in 1850.

Among other improvements in business was the opening of

CENTRAL HOSPITAL FOR THE INSANE.

the first wholesale dry good store in Indianapolis, by Joseph Little & Co. The three or four years following were uneventful, in the main, the city showing slow but steady growth, and another railroad or two began to make pretentions to public utility, and the Union Railway Company was organized, with the idea of bringing all the railroads into one central station. In 1848 the first telegraph line to the city was constructed, reaching to Dayton, Ohio. Two or three attempts were made to organize a merchants' exchange, but one after another failed from one cause or another, until 1866, when the Chamber of Commerce was organized on a permanent basis. In 1851 a company was chartered to furnish gas light to the citizens, but it was not until 1854 the city took any gas for the streets, and then only for a few lamps. In 1852 the legislature granted a charter for the Northwestern Christian University, and plans were adopted to raise funds for the construction of the necessary buildings. The same year the Grand Lodge of Odd Fellows began the erection of a building on the northeast corner of Washington and Pennsylvania street, and in the same year the city again changed its form of government, surrendering the special charter and accepting the general law. This change was mainly occasioned because the special charter limited the power of taxation to fifteen cents on the one hundred dollars, and it had been found totally inadequate to the needs of the city.

The year 1854 was made locally memorable by the intense excitement created by the attempt to take from the city a colored man by the name of John Freeman, on the ground that he was a fugitive slave. This case demands more than a passing notice from the fact that it displayed upon the part of certain public officers an overzealous effort to rob a man of his freedom. Freeman had lived in this city for a number of years and had been known as a sober, industrious citizen. One Pleasant Ellington, of Missouri, came here and claimed that Freeman was his slave and had escaped from him in Kentucky. He was arrested and hurried before the United States commissioner who for sometime refused to listen either to him or to attorneys who had volunteered to defend his cause. Freeman claimed that he had been born and raised in Georgia, and if permitted to send there could easily prove he had always been a free man, but it was determined to hurry him off to slavery.

The citizens, however, determined that this should not be done, and filled the streets with an angry mob. The United States marshal, John L. Robinson, armed himself and his deputies and declared his determination to escort Freemen to Mis-

VIEW ON FALL CREEK.

souri, but the temper of the citizens soon convinced him that he and his deputies would more likely become victims of their indignation. A stay of proceedings was at last forced, but Freeman was committed to jail where he had to employ guards to prevent his being run off south. Ellington's own brother, who was well acquainted with the real fugitive, gave his testimony that Freeman in no manner resembled him; that the fugitive was tall, straight, and a very robust man. Freeman, on the other hand, was a very short man with extremely bowed legs.

ENTRANCE TO CROWN HILL CEMETERY.

Even with this testimony the court would not release him, and General Coburn, one of his attorneys, went to Georgia and got the evidence of a number of planters and others as to Freeman being a free man, and then went to Canada where he found the real fugitive.

Freeman was kept in jail from May until August. The Georgia planters then came here to give their evidence. Their presence increased the excitement, and a meeting of citizens was held in Masonic Hall, where speeches were made severely arraigning the judge, who still refused to release Freeman. This meeting was attended and participated in by the Georgia planters, who were honorable men. At last the grand jury, on the evidence given by the Georgia planters, indicted Ellington for perjury. While the warrant was being prepared he fled from the city. Then, when there was no longer any one here to claim him, the judge reluctantly released Freeman. By his industry he had been able to get a little property, but the exactions forced upon him by the officers of the United States had caused him to expend it all.

The year 1854 was one of almost continued rioting. The legislature had enacted a law prohibiting the sale of liquor, and, in attempting to enforce it, a terrible riot occurred between the police and a large number of German citizens, in which quite a number of Germans were wounded, but none fatally. The police force conquered, but all during the year riotous demonstrations were kept up, and there were nightly conflicts between the police and the supporters of the traffic. The law was finally overthrown by the supreme court and quiet was restored.

In the earlier history of the city, at almost every recurring election, fights would occur, in which blood was shed to some extent, but they were seldom followed by any riotous demonstrations, the fighting at each occasion being confined to a few of the rougher element. In fact, Indianapolis has been peculiarly free from disturbances such as have cast blots upon the good name of so many cities. Political excitement has always run high, and it is a matter of wonder that many campaigns have not been accompanied by serious disturbances of the peace. The only serious election riot was on the evening of May 2, 1876, at the close of the election for municipal officers. For days the excitement had been most intense, and the contest for control of the city had been fought with much more than the usual feeling. The colored people had been admitted to the right of the ballot, but those who had opposed that innovation had not grown used to seeing them exercise the right, and a great deal of irritation followed. On the evening referred to, after the close of the polls, a riot occurred and one man was killed and several more or less injured. The riot would not have occurred had it not been for the police, and that department was wholly to blame. On several occasions when strikes were in existence the city has been filled with angry men, but the coolness of the better element of the citizens has always prevented any disastrous consequences.

Beginning with 1855 and continuing until 1860, the whole state,

MARION COUNTY JAIL.

and Indianapolis especially, suffered from "wildcat" money. The destruction caused by that wild experience in banking would have practically closed the doors to the growth and prosperity of the city for at least ten years had not the war intervened. There had been a demand for more currency and the legislature had enacted a law to provide for the establishment of banks of issue, without any adequate security, and it was not long until the state was flooded with bills issued by irresponsible persons, and an explosion soon came. Beautifully printed and engraved bills were issued, but when the holders went out to find the banks and have the bills redeemed no banks could be found. They never had any actual existence. When the crash came nearly all of the free banks closed their doors within the space of a few weeks. For some months their money had been hawked about at a discount that changed every day. A workingman would be paid off in money quoted at a certain discount by the note reporter of that day, and on the next morning, when he would appear at his grocer's or butcher's to pay off his weekly bills, he would find that his money had been shaved five or ten per cent. more.

This crash almost destroyed business. New enterprises were paralyzed, and there was a general want of confidence. The distress was even greater than that which followed the panic of 1837. The free banks were weeded out, and business began to brighten up a little before the war began.

Indianapolis had been generally fortunate in its selection of men to conduct its business, but in 1856 it had an experience which proved that all men could not be trusted. At that time the city debt had slowly increased until it had reached the sum of $15,000. To meet the pressing obligations it was determined to fund the debt, and Jeremiah D. Skeen was appointed an agent to negotiate the sale of $30,000 worth of city bonds in New York. Sometime afterward the banking firm of Winslow, Lanier & Co., of New York, notified the city that it had the bonds, purchased from Skeen. He had sold the bonds and kept the money. The city, of course, had to pay the bonds. It was charged that Skeen used the money to bet on the election.

By 1860 more railroads had been completed and Indianapolis was already attracting attention as quite a railroad center. The population had increased to about 18,000, and persons hunting for a location for some manufacturing enterprise or another began to consider the claims of the Hoosier capital. The state had gotten rid pretty generally of the wildcat money, and what was in circulation was considered as pretty good. Some

of the streets had been improved and a better class of buildings were being erected. The state also was getting a better name abroad. Its good name had suffered first by the disastrous failure of its internal improvement schemes, and again by the destruction of our school system by a decision of the supreme court. This latter had been rectified by a new opinion, but it took several years for the state to recover the good name it had lost by the first reckless decision. Indianapolis suffered with the state, but in 1860 it witnessed the dawn of a prosperity that

DAM AT BROAD RIPPLE.

has shone brightly ever since, meeting with a few clouds, but they did not long check the march of progress.

The year 1860 was marked by the most exciting political campaign that up to that time the city had witnessed. It was early seen that the issue of the contest might probably be civil war, and the feeling was intense. Three political parties were in the field, with Abraham Lincoln as the leader of the Republicans, Stephen A. Douglas of one wing of the Democratic party, and John C. Breckinridge of the other. The threat of civil war had aroused the military spirit of the people, and early in the year 1860 it could be seen that the people were beginning to prepare for war. Several military companies were organized and began drilling in an active manner. The Mexican war had left a little of the military feeling, but by 1852 it had died away, and was not revived until 1856. In February of that year the St. Louis Guards visited Indianapolis, and made such a showy figure that it at once fired the hearts of the young men of Indianapolis and they immediately organized the National Guards. The uniform was of blue with caps and white plumes. It maintained its organization until it went into the civil war as a part of the Eleventh regiment. The next year the City Grays organized. It also went into the Eleventh regiment. Two years afterward the Grays organized an auxiliary artillery company, but an explosion of a gun crippled its commander and the company soon went down. A cavalry company was organized in 1858, but, like that of the artillery, did not long survive.

On the twenty-second of February, 1860, the Montgomery Guards of Crawfordsville, under the command of Captain Lew Wallace, came to the city, and in connection with the city companies gave a parade. The Montgomery Guards used the zouave drill and its strange tactics created great enthusiasm, and at once a zouave company was organized, and afterward became a part of Wallace's Eleventh regiment. In June a military convention was held here and an encampment decided upon to be held in September. Two or three new companies were at once organized, and the military spirit began to pervade all classes. The result was that when Mr. Lincoln called for troops in April, 1861, Indiana was ready to furnish more than a regiment of well drilled men.

After the election, as one state after another seceded and began to prepare for war, the tension on the public mind was so great that nothing was talked about but the probabilities of war. Governor Morton sounded the key-note of opposition to secession in a speech at a great meeting of the citizens to jollify over the election of Mr. Lincoln. His patriotic words fired all hearts, and but one sentiment was manifested, that of armed resistance to secession.

When the news came that Major Anderson in Fort Sumter was being bombarded by the troops of South Carolina, the feeling grew in intensity. Business was abandoned, and the people gathered on the streets to wait for the bulletins and to discuss the situation. The question of the moment was what course the president would take. The people could not remain quiet, but moved around the streets in a feverish excitement. Party feeling was forgotten for the time. At night a meeting was held in the Metropolitan theater and several patriotic speeches were

SOUTHWEST SECTION MONUMENT PLACE.

made while waiting for the news. A little before ten o'clock the news came that Major Anderson had been compelled to submit to the inevitable and had surrendered. "War" was shouted from every lip, and the meeting broke up, the people crowding out on the streets, and all night long anxious crowds thronged around the newspaper offices to get every particle of news that came over the wires. Early the next morning the military companies began the work of recruiting, and it was kept up all day Sunday without intermission. The drum and the fife were heard everywhere, and the names of recruits were fast added to the rolls of the various companies.

On Monday came the proclamation of President Lincoln

calling for 75,000 volunteers. It was accompanied by an order of the war department assigning six regiments as the quota of Indiana. The next day the governor issued his proclamation and the Indianapolis companies at once hastened to camp, and companies from other towns and cities came pouring in. The change was like magic. From the restless, feverish anxiety of uncertainty all was changed to the bustle of armed men rushing to the defense of the imperiled Union. The trains came into the city loaded with men anxious to serve their country. Governor Morton and his staff were busy in preparing to accommodate the arriving hosts, and to procure clothing and arms for them. The government had neither, and if it had there were calls from other states. Governor Morton did not wait. He realized, more than any one else, the urgent need of promptness, and while his staff was busy in arranging for the new troops, and assigning them quarters where they could be housed and fed, he appealed to the patriotic citizens for aid in clothing them, and dispatched agents to eastern cities and to Europe to purchase arms and equipments. All Indianapolis was a military camp. Instead of six regiments Governor Morton offered thirty, and he had the men in camp.

Gen. Lew Wallace was adjutant-general of the state, but asked for a command that would take him to the field, and he was made colonel of the Eleventh regiment, the first regiment organized. It was made up mostly from Indianapolis recruits. It adopted the zouave drill and uniform. The Geisendorffs were then operating a large woolen mill here, and Governor Morton purchased all the gray jeans they had on hand, and hundreds of women of Indianapolis were soon busy changing it into short, baggy breeches and jackets for the regiment. Just before the Eleventh left for the front the regiment was marched to the statehouse to witness the raising of the stars and stripes over the dome. It was an impressive scene. Miss Caroline Richings sang "The Star Spangled Banner," thousands of citizens joining in the chorus. After the flag was raised over the state-

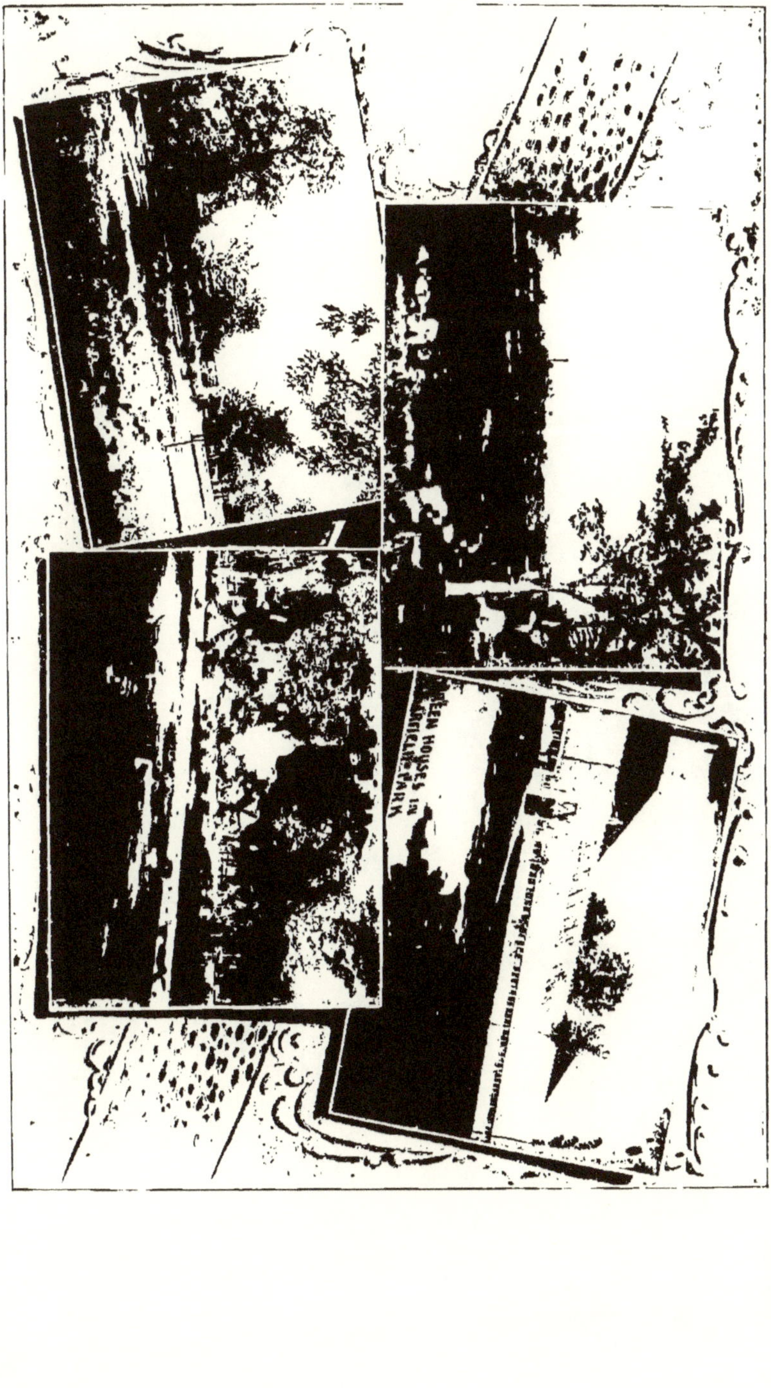
HOUSES IN
PARK

house, the ladies of Indianapolis presented the regiment with a magnificent silk banner bearing the coat of arms of the United States, while the ladies of Terre Haute gave them a fine silk flag. It was received on behalf of the regiment by Colonel Wallace, who at the close of his speech ordered the men to kneel and raise their right hands and swear never to desert the flag, and then gave them as their battle cry, "Remember Buena Vista." At the battle of Buena Vista an Indiana regiment was broken by a charge of Mexican lancers, and Jeff. Davis had

MASONIC TEMPLE.

affixed the stigma of cowardice on the regiment, and it had followed Indiana ever since.

The Eleventh regiment went first to Evansville and then to Maryland. In June a mounted squad of the regiment, doing scout duty, had a fierce battle with Ashby's black horse cavalry, and John C. Hollenbeck, of Company B, was killed. He was the first soldier from Indianapolis to offer up his life for the perpetuity of the Union. It has been claimed for him that he was the first soldier from Indiana killed in the war, but that honor belongs to Carroll county. A member of the Ninth Indiana,

Colonel Milroy's regiment, was the first soldier to fall in actual battle for the cause of the Union. The other five regiments of the state's quota were soon organized and hurried to the front, where they took part in the battles in West Virginia. They were under the immediate command of Gen. Thomas A. Morris, of Indianapolis, who was the real moving power of that campaign, but the credit was given to his superior, Gen. George B. McClellan.

Governor Morton, after having filled the quota of the state, did not dismiss the excess of troops that had offered, but put them into camp to be drilled for future service. He was not one of those who believed the war would end in a flurry, but saw that a long and desperate struggle was ahead of the government, and was determined that Indiana should not be a laggard in the contest. Several camps were formed in different parts of the city, and from the 22d of April, 1861, until after the surrender of the last of the Confederate troops, Indianapolis had the air of an armed camp. Regiments were either forming and being sent to the front, or were being received on their return home. On the 20th of April, 1861, the city of Indianapolis appropriated $10,000 to aid the cause, and before the war closed the city had given until its expenditures had reached more than $1,000,000. This vast amount had been raised mostly by taxation, but such was the spirit of patriotism that the people cheerfully submitted to the heavy burdens imposed. The war left the city with a debt of $386,000. It should be remembered that the city then had a population of less than 20,000. Nor did this vast sum of $1,000,000 represent all that the citizens of Indianapolis gave to the war, for large sums for the sanitary and Christian commissions were raised by private subscriptions.

Even a cursory history of Indianapolis would not be complete without referring to some of those who so ably seconded the efforts of Governor Morton. Especially should the services of Isaiah Mansur be mentioned. He was appointed commissary by Governor Morton. The state had no money, nor had the general government furnished any for the maintenance of the troops. Mr. Mansur did not wait. He served without pay, but threw his whole soul into the work, and his activity and energy were boundless. He furnished meat from his own packing houses, advanced his own money to purchase fresh bread, and other supplies, taking the chance of being reimbursed by the legislature. The recruits were not used to camp fare, and expected to have the same delicacies furnished them they were

HARRISON MONUMENT.

used to in their own homes, and many complaints were made. So loud were these complaints that the legislature, without examining into the facts, passed a resolution of censure on Mr. Mansur, but it was afterward revoked and he was complimented for his efficiency and patriotism. Mr. Mansur was not the only one who advanced money to the state during the war, but on several occasions the bankers furnished large sums. Notably was this the case when Kentucky was invaded by Bragg and Kirby Smith. The government had offered a bounty and advanced pay to troops, but the call from Kentucky was urgent, and there was delay upon the part of the government in sending the money necessary. The facts were reported to the banks by Governor Morton, when they promptly stepped forward and supplied the funds, and the troops were hastened to Kentucky to join in rolling back the tide of war.

The State Fair grounds, north of the city, were taken for camping purposes, and there the first regiments were organized. It was used for that purpose until the twenty-second of February, 1862, when it was first used as a rebel prison. The first prisoners were from those captured at Fort Donelson. About three thousand were brought here first, many of them suffering severely from pneumonia and camp diarrhea, induced by exposure in the ditches around Fort Donelson. On their arrival they slept the first night on the floor of the union depot. They were in a pitiable condition. The next morning the humane physicians of Indianapolis were attending on them, fully one-fifth of the whole number needing medical attendance. Two hospitals were established, and the men and women of the city acted as nurses, and greatly added to the hospital supplies from their own homes. Notwithstanding all this care several hundred died. For some time before their capture they had been insufficiently fed and clothed, and during the inclemency of the winter had been compelled to be a good deal of the time in the ditches around the fort. The dead were first buried in a part of Greenlawn cemetery, but were afterward removed to Crown Hill.

The other prisoners were taken to Camp Morton, where they were joined by several hundred others who had been cared for temporarily at Madison, Terre Haute and other places. They were kept in Camp Morton until exchanged in the September following The camp then remained unoccupied until after the surrender of Vicksburg when it was again used for a prison camp, and from that time to the close of the war it held from three thousand to five thousand prisoners. At one time a plan was formed by citizens of the state who sympathized with the

SOLDIERS' GRAVES IN CROWN HILL CEMETERY.

South, to overthrow the state government, release the prisoners and arm them from arms contained in the state arsenal, and march them to the South. The plan was discovered, and resulted in what has since been known as the "Treason Trials." Some very ludicrous incidents came from this abortive attempt, among them being the celebrated "Battle of Pogue's Run." To hide the attempt from the eyes of the authorities and to furnish an excuse or explanation for the presence of such a great number in the city, a mass meeting of those opposed to the

ST. VINCENT'S INFIRMARY.

war was called. The intention was that under the guise of this meeting a raid should be made on the camp by armed men, the guards overpowered and the prisoners released. The prisoners had been fully advised of the effort that was to be made in their favor and were ready to do their part.

The authorities, however, were fully informed of the whole matter and were on the watch. The mass meeting was being held on the state-house grounds, and by some means a rumor was started that troops were on their way to disperse the meeting. A panic ensued, and those in attendance hastily scattered in every direction. Troops had been placed in various parts of the city prepared to suppress any violence and to nip any effort to carry out the plan of releasing the prisoners. As the soldiers saw the crowds hastening through the streets toward the union station they added to their terror by shouts of derision. The crowd of panic stricken visitors clambered into the cars ready to leave the city. They might have been permitted to go in peace, if some of them in passing the Soldiers' Home had not fired their revolvers from the car windows. The trains were immediately stopped, and soldiers went from car to car searching for arms. This added to the fright, and many of those who, a few moments before, had been boldly exhibiting their revolvers hastily threw them from the car windows. A large number of revolvers and knives were taken, and for several weeks were kept on exhibition at the headquarters of the general commanding.

This opposition to the war soon developed a number of secret organizations, whose object was to furnish aid and comfort to the South. At last the leaders in this movement were arrested and brought to Indianapolis for trial before a military commission. The leading prisoners were H. H. Dodd, of this city; William Bowles, of Orange county; Lamdin P. Milligan, of Huntington county, and Stephen A. Dorsey, of Martin county. Several others were arrested at the same time but afterwards released, either because of the want of any evidence connecting them with the conspiracy or that they might become witnesses against the others. During the trial Dodd escaped from prison and fled to Canada. Bowles, Milligan and Dorsey were sentenced to death, but the sentence was commuted by President Johnson to life imprisonment in the Ohio penitentiary. They were afterwards released by the supreme court of the United States, on a writ of habeas corpus.

While Camp Morton was still occupied, Camp Burnside was formed just south of it. It was here while it was occupied by the Seventy-first regiment in the summer of 1862 that the first

GARFIELD PARK.
GARDEN IN GARFIELD PARK.
PLEASANT

military execution that ever took place in the state occurred. Robert Gay had been charged with desertion and as being a spy. He was tried and convicted and sentenced to be shot, although hanging was the penalty for being a spy. He was shot in the old Henderson orchard, between Camp Morton and Camp Burnside. The regiment and spectators formed three sides of the square, the open side being to the east. Gay was brought out by the guard and placed in front of his coffin. He made a speech protesting that he had no guilty purpose in deserting. He told the firing party to aim at his heart. He then sat down on his coffin and was blindfolded. The signal to fire was given. The firing party consisted of ten, but one of the guns was loaded with a blank cartridge. Eight of the nine balls struck him in the heart while one went through his neck. In 1864 three "bounty jumpers" were shot on the same ground. In 1864 General Hovey, who was then in command, prepared a scaffold on the same ground for the hanging of Bowles, Milligan and Dorsey, but the sentence, as mentioned before, was never carried out.

Almost as soon as the war began Governor Morton, was satisfied that the federal government would be unable to supply the demand for ammunition and he determined to establish here an arsenal for the manufacture of catridges. He secured the services of Gen. Herman Sturm, and throughout the war this arsenal not only supplied the state troops, but many times furnished the federal government with ammunition for the troops at the front. The supplies thus furnished on several occasions saved the Union armies from defeat. At the close of the war, upon a settlement with the government, it was found that the arsenal had not only paid its expenses but had a large surplus of money, which was turned over to the state treasury.

Among other camps established near the city during the war were Camp Carrington, which was considered the best arranged, and best managed military camp in the United States; Camp Noble, which under command of Col. W. W. Frybarger, was used for artillery purposes, the practice ground being between the Bluff road and the river bottom, and Camp Fremont used by the colored troops.

Governor Morton, early in 1861, became convinced of the necessity of some extraordinary effort to supply the troops with good winter clothing, and he devised a system which afterward proved the foundation of the great sanitary commission. He purchased through his agent at New York nearly thirty thousand overcoats. Some of these overcoats were purchased at a cost of $1.25 more than the regulation price, and United States Quartermaster Meigs refused to pay this extra price. Governor Morton at once announced that Indiana would bear the burden. Socks, shoes and blankets, together with underclothing of all kinds, were greatly needed, as well as mittens, sheets, pillows, bandages, dressing gowns and other things for hospital use. On the 10th of October, 1861, the governor issued an appeal to the women of Indiana. The response came very quickly, and many thousands of dollars worth of these supplies were contributed. Competent agents were appointed and sent to the best points to carry on this work of furnishing relief to our soldiers, especially to the sick and wounded. The sanitary stores were sent to them for distribution. Surgeons and nurses were sent to every place where Indiana troops were to be found. Combined with the sanitary service agents were sent out to take care of the pay of the soldiers and bring it home to their families without cost, to write letters for the soldiers, to see to the burial of the dead, and keep registers of all men in the hospitals and to assist returning soldiers to get transportation home. The headquarters of the commission was in Indianapolis, and during its existence, from February, 1862, to the close of the war, collected in cash $247,570.75, and in goods $359,000, making a total of sanitary contributions in the state of $606,570.75. This was the first sanitary work done by any state.

Indianapolis was the main depot and recruiting station for the state, and was the chief resting place of all troops passing

to the front. Governor Morton, in his solicitude for the soldiers, early in the war determined to make some arrangements whereby the troops passing through the city, or coming into it, could be temporarily provided for without cost to them. During the first months of the war the sanitary commission had agents at the union depot to supply passing troops and to take care of the sick at hotels, but this was expensive and inconvenient, and a camp was established on the vacant ground south of the depot with hospital tents and other conveniences, and maintained until 1862, when the governor determined to establish a permanent home. The grove on the west side of West street, just north of the Vandalia railroad, was selected and temporary frame buildings erected, which were enlarged from time to time until they could accommodate about two thousand with beds and furnish eight thousand with meals every day. From August, 1862, to June, 1865, the home furnished 3,777,791 meals. The bread was supplied by a bakery maintained by the quartermaster with such economy that the rations of flour, to which the men served in the home were entitled, sufficed for all they needed, and for thousands of loaves distributed among the poor. The saving of flour, after all bread supplies were completed, the sale of offal and a suttler's tax paid $19,642.19. The saving in the rations of other articles amounted to $71,130.24. Thus the home was sustained in all its expenses almost wholly by the rations of the men provided for in it. On holidays the ladies of the city furnished festival dinners of their own preparation, and waited on the tables. A Ladies' Home, for the care of soldiers' wives and children, was opened in a building near the union depot, in December, 1863, and was maintained until the close of the war, taking care of an average of about one hundred a day.

The good people of Indianapolis did not stop at these extraordinary provisions for the comfort and care of the soldiers, but the families left behind by the soldiers were equally well cared for, the city itself on several occasions appropriating large sums for the purchase of fuel and other necessaries for soldiers' families. On one occasion a fair was held that netted $40,000 for this purpose. Other fairs were held at different times, but none of them realized so great an amount. The good people of the county outside of Indianapolis were not behind in their patriotic offerings, and it was no uncommon sight to see long processions of wagons loaded with fuel and food contributed by the farmers of Marion county. They frequently turned the occasion into a holiday, parading the streets behind a drum and a fife.

During the war the city was not at all times peaceful and quiet. The excitement at all times was very high, and on the receipt of news from the front of some great battle it became intense. At the beginning of the war there was no open division of sentiment, but as the war went on, and taxes increased, and the call for troops became more urgent, a strong opposition to the further continuance of the war grew up. The city was always full of soldiers, and they could bear with but little patience words of opposition to the government, or of sympathy with the South. On a number of occasions it required the coolest and most determined efforts upon the part of the authorities to prevent violence and bloodshed. On one occasion, especially in 1862, some of the speakers at a county convention indulged in some very bitter denunciations of the war, the government and the soldiers. There were many soldiers in the crowd and a riot followed, some of the speakers and those sympathizing with them barely escaping with their lives. At the October election of that year the opponents of the war were excluded from the polls by threats of violence. In 1864 while one of the regiments was here on furlough, an attempt was made to mob the Sentinel office, but it was prevented by Col. Conrad Baker, provost marshal.

On two or three different occasions rebel raids were made into the state, and on such occasions the excitement grew in intensity. This was especially the case in 1863 when Gen. John Morgan crossed the Ohio river with about three thousand men,

THE COMMERCIAL CLUB.

and the news was flashed that his aim was to reach Indianapolis, and to overturn the state government and release the rebel prisoners at Camp Morton. Volunteers were called for, and the troops that were already in the city were hastened forward to intercept him. A horrible catastrophe accompanied this sudden movement of the troops. A Michigan battery which had been stationed here was hastening one day from the artillery camp to the depot when the jolting caused a shell to explode in one of the caissons. This exploded all the contents of the caisson, blowing two of the men over the tops of the shade trees along the sidewalk, killing them instantly. A man and a boy who were on the street watching the movement of the battery were also killed. This was the first catastrophe of the kind that had ever occurred in the city.

Since then the city has been visited by three catastrophes, each of which for the time being spread a pall of gloom over the entire city. The first occurred during the state fair of 1869. Two saw-mills were running a race on the first day of October of that year, receiving their power from the boiler in power hall. The boiler exploded and killed and wounded nearly one hundred people. The disaster would have been far more terrible if it had not been for the fact that a great part of the crowd had left the vicinity only a few moments before to witness one of the races. A large amount of money was soon after subscribed, and a committee of prominent citizens appointed to distribute it. The second occurred on March 17, 1890. On the afternoon of that day a fire broke out in the great book house of Bowen & Merrill, and while the fire was fiercely raging the roof and floor fell in, carrying to death ten of the gallant firemen. Nineteen others were injured at the same time, two of whom afterwards died. The news of the terrible accident soon spread throughout the city and thousands of anxious citizens crowded to the vicinity. The work of rescue began at once, but was materially interfered with by the fire and falling walls. On the second day after the fire, while a score or more of men were engaged in hunting for the bodies, one of the walls toppled and fell, covering the bodies with an additional depth of debris. Fortunately those engaged in the work of rescue received timely warning and all escaped without danger. In a very few moments, however, the news went abroad that they too had met their death, and it looked as if the whole city was rushing to the scene. The fire occurred on Monday, but it was not until Friday that the last body was removed. A relief fund for the benefit of the families of the killed and the wounded was immediately started, and soon reached the sum of about $70,000.

About midnight, on January 21, 1892, it was discovered that the Surgical Institute, which then occupied several old buildings on the corner of Illinois and Georgia streets, was on fire. It was filled with crippled men, women and children, the children largely predominating. When first discovered it was seen that Indianapolis was to have a night of horror. The buildings were soon wrapped in flames, and it was found imposible to rescue the alarmed inmates. Nineteen perished in the flames, and a large number of others were more or less seriously injured. Even the fatal Bowen & Merrill fire of two years before did not create such intense excitement.

Before the war ended, volunteering became so slow that it was necessary to resort to a draft to fill the ranks of the armies at the front. In several parts of the state the draft was resisted, and enrolling officers were assassinated, but nothing of that kind occurred in Indianapolis. In 1864 the city council appropriated $132,000 as bounty money for the city's quota of the draft, and on two other occasions appropriated $125,000 for a like purpose. When this money was about all paid out, and the quota was nearly full, it was discovered that by a blunder the war department had failed to give proper credits to the city, and the city's quota under all calls had already been more than filled, she having several hundred still to her credit.

While the city was rejoicing over the fall of Richmond and the surrender of Lee, the news came that President Lincoln had

INDIANAPOLIS BOARD OF TRADE.

been assassinated. Never within the history of the city had such excitement existed as was occasioned by this news. In almost an instant the news was spread over the whole city, and in another instant the streets were filled with an excited throng. Tears coursed down the cheeks of strong men as they stood on the streets discussing this terrible event. Deep anger was at once aroused against all who had been known to be opposed to the war, and it required the most strenuous exertion of Governor Morton and other high officials to prevent a riot that would have destroyed the property and lives of the known Southern sympathizers. A meeting was called of the citizens to take some appropriate action, and among others Senator Hendricks was called upon to address the crowd. During his remarks he began a sentence the first words of which did not please the audience, and a rush was made for the platform while a thousand men uttered cries of vengeance. Governor Morton and others stilled the angry crowd, and Senator Hendricks completed his sentence, showing that what he was saying was not offensive but on the other hand highly commendable. This incident is related simply to show how sensitive the people were in that time of excitement.

The city was dressed in mourning from one end to the other. The funeral cortege of the dead President was to pass through the city on its way to Springfield, and extensive arrangements were made to suitably receive it and pay due honor to this great statesman. The funeral train was expected to arrive here on Sunday morning April 30, 1865. Governor Morton, together with his staff, members of the legislature and the city council went to Richmond to meet the train and escort it to the city. Sunday morning came bringing with it a cold, drizzling rain, but before daylight thousands of people had congregated in and around the union depot to await the coming of the train. The immense crowd stood for hours talking in whispers. It seemed as if every one felt the awful solemnity of the occasion. At about seven o'clock the train slowly pulled into the station.

The coffin was tenderly lifted from the car in which it had rested, and was slowly borne to the catafalque which had been constructed for the purpose of conveying the body through the streets and to the state-house where it was to lie in state. A procession followed in solemn silence except the funeral music discoursed by the band, and the low sobbings of the multitude who lined the streets. The whole city was elaborately decorated with funeral emblems.

The body was placed on a platform erected under the dome of the capitol, and the citizens for hours marched through the great hall of that building, and gazed upon the face of the man they had learned to love, and whose guiding wisdom they would miss in the days to come. All day long and far into the night the throng continued its slow, and solemn tread. The falling rain seemed to have no influence in keeping any one away from the solemn scene. One of the most touching incidents of this occasion was the visit of the Sunday-school children of the city to view the remains. Proper arrangements had been made for their visit, and several thousands of them marched through the state-house and poured out their tears as a loving tribute to the memory of the martyred president. At one time the procession of citizens desiring to see the remains reached from the state-house doors for many squares up Washington street, and thousands stood in line, in the pouring rain, for several hours, waiting for their turn to enter the portals of the state-house. While this vast throng of citizens was viewing the remains funeral music was alternated between a band on one side and a choir of voices upon the other. A guard of honor, composed of the leading citizens and of army officers who were in the city, watched over the body. A little after midnight the doors of the state-house were closed and the body was taken again to the funeral train. It was estimated that fully 50,000 strangers were in the city on that day and that more than 100,000 persons passed through the state-house.

This was the last great scene of the war in Indianapolis.

INDIANA TRUST BUILDING.

The war soon ended and the troops came marching home. They were received into the city by Governor Morton and all honor paid them. It was not, however, for several months after the final surrender of the Confederate forces that the last of the troops arrived at home.

The close of the war found Indianapolis budding out into a real city. Its population had largely increased, and the impetus given to business put the city on a firmer foundation. The heavy taxes during the four years of war made necessary by the vast sums voted in aid of the soldiers and their families, and to encourage enlistments, had prevented anything like a systematic improvement of the streets and sidewalks, and at that time Indianapolis was about as dirty a town as could be found on the continent. Some new business houses and some residences had been built, and there was some little more pretentions to architectural effect than had been manifested in previous years. The influx of visitors, and the great number of soldiers that had been here at one time or another, had largely increased the volume of trade, and then, too, it had grown into a sort of a habit with many of the merchants in the smaller towns around Indianapolis to depend upon the merchants here for their supplies during the war, and that habit remained with them when peace came.

Up to the close of the war there had been no steps taken by the city to mark the growth of the city in any way, but in 1864 the council passed an ordinance requiring those proposing to build to take out permits, and since then there has been a record by which the changes could be noted. The war practically ended in May, 1865, but the doom of the Confederacy was certain before then, and as soon as spring opened the work of building began. The record shows that during the year 1865, 1,621 houses were built, at the cost of $2,060,000. That year the city began to improve the streets and sidewalks, and nine miles of streets and eighteen miles of sidewalks were graded and graveled. The next year 1,112 buildings were erected at a cost of $1,065,000. More of the streets and sidewalks were improved. In 1867 the street lights were largely extended, and the work of improvement continued. Since then the city has grown steadily, meeting with only one or two backsets.

In 1863 it became apparent that the existing cemetery for the disposal of the dead would very soon prove inadequate, and an organization of citizens was effected to purchase ground for a new cemetery. Mr. S. A. Fletcher, Sr., proposed to advance whatever money might be needed for such a purpose, and the grounds now known as "Crown Hill" were purchased. In 1864 the new cemetery was dedicated, Hon. Albert S. White delivering an oration.

Among other necessities occasioned by the growth of the city and the evil effects of the war was some house or home for abandoned women, and in 1863 an effort was made to establish one, Mr. Fletcher giving the ground, but after part of the work of constructing the building had been completed it was abandoned. In 1866 the ladies of the city formed an association to operate a Home for Friendless Women. They at first rented a house for their purposes, but not long afterward received gifts and help enough to erect a commodious building on Tennessee street, now Capitol avenue. In 1870 the building was partly destroyed by fire, but it has always been well managed and very successful.

Other charitable organizations have at different times been perfected, until now the poor and unfortunate of Indianapolis are well looked after and taken care of. In addition to what the city has done the state has erected, in connection with a female prison, a reformatory for girls, and so well has it been managed that it is ranked as the foremost institution of the kind in the United States.

In 1863 the first attempt was made to construct a street railroad. Two companies applied for a charter, and after a long delay and a bitter fight a charter was granted to the Citizens' Company, and by 1866 about seven miles of track was com-

BIRD'S-EYE VIEW LOOKING NORTH-EAST FROM MONUMENT.

pleted. The first line was that on Illnois street, and this was opened in June, 1864, the mayor of the city driving a car over it.

The close of the war also brought an era of railroad building, and by that time the citizens of Indianapolis were thoroughly alive to the advantages of such means of transportation, and in 1865 the council voted about $200,000 to aid in the construction of four roads.

Before the era of railroads the farmers of Indiana fed their corn to hogs and then drove the hogs to market, Cincinnati and Louisville being the chief markets, but in 1864 an enterprising firm of brothers, from Belfast, Ireland, concluded that Indianapolis was a good point for the establishment of a packing house on an immense scale. This introduction of the Kingan Brothers to Indianapolis proved to be an epoch in its growth and development. They erected immense buildings and opened business by the beginning of the season of 1864–5. In the spring of 1865, however, a fire destroyed a great part of their buildings, together with a large stock of lard, bulk meat and hams. The loss was about $240,000. They immediately rebuilt. In 1868 Mr. J. C. Ferguson erected a packing house but a little smaller than that of the Kingans, and from that time the business of packing meat has steadily grown until now it is one of the great industries of the city. Out of this increase of the packing industry grew the stock yards.

Among the lost opportunities of the city was one in 1868. At that time the Circle, University Square and Military Park, were the only spaces in the city for park purposes, and the city owned neither of those. They were anything but inviting at that time for parks, but as they did not belong to the city no one felt like having the city expend any money on them to improve them in any way. In 1868 the heirs of Calvin Fletcher offered to give the city thirty acres in the northeastern part, for park purposes, on the condition that the city should expend $30,000 to improve it, and keep it forever as a park. Most cities would have jumped at the chance of getting such a park on such easy terms, but, strangely, the proposition raised a storm of objections, even some of the newspapers joining in fighting the project. About the only ground of opposition was that the Fletchers owned other real estate in that vicinity and if a park was established there it would enhance the value of the other property. It was a sort of a dog in the manger policy that was a disgrace to the city then and will always remain a disgrace. Now the city is trying to purchase grounds for the establishment of parks, and will have to pay out large sums before they are obtained.

The growth of the city had begun before the close of the war, and continued steadily. Manufacturing establishments were erected, and wholesale houses opened. New streets were laid out and old ones improved. The residence portion of the city spread out on every hand. In 1870 the county had outgrown the old court-house, and it was determined to erect a new one, but a strong opposition arose among the citizens. All admitted that the old court-house was inadequate, but they objected to the heavy expense of erecting a new one. The work went on, however, and the present house was constructed. At the session of the legislature in 1875, steps were taken for the erection of a new state-house. The old one was too small, and besides had become very much dilapidated. After a considerable opposition from members from the out counties, it was ordered that plans and specifications be advertised for. In 1877 it was finally decided to erect a new building and the present handsome structure was the result. It was first used by the legislature at its session of 1887.

The growth of the city during 1869 and 1870 was so rapid that it created an era of real estate speculation which, in the end, proved disastrous not only to the city but to a large number of persons who engaged in it. Additions were laid out, in every direction, some of them being several miles from the then city limits. Not content with this, several suburban towns were started. For a while the people went wild and the prices of all

BIRD'S-EYE VIEW LOOKING WEST FROM MONUMENT.

real estate, both in the city and around it, rapidly advanced, until in some cases they reached enormous figures. The panic of '73 soon brought an end to this era of speculation, and it was several years before the city recovered from its effects. In fact even after affairs began to resume their normal condition the bad effects of this real estate boom remained and dragged down one or two of the oldest banking institutions in the city.

By 1884, however, the general tone of all business began to revive, and Indianapolis started out on an era of rapid growth, such as it had never experienced before and such as has been exceedingly rare even among "boom towns" in the West. Its growth since that time has not only been very rapid but has been permanent. The character of the architecture materially changed and it now can boast of as handsome business blocks, hotels, public buildings and residences as any city west of the mountains. Among its public buildings that of the Young Men's Christian Association may take high rank. This association was first organized on the 21st of March, 1854. It at once made arrangements to secure a regular course of lectures. It had many ups and downs until 1884, when it erected its present handsome building.

Among the generous citizens of Indianapolis some years ago was Mr. Daniel Tomlinson. After his death, on opening his will, it was found that he had devised a large amount of real estate and other property to the city for the erection of a public building, providing in his will that the building should be erected on the west end of what is known as East Market Square. The devise was accepted by the city and the bequest taken possession of Nothing was done, however, toward carrying out the wishes of the testator for several years. Some attempts were then made to use the money as intended by Mr. Tomlinson, but at every effort hostility was aroused, until at last the matter was made an issue at a city election. The council then took steps and the present Tomlinson Hall resulted.

Among the public buildings erected during the era of prosperity may be mentioned the English Opera House and the Grand Opera House. By these two structures the amusement loving public have been well accommodated. Old Washington Hall, which for many years stood as the great hotel of the city was opened in 1824. In 1841 the Palmer House, now known as the Occidental, was erected. It became at once the democratic headquarters and remained so for many years. Several other smaller hotels were built, and in 1853 Mr. Hervey Bates erected the Bates House, that since that time has stood as one of the best hotels in the country. In 1870 a stock company undertook to erect a large hotel on the southeast corner of Pennsylvania and Ohio streets. The work was not vigorously pushed, however, and the property fell into the hands of Harry Sheets. It was then an incomplete four story brick. It remained in this unfinished condition until 1874, when it was nearly destroyed by fire. A few years later John C. New and Mr. Denison purchased the ruins and completed the building in a much better style than had been originally contemplated. It was opened in January, 1880. In 1894 it was again damaged by fire, and was then enlarged, until now the Denison House ranks as one of the finest and most complete hotel buildings in the country. The Grand Hotel was begun some years after the Denison, but completed much sooner. It is not so large as the Denison, but is a very popular hostelry. The Denison is the Republican headquarters while the Grand is that of the Democrats.

Very early in the history of its railroads, the importance of having a union passenger station for all the roads became apparent to some of the enterprising citizens of Indianapolis, and steps were taken to erect one. This was the first station of the kind erected anywhere in the country. It served its purpose until 1887 when it became entirely too small, and it was determined to erect a larger and finer structure. This was completed in 1888, and was then thought to be large enough to supply all demands for many years. Its projectors, however, did not dream of the rapid growth of Indianapolis that was just then fairly

BIRD'S-EYE VIEW LOOKING NORTH-WEST FROM MONUMENT.

starting on its new era of prosperity, and now it is seen that a building of almost twice the size of the present one is as badly needed as a new and larger one was in 1887.

Not very long after the war Dr. H. R. Allen, and some others opened a surgical institute on the corner of Illinois and Georgia streets. In 1892 it was destroyed by fire and several of the patients burned to death. The institute company at once decided to construct a new building, and now one of the handsomest and most imposing structures in the west stands just north of the state-house and is occupied by the institute. It may well be mentioned among the public buildings of Indianapolis.

While Indianapolis can not boast of as costly residences as may be found in Cleveland, Cincinnati, Chicago, or St. Louis, yet neither of those cities can present more homelike or attractive residences than Indianapolis. Indianapolis may well be styled "the city of homes." Visitors always speak in the most glowing terms of the beautiful appearance of the Indianapolis residential streets. The architecture is varied, presenting a most pleasing appearance to the eye, while the well kept and well shaded lawns give an air of comfort seldom found in the limits of cities. These shaded lawns in some part do away with the necessity of parks, as even the homes of the working classes can boast of their lawns.

Indianapolis is a city of churches. A bird's-eye view of the city will show tall spires rising like forest trees in every direction. Every denomination is represented, and Indianapolis can boast of a church-going people. The Catholics, Methodists and Presbyterians predominate, but all other denominations have good congregations, and some have very fine church buildings.

The literary, musical and art culture is not behind its religious and moral standing. The state library has elegant quarters in the state-house, and for several years has been liberally dealt with by the legislature, in furnishing money for the purchase of new books, and is now rapidly becoming an institution the state can take pride in. The city library occupies a handsome and imposing new building on the corner of Meridian and Ohio streets, and is very popular with the public. Its reading-rooms are almost constantly filled with persons consulting the papers, periodicals, and other works. In music Indianapolis is rapidly forging to the front. On the completion of Tomlinson Hall, a May Festival Association was formed by some of the enterprising citizens, and now annually a musical festival of the highest order is held. In 1895, John Herron, a public-spirited citizen, by will devised to the city a large amount for the establishment of an Art Academy. This fund has not yet been made available, but there is no doubt that in the near future the city will have a handsome structure for the use of students of art.

Indianapolis is fast developing into a club city. The most important of the clubs, as it is the most potent aid for the rapid growth of the city, is the Commercial Club. It was organized to promote the growth of the city, and its membership is composed of the leading business men. It was organized in 1890, and soon after erected a handsome building on South Meridian street. Much of the rapid advance of the city within the last six years has been due to the efforts of this association. The Columbia Club is a political organization of Republicans, and has a handsome building of its own on Monument Place. The ladies, not to be behind, in 1889 determined to erect a club house, and now have as handsome a structure as there is in the city. There are a number of other clubs, for literary, musical or other purposes, but none own their own buildings.

When the war ended, the military spirit died out. The old soldiers had had enough of marching, of camping, of actual war, and did not feel inclined to engage in the imitation of the actual thing. The younger people did not show any desire to play at soldiering. An attempt was made to revive a military spirit, a few years after the war, but it was not until 1881 that much was done. A number of companies were soon formed, and in 1882

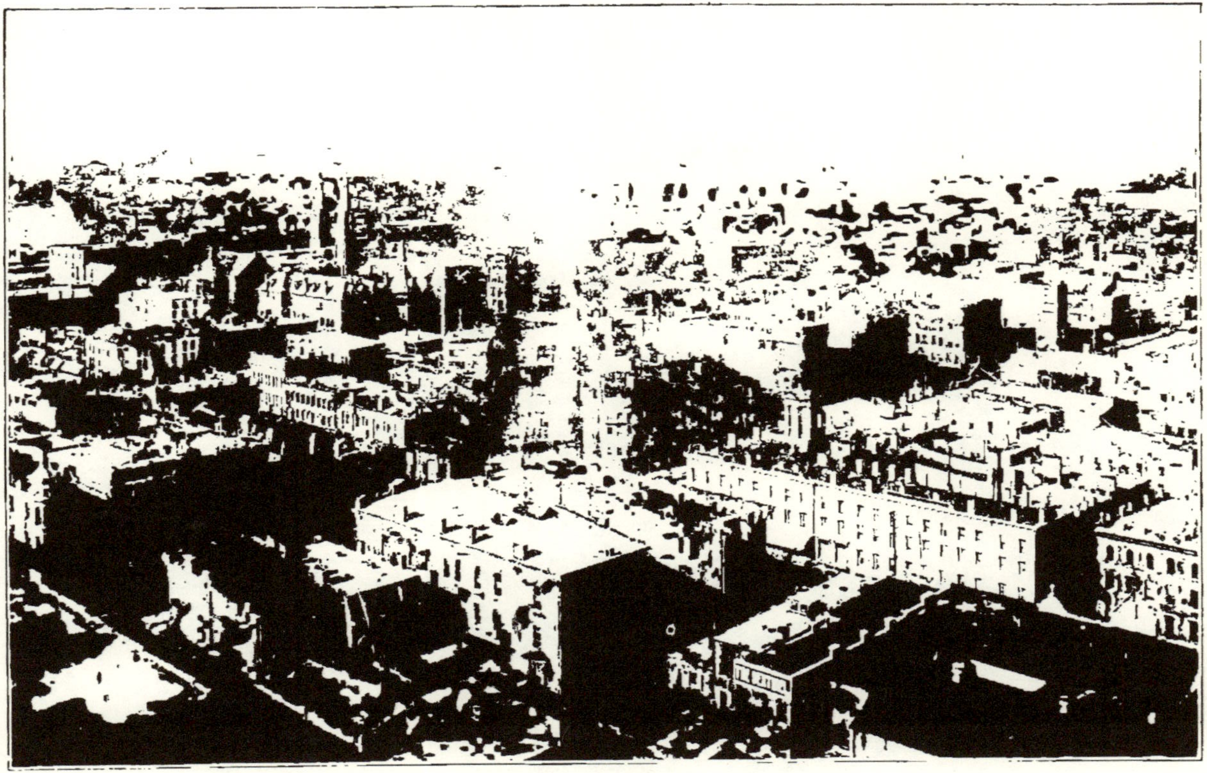

BIRD'S-EYE VIEW LOOKING SOUTH-WEST FROM MONUMENT.

a grand encampment and prize drill was held, under the auspices of the "Raper Commandery" of the Masonic order. A number of famous companies from other states took part, among them being the Crescent Rifles, of New Orleans; the Louisiana Rifles, of the same city; the Chickasaw Guards, of Memphis; the Porter Rifles, Nashville; the Quapaw Guards, of Little Rock; Company G, First Missouri, and two other companies from the same state; one company from Geneva, New York; four from Illinois; three from Ohio; two from Michigan; two batteries from New Orleans; one from Nashville; one from Louisville; one from Danville, Ill.; one from Chicago and two from St. Louis. Twenty companies from Indiana took part. The following year another encampment and prize drill was held, in which thirty-six companies from Indiana participated, with several from other states. The Indianapolis Light Infantry, and the Indianapolis Light Artillery have participated in a number of prize drills in other places, and have taken a large number of prizes. In addition to this, the Raper Commandery of Knights Templar carried off the second prize at the great contest at San Francisco.

In 1882 the G. A. R. held its annual encampment in the city, and many thousand old soldiers participated. In 1893 the encampment was again held here, the attendance being estimated at 75,000. On that occasion the city appropriated a large sum of money to properly care for and entertain the veterans. The state camps of the G. A. R. early took up the idea of erecting a monument to commemorate the story of the war, and quite a sum was raised for that purpose. This idea was first broached by Governor Morton in a message to the legislature in 1867. He wanted it placed on the high hill in Crown Hill cemetery. He said:

"I recommend that upon this hill the state erect a monument in memory of her brave soldiers who perished in the rebellion. We can not pay too much honor to the memory of the men who died for their country. This monument, overlooking all the country around, would be the first object to greet the eye of the traveler as he approached the capital, and in the language of the great Webster, when he laid the corner-stone of the Bunker Hill monument at Boston, 'Let it rise! let it rise! till it meets the sun on its coming; let the earliest light of the morning gild it, and parting day linger and play upon its summit.'"

The movement did not take shape, however, until 1887, when the legislature was asked to appropriate $200,000 for that purpose. The appropriation was made and a commission appointed to carry out the plan, the Circle being selected as the site. The monument proper has been completed, but some of the accompanying figures are yet to be put in place. Prior to this, however, a statue had been erected to Governor Morton by private subscription. The city has two other statues, one of Hon. Schuyler Colfax in University Park, erected by the Odd Fellows, and one of Hon. Thomas A. Hendricks, in the state-house grounds. Around the monument in the Circle are grouped statues of Gen. William Henry Harrison, Gen. George Rogers Clark, and Governor James Whitcomb.

INDIANAPOLIS AT PRESENT.

A COMPREHENSIVE OUTLINE DESCRIPTION OF THE WHOLE CITY—AREA, POPULATION, WEALTH, STATISTICS, ETC.

Indianapolis is to-day the largest inland city on the American continent, and one of the most important railroad centers in this country. It is, too, one of the handsomest cities, and one of the most prosperous and progressive. Its growth has been practically that of only two decades. Within that time it has emerged from a rambling village-like town, into a city of magnificent business blocks, public buildings, and handsome residences—in short, has become a progressive, prosperous city, recognized as such in all parts of the United States.

The Area actually within the city is about twenty square miles. The original plat was one mile square, and for many years after the first laying off of the town it kept within those bounds. Now and then an adventurous citizen, wanting more room, or desiring to have the advantages of the city, without paying tax therefor, would erect a residence on an out-lot, but it looked as if it was hard work to fill up the original square mile. When the war came it found Indianapolis still within the original limits, and with plenty of room vacant therein. The war brought many changes. It brought Indianapolis into notice through the activity of its citizens in raising troops, and their generosity in caring for them and their families, and when the war ended, and people began to look around for new locations, the situation of Indianapolis attracted attention. It was already quite a railroad center, but the usefulness of those great highways was not thoroughly appreciated. The city began to grow, and in growing widened out. The old plat was filled and additions began to look forward to a time when their vacant lots would also be filled with a thriving, bustling population. It was not until 1870 that the city really began to reach out with a conception that it might become in time a great commercial and manufacturing center. Then an era of speculation seized upon the people, and discretion fled to the woods. The result was a set-back, that took years to overcome. By 1880, however, the tide had again turned, and since then the growth of the city has been rapid and steady. While not under the jurisdiction of the city, yet several outlying suburbs are, to all intents and purposes, parts of Indianapolis. They contain a large population and much wealth, and it will only be a matter of time when they will be integral parts of the city.

The Population has grown in a wonderful manner during the last twenty years. In 1870 the population was 36,565; in 1880 it had grown to more than double that, reaching 75,074. In 1890 it showed another great advance, the returns showing 128,000, and it is now believed that by the time the next census is taken it will have passed the 200,000 mark. All this marvellous growth has been made by an actual influx of people, and not by reaching out and taking in towns, cities and villages, as has been done by other cities. This population is legitimate, it is the population of Indianapolis. The people have come here to go into business, to become a part of the great inland city. Nearly every nationality on the globe is represented in this population. Of the foreign born the Germans predominate, closely followed by the Irish. The population is industrious and thrifty, there being fewer idle men in Indianapolis than in any other city of its size. Hundreds of workingmen own their own homes, and while there is not in the city any great aggregation of wealth, as is found in the other large cities of the country, there is not that depth of poverty to be found. Indianapolis is a happy medium between great wealth and great poverty.

Greater Indianapolis will soon begin to be talked about. Around the city are West Indianapolis, Haughville, North Indianapolis, Irvington and Brightwood, that are now closely connected by rapid transit, and in fact it is almost one continuous city from West Indianapolis to Irvington. All those thriving suburbs are closely identified with the capital city, and it will not be long before they will of themselves be asking for the fire, police and other protection of the city. The question of uniting them all under the same postal system has already been discussed by the Postmaster-General, and when they are brought into the corporation limits of the city, Indianapolis will rank in population among the first cities of the country.

The Surroundings of Indianapolis are not so picturesque as those of many of the other cities of the country, but as it is the political center of the state, so is it the business center, and its admirable system of railroads makes the territory for seventy-five or a hundred miles in every direction tributary to it. It is in easy reach of the great coal fields, of the gas belt, and of the stone quarries that have made Indiana famous. It is in the very heart of an agricultural region unsurpassed anywhere. It has no navigable river, nor great lake to bring the commerce of the world to its doors, but without such adventitious aid, its manufacturers are now shipping their wares to every civilized nation.

The Municipal Administration is conducted by a mayor and the heads of various departments. The mayor is elected by a popular vote for the term of two years, and he appoints the members of the various boards. Municipal

BIRD'S-EYE VIEW LOOKING SOUTH FROM MONUMENT.

legislation is in the hands of a council composed of twenty-one members. fifteen of whom are elected by wards and the other six by the city at large.

Public Buildings—Indianapolis deservedly ranks high, although the city proper owns but three. Being the capital of the state it has had the benefit of the state's bounty in the direction of public buildings. The state-house is an elegant structure, covering about two acres of ground. It is built of Indiana Oolitic limestone, the interior being finished in marble. It was erected only a few years ago, at a total cost of about $2,000,000, being the only public building in the country completed within the original estimate of the cost. It stands on a plot of ground of about eight acres in extent, and has four broad entrances. It is three stories high, and contains elegantly appointed rooms for all of the state officers, halls for the two houses of the general assembly, with a sufficient number of committee rooms, rooms for the state library, the supreme court of the state and its library, and for the state board of agriculture. It is heated by approved devices and lighted by electricity. The state also has here a large hospital for the insane, accommodating about one thousand five hundred patients; an asylum for the blind, and one for deaf mutes, and a reformatory for girls. These

ENGLISH MONUMENT, CROWN HILL.

buildings are all capacious and handsomely constructed, and the grounds around them are cared for with great attention. The county court-house, costing about $1,750,000, is also located here. Tomlinson hall, owned by the city, was the gift of the late Daniel Tomlinson. It is an imposing structure and is capable of seating about 4,000. The city library is in a very handsome new building located in the very heart of the city. The city hospital is one of the best arranged buildings for such a purpose in the country. All the school houses are of modern structure and most of them are ornamental. The two high school buildings are especially attractive.

The City Finances, according to the last report of the comptroller, for the year ended December 31, 1895, shows the receipts, from taxes, $648,975; from all other sources, $438,545, making the total receipts, $1,086,975. The total expenditures were $1,072,952. The total bonded indebtedness January 1, 1897, was $1,434,500. This bonded indebtedness bears a low rate of interest. The expenditures for 1896 were: Police, $116,824.26; fire department, $187,-523.47; public works, $395,348.06; miscellaneous, $229,324.61. The estimated expenditures for the year 1897, $929,015.40.

The Judiciary is partly under city authority, and partly under that of the state. It is all elective. The police judge is elected for a term of two years, and has a salary of $2,500. He has exclusive jurisdiction of all cases for violations of the city ordinances, and concurrent jurisdiction with the county criminal court in cases of petit larceny and other violations of the statutes of the state where the punishment does not exceed a fine of $500 or imprisonment for more than six months. The judge of the criminal court is elected by the people, for a term of four years, and has a salary of $2,500 per year. It has original jurisdiction in all cases arising from violations of the state laws. The superior court has three judges, each elected for four years, at a salary of $3,000 per annum. It has jurisdiction in all civil cases, except slander and probate matters. The circuit court, having similar jurisdiction, but including slander and probate matters, has a judge elected for six years with an annual salary of $2,500. There are also a number of justices of the peace, having limited jurisdiction.

The Police Department is under the control of the board of public safety, and comprises one chief, two captains, eight sergeants, and one hundred patrolmen. In addition there is a detective force, consisting of one chief and eight detectives. The arrests average about 6,000 yearly.

The Fire Department has one hundred and thirty-one employes; six steam fire engines, three hook and ladder trucks, three chemical engines, one water tower, and sixty-eight horses, fourteen wagons and hose reels. There are 145 miles of wire and 172 signal-boxes for the fire alarm telegraph.

The Executive and administrative authority of the city is vested in the mayor, city clerk, and certain boards. The mayor receives a salary of $4,000 per annum.

The Department of Finance is under the charge of the comptroller, who

STATE HOUSE.

is appointed by the mayor, with a salary of $3,000. All warrants on the treasury must be drawn by him.

The Department of Law is under the charge of the attorney and counsel of the city, appointed by the mayor. He has a salary of $4,000 per annum.

The Department of Public Works consists of three commissioners appointed by the mayor. The board has control of the streets and all public buildings of the city. Each commissioner has a salary of $2,000 a year, and their expenditures amount to $395,348.06 per annum for 1896.

COLFAX STATUE.

The Board of Public Safety consists of three commissioners appointed by the mayor, at a salary of $600 each. This board has control of the police and fire departments.

The Department of Health and Charities consists of a board of three commissioners appointed by the mayor. The board has direct control of all regulations for public health. The members of the board must be physicians.

The Department of Parks is composed of five commissioners appointed by the mayor. for five years, and who serve without compensation. They have charge of all the public parks.

The Number of Buildings, including dwelling houses, in the city, and business houses, makes a total of 35,000. In 1895 nine hundred and ninety-three residences were built, fifty-three business blocks, five churches, seventeen factories and nine warehouses, besides a number of other structures, at a cost of $2,868,695. In 1896, 651 residences, 81 business blocks, and the total value of building permits was $2,241,758.

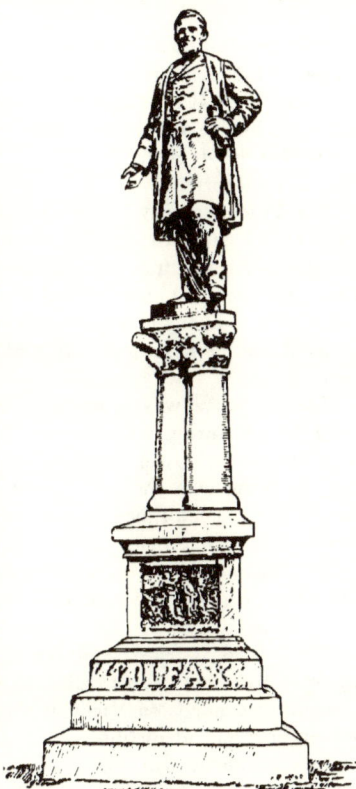

Streets and Sewers—The total length of the streets of the city is about 335 miles, of which forty-five miles are paved with asphaltum, brick or cedar blocks, and the rest is graveled. There are seventy-one miles of sewers, of which fifty miles have been constructed within the last five years, at a cost of more than $4,000,000. The streets are lighted by gas and electricity, there being about 850 electric lights.

The Water Supply comes from deep wells, some few miles from the city, and is brought to the city through large iron mains, and supplied to the houses by direct pressure from the pump house. The supply is abundant for all purposes. Coming from deep wells it is as pure as can be furnished in any city.

The Railways of Indianapolis reach to every part of the country. They number sixteen, and all enter and leave from the same passenger station Over one hundred and thirty passenger trains enter and depart every twenty-four hours.

The Belt Railroad—One of the most important features of the railroad system of Indianapolis is the Belt line which connects all the railroads which enter the city. It runs about three-fourths of the way around the entire city, and along its line are many of the most important manufacturing establishments, and the stock yards. Over it all freight passing from one road to another is transported.

The Union Railway Lines—Early in the railroad history of Indianapolis some of her enterprising citizens and railroad managers conceived the idea of bringing all the lines into one central passenger station. To this end the Union Railway Company was chartered, and tracks through the city were laid. This company now owns and manages the great Union Station, wherein about one hundred and fifty trains enter and depart every twenty-four hours.

The Street Railway System—Electricity is used as the motive power for rapid transit through the streets. The system reaches to every part of the city. The electric roads extend to all the suburbs, giving ready access to the city for those who dwell in the outlying districts. Strangers arriving in the city can reach all the hotels or any point of interest from the Union railway station by street cars, either direct or by transfer, for one fare.

The Custom House is a very important adjunct to the trade of the city. The value of goods imported into the district of Indianapolis for the fiscal year ending June 30, 1896, was $456, 625.

The United States Arsenal Grounds comprise seventy-six acres, extending from Michigan street to Clifford avenue at the eastern limit of the city. The entrance gate is on Michigan street at the head of Arsenal avenue. The present government institution was laid out in 1863 and finished in 1868. The seven buildings of the arsenal are of brick and stone. The most important are the main storehouse, the artillery storehouse and the barracks. There are also residences for the officers stationed there.

The Banks include three national banks, with a capital of $1,600,000. and resources of $9,413,554.83; two private banks, with a capital of $1,200,000, and resources of $5,155,867,44. and three trust companies with a capital of $1,900,000 and resources of $2,816,682.14.

The Indianapolis Clearing House Association showed bank clearings for 1896 amounting to $204,576,890.29.

Office Buildings—There are several very fine office buildings, with all the modern conveniences. Among the most notable are: The Majestic, the

MARION COUNTY COURT HOUSE.

Lombard, the Fitzgerald, the Lemcke, the Thorpe, the Ingalls, the Indiana Trust Building, the Stevenson, and others.

Manufacturing—Every railroad on the continent has transported manufactured wares from Indianapolis, and every line of ocean steamers touching the shores of the United States has borne to foreign lands the product of her industries. Various manufactories in the city have built up a large and steady trade in foreign countries. Shipments of flouring mills, engines, chemicals, canned goods, bicycles, pork, woodenware, woolen goods and other products of our factories to Canada, Mexico, the South American States, Australia, Europe, the Sandwich Islands, South Africa and Asia as well, are of so frequent occurrence as to have become common and are no longer thought worthy of special note. There are eleven hundred separate manufacturing establishments located here, the number of employes in the different lines of production ranging from scores to thousands, and the total number of persons employed in manufacturing in the city reaching at least twenty-five thousand. The value of the combined production of all the manufactories in the city is estimated at about $70,000,000 a year.

DRINKING FOUNTAIN, FOOT OF VIRGINIA AVE.

The Wholesale Trade—Indianapolis, with her sixteen railroads, is brought into direct and prompt communication with fully a thousand cities and towns for which she is the natural base of supplies. The thickly settled and prosperous agricultural communities which form a zone a hundred miles wide all around, send up a never satisfied demand for the necessaries and comforts of life. Millions of people are to be fed, and clothed, and housed, and every law of trade and geographical consideration fix Indianapolis as the place.

As a natural course of events the wholesale and jobbing business of Indianapolis is in a flourishing state. A trip through the wholesale district, along South Meridian, South Pennsylvania, South Delaware, Maryland, Georgia or McCrea streets, will impress this deeply on your memory. The rumble of heavily laden drays, the sidewalks blocked by mountains of boxes and crates and bales, the hurry and confusion of porters rolling the goods about, the short, sharp commands of men directing the work, all together impart a sense of an important business movement. That this impression is not a mistaken one is proven by the fact that the sales of the wholesale merchants of Indianapolis aggregate, in round numbers, $45,000,000 a year. There are in the city over three hundred wholesale and jobbing houses, and, in their employ, over one thousand traveling salesmen. It is a noteworthy fact that Indianapolis merchants have carried their trade into the very gates of surrounding cities, and have established strong business connections beyond them. They have gone beyond Louisville and Cincinnati, and built up a strong trade in the South. They have gone into Michigan and found permanent patrons within a few miles of Detroit. They have beaten Chicago in Michigan. They have invaded Ohio and Illinois, and a large per cent. of their entire business is done in these two states. They have pushed beyond St. Louis and Kansas City, and annually send large quantities of goods west of the Missouri river. The city is especially strong in its wholesale dry goods, millinery, drugs, hardware, grocery and confectionery trades. The volume of business done in these lines is enormous. The summing up of all is, that whatever is to be purchased for the retail trade may be obtained in Indianapolis cheaply and promptly, and with the smallest amount of risk in transportation.

Papers and Periodicals—There are seven daily newspapers, two of which are printed in German. There are twenty-eight weekly and thirty monthly and semi-monthly periodicals. All the varied social, religious, literary, political and business interests are served by the periodicals.

Amusements—Indianapolis has two opera-houses, first-class in appointments and of a high grade. It also contains several theaters of the vaudeville class.

Clubs—A number of social, political, and professional clubs are maintained. The most prominent is the Commercial club, composed of the business men and occupying a magnificent eight-story building of its own. Among the noted political clubs are, The Columbia and Marion, Republican, and Gray, Democratic. The ladies have a club and occupy their own building, the Propylæum, a beautiful stone structure. Das Deutsche Haus is the finest club building in the city. There are a number of literary clubs, but none of them owning their own club house.

Hotels and Cafes—For a city of its size Indianapolis is well supplied with hotels. Three of them, at least, have a reputation throughout the entire country. The Denison, for several years, has been known as the Republican headquarters, while the Grand has been that of the Democrats. The Bates

TOMLINSON HALL.

house has long been known as one of the first hotels in the West. Hotel English, which has just been remodeled, is now one of the most attractive hotels in the state. There are also the Spencer House and Hotel Normandie, which are also popular hostelries. Prominent among a large number of restaurants may be mentioned the Commercial Club restaurant and the Normandie Cafe, where the service is good and at moderate rates. In addition to these are a number of smaller hotels, all well kept and well patronized.

Thoroughfares, Parks and Adornments—Indianapolis is yet too young a city to be expected to have done very much in the way of adornment, but it can lay claim to some as handsome streets as any city in the country. At the original platting, with the evident intent to give the people plenty of light and air, the streets were made very broad. In some of the later additions to the city the streets have been somewhat narrowed, for the purpose of reducing the cost of maintaining them, but still they are broad enough to give plenty of room for abundant shade and adornment.

CROWNING FIGURE SOLDIERS' AND SAILORS' MONUMENT.

Washington Street is the main street of the city running east and west. It is 120 feet from curb to curb, with sidewalks of proportionate width. Along this street from Capitol avenue, on the west, to Alabama, on the east, is conducted the leading retail trade of the city. It is crossed at right angles by numerous streets and from it running to the southeast and to the southwest are two broad avenues. Many of the business blocks are of modern style and structure and some of them are very imposing in appearance. The extreme width of the street and the sidewalks makes it a grand avenue for parades. Notwithstanding the retail business transacted on the street is very large it never has the appearance of being crowded. This, with nearly all the principal streets of the city, is paved with asphaltum, but some of the residence streets are paved with cedar blocks, and a few with brick.

Meridian Street is divided into two parts, north and south, the dividing line being Washington street. It is the center street of the original plat of the city, and extends from the extreme southern part to the extreme northern, a distance of nearly five miles. South Meridian street from Washington to the Union railway tracks is devoted almost exclusively to the wholesale trade. Nearly all the buildings are of modern style and conveniences. North Meridian street from Ohio to the extreme northern limit of the city is devoted to residences and churches. It is beautifully shaded throughout its entire length, and in the summer time presents a beautiful woodland scene. The residences are all set back some distance from the street, having well shaded and well cared for lawns in front of them, giving to each one of them a villa-like appearance. Other notable residence streets are Pennsylvania, Delaware, Alabama, Broadway, Park avenue, College avenue and Capitol avenue North.

Adornments—We might well class the beautiful shade trees of the streets and the picturesque lawns of the residences as a part of the adornment to the city. In these two particulars no city in the country surpasses Indianapolis. Washington surpasses it in shaded streets, but that beautiful city woefully lacks the lawns in front of the residences. Nowhere in Indianapolis are found those long rows of houses, built all alike, and fronting directly on the street, but nearly every residence sits on a lawn of its own with fresh air and light all around it, thus adding to the health and comfort of the people and the beauty of the city.

The Indiana State Soldiers' and Sailors' Monument—Indianapolis has the proud distinction of containing the first monument ever erected directly in honor of the private soldier. It is also one of the few real works of art in this line to be found in America. It is not a plain and unsightly shaft like that on Bunker Hill or in Washington City, but is a beautiful obelisk of artistic design. It was designed by Bruno Schmidt, the great German architect. Its construction was authorized by an act of the general assembly of the state of Indiana, and passed at the session of 1887. This act appropriated the sum of $200,000 to defray the cost of erection, and empowered certain of the state officers to appoint five commissioners who should have charge of the work. In addition to the amount appropriated by the legislature, the sum raised by the monument committee of the G. A. R. was paid over to the commissioners to be expended by them. In 1891 the state legislature made a further appropriation of $100,000 to aid in the construction. The monument is situated in the very heart of the city on a circle of ground that was originally designed for the residence of the governor. It is constructed of Indiana oolitic limestone. The park in which it stands has an area of 3 and $\frac{12}{100}$ acres, and lies at the intersection of Meridian and Market streets. It is surrounded by a circular street, paved with asphalt. There are four approaches to the monument from the surrounding street, the approaches on the north and south sides leading directly to the stairway by which the terrace surrounding the base of the pedestal shaft is reached. The monument, including crowning figure, is 268 feet in height. The top of the monument is reached by an elevator and stairway from the base of the interior of the

shaft. A magnificent view of the city of Indianapolis and the surrounding country is obtained from the top of the monument.

Morton Statue—In front of the soldiers' monument and facing southward stands a fine bronze statue of Oliver P. Morton, the great war governor of the state. It was erected by the voluntary subscriptions of the people in 1884. The designer was Franklin Simmons, of Rome, Italy, and it was cast there.

Geo. Rogers Clark Statue—At the western entrance of Monument Circle is a bronze statue of Gen. George Rogers Clark, the great hero of Kaskaskia and Vincennes. It was erected by the state as an accompaniment of the soldiers' monument.

DEITCH MAUSOLEUM—JEWISH CEMETERY.

James Whitcomb Statue—At the North entrance of the circle stands a bronze statue of Governor James Whitcomb, who was governor of the state during the Mexican war, and was long one of its most distinguished citizens. It was erected at the expense of the state.

William Henry Harrison Statue—Facing the east is another of the group of the four distinguished citizens chosen to accompany this great monument to the Indiana soldiery. It is a bronze statue of Gen. William Henry Harrison, who for many years was governor of the Indiana Territory, and who commanded at the battle of Tippecanoe, and who afterwards became president of the United States. The designer of this, the Harrison and Clark statues, was John H. Mahoney, of Indianapolis.

Schuyler Colfax Statue—The first citizen of Indiana to reach the vice-presidential chair was Schuyler Colfax, who had served three terms as speaker of the national house of representatives. He was a leading member of the Odd Fellows, and to his memory that organization has erected a bronze statue in University Park. It was erected in 1887. The designer was Laredo Taft of Chicago.

Thomas A. Hendricks Statue—Governor, senator and vice-president of the United States, Thomas A. Hendricks was one of the distinguished sons of Indiana, and to him the people of the state have erected a bronze statue in the southeast corner of the state-house grounds. It was erected by popular subscription, and unveiled in July, 1890. The statue itself is fourteen feet six inches high, and the monument as a whole has a height of thirty-eight feet six inches. The statue is of bronze; the pedestal is of Bavano granite from the quarries at lake Maggiore, Italy. Two allegorical statues representing "History" and "Peace" stand upon the base of the monument to its right and left. The monument was designed by R. H. Parks, of Florence, Italy.

Military Park lies between New York street and the Indiana Central Canal on the north and south, and West and Blackford streets on the east and west, and includes fourteen acres. In the early days of the city's history it was known as the "**Military** Reservation," and was the place where the militia musters were held. All the military companies of the city during the pioneer days camped and drilled there, and at the time of the Blackhawk outbreak 300 Indiana militia camped there before marching to Chicago. It was also the first camping ground of Indiana's quota of six regiments under President Lincoln's first call for troops, and throughout the war it was used as a camp ground. The park was then known as Camp Sullivan. Many of the old forest trees still stand, with some hundreds of younger growth. A large fountain is situated in the center of the park at the meeting place of the converging pathways. Reached by Blake street and Haughville cars.

University Park comprises four acres, lying between Pennsylvania and Meridian streets on the east and west, and Vermont and New York streets on the north and south. It was the site of a university that flourished from 1834 to 1846, and thus acquired its name. A statue of Schuyler Colfax stands in the southwestern side. Reached by North Pennsylvania street cars.

St. Clair Park adjoins the grounds of the Institution for the Blind on the north, from Meridian to Pennsylvania streets, extending to St. Clair street. It is four acres in extent, and in its center there is a fountain. Reached by North Pennsylvania street cars.

Garfield Park is the largest park within the limits of the city. It lies to the extreme south, and covers 110 acres. It is the most pleasing bit of landscape in the immediate neighborhood of Indianapolis. The principal driveway is over what was once one of the best known race tracks in the country. A small stream winds through the park. Reached by Alabama street and Garfield Park cars.

Fairview Park, seven miles northwest of the city, is a beautiful expanse of about 200 acres of wooded hills and ravines overlooking White river and the Indiana Central Canal. It is reached by two lines of electric cars running at intervals of five minutes, and is a favorite outing place on summer

WASHINGTON STREET LOOKING EAST.

evenings. A restaurant is located there, with bowling alleys, boat livery and various other means of amusement. Concerts are given in the park several times a week during the summer months.

Woodruff Place, nominally a town, but really a park, lies within the limits of the city, yet is not a part of it. It adjoins the Arsenal grounds on the east, and stretches from Michigan street to Clifford avenue. It is a most beautiful residence park. Many fountains and pieces of statuary are in it. Reached by Clifford avenue street cars.

The State Fair Grounds embrace a tract of 160 acres, three miles northeast of the city. Reached by street cars.

Armstrong Park is two miles northwest of the city, upon the bank of the canal. It is beautifully wooded, and a favorite boating resort. Reached by North Indianapolis street cars.

Churches and Missions—There are in all in Indianapolis 175 places of worship, including regularly organized churches and missions representing almost every denomination and creed. Millions of dollars have been expended in the erection of church property, and many of the buildings are the most elegant types of church architecture. The strongest denominations are the Methodist Episcopal, Presbyterian, Baptist, Roman Catholic, Protestant Episcopal, Christian, Lutheran and Jewish, and there are numerous others which have one or more congregations each in the city. Some of the most eminent divines which the country has produced have passed a part of their lives in Indianapolis. One instance is the years of Henry Ward Beecher's pastorate, also that of Myron W. Reed.

GEORGE ROGERS CLARK.

The Charities—Several organizations are maintained for charitable work, and labor very effectively in relieving the poor and suffering. Homes are maintained for orphan children, for friendless women, and for the aged, besides hospitals for the treatment of the afflicted. In addition there is a summer sanitarium for the purpose of furnishing fresh air, nourishment, and medical treatment to sick children. These charities are all maintained by private contributions, with the exception that the city makes an annual allowance to the Orphan Homes and to the Home for Friendless Women.

Religious Work is carried on by several societies outside of the churches.

The most prominent society is the Young Men's Christian Association, which has a fine building of its own, and a large membership. It occupies a broad field of usefulness in promoting the spiritual, intellectual, social and physical welfare of the community. It supports one branch especially for railroad employes.

The Hospitals of Indianapolis rank with those of any other city in their care and management. The city maintains one at which about 1,500 persons are treated annually. A regular corps of physicians and surgeons is maintained at a total cost of about $35,000 a year. In addition to this the city maintains a free dispensary, where patients are treated and medicines furnished free. About 14,000 persons are treated annually. The Sisters of Mercy also maintain a hospital where large numbers are treated each year.

Crown Hill Cemetery, covering 400 acres of ground, three and one-half miles northwest of the city, in which is the national cemetery in which are buried the Union soldiers who died in Indianapolis, and also those whose bodies were brought here for interment. There, among the soldiers for whose welfare he worked so tirelessly, lies the body of Governor Morton. No more beautiful cemetery can be found in the country than Crown Hill.

Other Cemeteries are the Roman Catholic, Greenlawn, German Lutheran, Jewish and Lutheran.

Schools and Libraries—The streets and highways of Indianapolis had hardly been staked off by the surveyor, when the few people who had gathered here at this embryo capital of the state began to look around and make some arrangements for the education of the children. At that time there was no provision for public, or free schools, and the only means for education were by private or "subscription" schools. The first building devoted to education in the city was erected at the intersection of Kentucky avenue and Washington and Illinois streets. From that little beginning has developed the great school system of Indianapolis which has made the Indiana capital take high rank in educational matters among the cities of the country. The magnificently endowed school fund of the state of Indiana, and the open-handed liberality of the people of Indianapolis, have united in building ud the present great free school system. Just when Indianapolis first began to feel the impetus of the legislation in favor of free schools it received a severe set back by an adverse decision of the supreme court. It was just emerging from the first crude efforts to establish free schools, and was getting on a higher place when this decision came. Graded schools were being established in different parts of the city, and the "old seminary," wherein many of the youth in the early days of the city had been prepared for college, had been changed into a high school under the jurisdiction of the city. Hope was bright, and the young city was buoyant with expectations of the future of the new school system, when the courts decided that the taxation provided for by the legislature was illegal, and the schools were compelled to depend for their maintenance on what was received from the general school fund. In consequence of this decision the schools languished for some years, but

HIGH SCHOOL NO. 1.

after awhile a brighter day dawned, and once again the people were permitted to tax themselves to maintain schools for the general education of their children. From that day the progress has been steady and rapid. The city has been fortunate in its selection of those chosen to have general management and control of this great interest. One idea has been steadily before them, and that was to bring the schools up to the highest grade possible while at the same time furnishing ample provision to accommodate all the

HIGH SCHOOL NO. 2.

children. For the school year of 1895–6, the number of school children enrolled in the city was 27,663. Under the law all persons between the ages of six and twenty-one are entitled to school privileges. During the school year of 1895–6, there belonged to the schools 17,094. The average daily attendance during the year was 15,939. The school year opens in September and closes in June. The number registered for the year 1896–7 was 20,083. The average attendance in October, the second month of the school year was 17,340.

The schools are under the management of a board of eleven school commissioners elected by the people, with terms so arranged that a part of them expire every two years. The system embraces forty-five graded schools, two high schools, one training school, and one manual labor school, occupying forty-nine buildings, all of them arranged with modern improvements and well adapted for their various purposes. The two high school buildings are especially elegant in all their appointments. The direct management of the schools is under the charge of a superintendent with one assistant. Special branches, such as German, drawing, music, penmanship and physical culture are each under the charge of a supervisor; of these there are seven. Four hundred and fifty-eight teachers are employed, twenty-eight of them being in the High School and six in the Industrial Training School. The amount paid the teachers for the year 1895-6 was $296,034.02. The total cost of the schools for the same year was $434,372.45. The school system embraces a course of study extending over twelve years, or twenty-four half years. The years begin at one and run up to twelve. In the High School the course of study covers four years. Students graduating at the High School are admitted to any of the colleges of the state on their certificates.

Other Schools—The efficiency and number of schools which Indianapolis possesses in addition to those belonging to the public school system is also a matter of pride and importance. Several schools of music are conducted where pupils are brought by eminent instructors to the highest degree of skill and knowledge to which they are capable. In the Indianapolis School of Art, painting, sketching, pen-drawing and modeling are taught by capable artists. This school is maintained and controlled by an association of liberal citizens. The schools which are connected with the Catholic churches are popular and attended by many pupils from distant parts of the country, notably. St. John's and St. Mary's academies. The Knickerbacker Hall, diocesan school for girls, is also a high class academy, and there are schools of elocution, of stenography, telegraphy, business colleges and others in great number. For literary culture the people of Indianapolis have the advantage of two large and several small but very valuable libraries.

The State Library was started soon after Indiana became a state, but for several years it met with but little encouragement from the legislature, and through carelessness and neglect many of its most valuable books were lost or destroyed. Within the last few years, however, the legislature has been much more liberal in furnishing means for the purchase of new books and caring for the library. The library occupies several elegantly appointed rooms in the state-house, and ample accommodations are provided for those who desire to consult the works contained therein. It has been unfortunate that the position of state librarian was for many years made a political matter, the librarian being elected by the legislature, thus making frequent changes. The authorities of the state have at last been brought to recognize that competent librarians are very scarce, and that when one is obtained it is much better to hold on to that one than to change because of political prefer-

PUBLIC LIBRARY.

ences. The library contains 26,000 volumes, and a large number of pamphlets.

Public Library is of much more recent origin than the state library, and has already reached proportions which make it one of the best in the west. It was established in 1873 under the authority of the school commissioners. It occupies a handsome stone building erected for its use by the city. It has connected with it a reading room for consulting the books, and for the use of those who desire to read the papers and periodicals kept there for that purpose. The reading room is well lighted and ventilated, and is kept open from 9 A. M. until 9 P. M. on each day of the week. Any citizen is entitled to withdraw books from the library for home reading. The whole is under the control of the board of school commissioners. Sub-libraries were established the latter part of 1896 in various parts of the city, each being supplied with 1,000 volumes, and the newspaper and magazines and reading room accommodations for 150 persons. Beside these there are ten delivery stations where books are delivered to and received from the patrons of the library. There are 65,000 volumes in the library. Additions are made monthly by the purchase of new books, about $6,000 being expended annually for this purpose,

Agricultural Library of the state board of agriculture, located in the state-house, contains about 1,200 volumes.

Law Library of the Indianapolis bar association, established in 1880, contains about 3,000 volumes. It is located in the Marion county court-house.

Marion County Library, located in the court-house, was established in 1844, and contains 3,800 volumes. It is open on Saturdays.

State Law Library, which was separated from the state library in 1867, contains 35,000 volumes. It is located in the state-house.

Horticultural Library, of the State Horticultural Society, in the state-house, contains over 500 volumes.

Other Libraries are Butler University library, at Irvington, the St. Aloysius, St. Cecilia, Y. M. C. A., and excellent special libraries in the different medical colleges.

Mayors of Indianapolis were as follows: Samuel Henderson, 1847–1849; Horatio C. Newcomb, 1849–1851; Caleb Scudder, 1851–1854; James McCready, 1854–1856; Henry F. West, 1856; Charles Conlon, 1856; William J. Wallace, 1856–1858; Samuel D. Maxwell, 1858–1863; John Caven, 1863–1867; Daniel Macauley, 1867–1873; James L. Mitchell, 1873–1875; John Caven, 1875–1881; Daniel W. Grubbs, 1881–1884; J. L. McMasters, 1884-1886; Caleb S. Denny, 1886–1890; Thomas L. Sullivan, 1890–1893; Caleb S. Denny, 1893–1896; Thomas Taggart, 1896.

A Convention City—Indianapolis is fast taking high rank in popular favor as a place for holding conventions. Its railroad facilities make it readily reached from all parts of the country, and its fine hotel accommodations eminently fit it for taking care of delegates and others who attend conventions. At one time or another all the great organizations of the country, those of labor and of the various branches of business, have held their meetings here. Scientific and educational, religious and professional bodies look to Indianapolis as the most desirable place in which to hold their annual gatherings. It has also assumed importance with political parties for convention purposes. In 1884 the Greenback-Labor party held its national convention here, and nominated Gen. Benjamin F. Butler as its candidate for president. Four years later the Prohibitionists selected Indianapolis as the place for holding their national convention. The most important political gathering ever held in the city, and in some respects the most important ever held in the country, was that of 1896, when a great division of the Democratic party declared it could not support the party candidates for president and vice-president, and determined to put forth a new ticket. The party proper had declared in favor of the unlimited coinage of silver, and against that declaration a large number of the leaders of the party revolted. The revolt finally assumed shape, those of Indiana taking the lead. After numerous consultations it was determined to hold a national convention, adopt a platform and nominate a ticket. Indianapolis was chosen as the place for holding the convention, and it is doubtful if ever a political gathering called together more distinguished men than did the sound money convention of 1896. There was no concealment of the object of the gathering. It was not claimed that the ticket to be nominated would have any reasonable prospect of success, and the only object in putting it forth was to secure the defeat of their party candidate who stood on a platform they believed to be dangerous to the prosperity of the country.

In January, 1897, the Monetary Convention was held in Indianapolis. It was not of a party nature, but was practically the outgrowth of the late political contest. It was a gathering to take into consideration the best method of reforming the currency and banking system of the country, and thereby putting the business of the country on a stable foundation. It was attended by the ablest financiers and business leaders of the country, and a plan was developed for submission to the consideration of congress. All these gatherings liberally advertise Indianapolis, and tend to advance her growth and prosperity. Nearly 400 conventions are held every year in this city.

The Indianapolis Light and Power Co.—In June, 1881, the Indianapolis Light and Power Company commenced the erection of an arc light plant on South Pennsylvania street, with an immediate capacity of 180 lights and room for as many more. This was the first central station in Indiana, one of the first in the west, and, indeed, among the first in the world. The company had great difficulty and delay in procuring a franchise from the city, as the council had but little confidence in it, and when the franchise was finally granted it was cautiously termed: "The So-Called Electric Light." The first lights were turned on in the Union depot, January 12, 1882. In June, 1881, the company proposed to the council to light the entire city with electricity, agreeing to furnish six times the light it was then receiving, for ten

LEMCKE BUILDING.

per cent. less than the city was then paying, but the offer was rejected, and in August of the same year, nearly the same offer was made and again rejected. This was the first offer ever made in the world to light an entire city with electricity. In August, 1882, the company made a third offer to light the city, agreeing to furnish ten times the light it was receiving for 16 per cent. less than it was paying, and this offer was also rejected. Had it been accepted in the very infancy of electric lighting, Indianapolis would have had the distinction of being the first city in the world to be entirely lighted by electricity, at the same time saving over $10,000 a year by so doing. In 1886 the company erected five towers, one in the circle, 153 feet high, and one

POWER PLANT INDIANAPOLIS LIGHT AND POWER CO.

each at the corners looking out the four avenues, and lighted them several months without charge. Experience proved that the practically useful way to light a city is by lamps suspended from mast-arms at each street crossing, and Indianapolis is so lighted. In 1892 the company obtained a ten-year contract for lighting the city, and the city now has 824 lights; West Indianapolis, 57; Haughville, 30; Mount Jackson, 7. The price paid is $85 per lamp per year, and the company pays a special tax of five per cent. on its gross receipts, which makes the lights cost only about $78 per year, which makes the cost of each light about $69 per year less than the average price paid in the United States in other cities of like rank, and twenty per cent. less than what it costs some cities lighting themselves, merely for labor and consumable supplies, leaving out water supply, insurance, taxes not received, interest on the investment and that important factor of loss, depreciation, so often lost sight of.

In some recent investigations in other cities to determine the advisability of municipal ownership, they all select Indianapolis as obtaining its light on more favorable conditions than any other of its rank, and much more so than most. It is now costing the city only about as much while receiving about thirty times the volume of light as it did to light with gas when the city contained only about one-third its present territory, and, in addition, the electric

INTERIOR VIEW OF POWER HOUSE INDIANAPOLIS LIGHT AND POWER CO.

lights are promptly turned on when cloudy, even though the moon be full. The company's new station on Kentucky avenue is about seven hundred yards from the business center; is one of the finest in the world, and among the largest, and with capacity for almost indefinite expansion. Owning the entire block, and surrounded by wide streets effectually protecting it from external fire, and internally is almost entirely fire-proof, and, with perfect light and ventilation, securing the greatest comfort to the employes—something so frequently neglected. It is equipped with everything of the best to date—with Sterling non-explosive boilers, three Hamilton-Corliss compound condensing engines of the most perfect type, and with a combined power of 2,000 horse-power and a capacity of 2,100 2,000-C. P. arc lamps and dynamos

STEVENSON BUILDING.

with a capacity of 2,100 lights and ample room for more; three self-connected, upright Lake Erie engines with a combined power of 2,000 horse-power and 20,000 sixteen-candle incandescent lamps. The lines of two natural gas companies run into their premises, and coal can be thrown from cars on their own switch to the furnace doors, and having a storage capacity of 2,500 tons, and a two-months' supply is kept continually on hand. The company recently completed a three-foot conduit to White river forty-one feet deep and lower than low watermark in White river, and capable of supplying condensing and feed water for 30,000 horse-power. The engines are all compound-condensing engines, and while it might sound a little paradoxical to allege that cold water is a fuel, yet with condensing engines this is true, and the colder the better, saving at least 40 per cent. at the coal pile. The company commenced putting in under-ground conduits in 1889, and are now under ground in the central square mile. It was the first to adopt the vitrified tile, laid in cement, which will neither rust nor rot, and is acid proof and a non-conductor and not affected by electrolysis, a combination of merits possessed by no other conduit, and is now being generally adopted. Indianapolis has now twice as many street-lights as London, England, and three

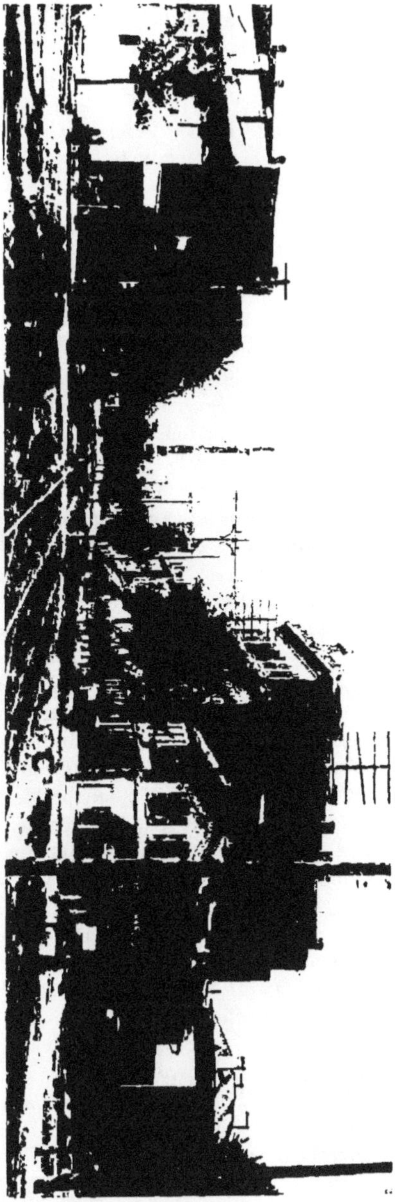

MASSACHUSETTS AVENUE.

times as many as Cleveland, where it was invented, and there are few plants in the world that equal the present capacity of Indianapolis. Its underground conduits will accommodate the city for a century, and can add to its buildings and power almost indefinitely. Statistics prove that in proportion to effective output of results, lighting, heat and power are obtained in no other way with anything like so small a percentage of loss of life and property. The company is purely a local one—the stock and bonds being owned entirely by Indianapolis citizens. Daniel W. Marmon is president; John Caven, vice-president; Charles C. Perry, secretary and treasurer, and Thomas A. Wynne, superintendent.

The Citizens' Street Railroad Company was chartered December 8, 1863, with a capital of $100,000, and operated lines of horse cars for twenty-five years. The company was again chartered in April 23, 1888, with a capital of $1,500,000, when the franchise of the original company was purchased, and the lines were rebuilt and extended. In 1893, the capital stock was increased to $5,000,000. The company began putting in an electric power plant in 1891, and finished the work in 1895. This included relaying the track with heavy rails, the purchase of new cars and the installing of two power plants with the most modern equipments throughout. The company now has over 100 miles of single track, 4 feet by 8½ inches gauge, laid with 38 to 95 pound Johnson girder rails; nearly 350 cars of the very finest pattern, two power houses. Nearly 1000 men are employed in the various departments and operating the cars. The equipment and service of this company is not surpassed in any other city in the United States, and all parts of the city are served, as well as furnishing convenient and rapid communication with Brightwood, Irvington, West Indianapolis, Haughville, Mount Jackson, Mapleton, and, by a traffic arrangement with the Broad Ripple line, also reach Broad Ripple. The Citizens' Street Railroad Company also owns and manages Fairview Park, the most beautiful outing place that is patronized by the citizens of Indianapolis. The park is located about six miles northwest of the city, and is reached by the College avenue and Illinois street lines. The officers of the company are Augustus L. Mason, president; William L. Elder, vice-president, and W. F. Milholland, secretary and treasurer. The office of the company is located at 750 West Washington street.

The Indianapolis Gas Company, 49 South Pennsylvania street, in the Majestic building, is an outgrowth of the Indianapolis Gas Light and Coke Company and the Indianapolis Natural Gas Company, which was chartered in 1876, succeeding to this business in 1890. The artificial plant of the company is situated on South Pennsylvania and Louisiana streets and covers an entire square, also owning and operating nearly 200 gas wells in Hamilton, Madison, and Tipton counties, Indiana, with an output of nearly three millions and a half feet of gas per day. The company is also owner of the Majestic, the finest office building in the city. The officers of the company are Charles F. Dieterich, president; E. C. Benedict, vice-president; John R.

MAJESTIC BUILDING.

MARION BLOCK.

Pearson general manager; A. B. Proal, assistant secretary and treasurer, and S. T. Pray, secretary.

The Western Union Telegraph Company is associated with the earliest history of Indianapolis, and to record its growth is to write a business career of its present manager, Mr. John F. Wallick. The first telegraph company that operated from this point was known as the Ohio, Illinois and Indiana Telegraph Company, and the line was constructed from Cincinnati to Chicago, *via* Lafayette, over the highway. This was before any railroads had been projected in that direction. The office was opened in 1848, and the first manager was I. H. Kiersted, who is still a resident of Indianapolis. Dennis Gregg succeeded Mr. Kiersted as manager, in 1849, and W. J. Delano was superintendent, located at Dayton, Ohio. In 1850 Mr. Henry McNeeley, now editor and proprietor of the Evansville, Indiana, *Journal*, became manager of the office. In 1891 a new line was built from Cincinnati, known as the Cincinnati and St. Louis Telegraph Company, or Wade lines, with Mr. John F. Wallick, the present superintendent of the Western Union Telegraph Company at this point, as manager. The lines were operated under this name until 1856, when the title changed to the Union Telegraph Company, and soon after became what is known as the Western Union Telegraph Company. At this time Mr. Wallick operated the office with the assistance of one man. Prior to that time he managed the office alone. As the town grew, the business of the company kept pace with it, and more operators were added to the force under Mr. Wallick, and, in 1867, we find the distinguished name of Thos. A. Edison on the pay-rolls of this office. He had just entered on the career that has since made him world famous. About this time the office was located on the second floor of the building at the northwest corner of Meridian and Washington streets. Mr. M. D. Butler, the present manager of the Western Union Company's main office, has acted continuously in that capacity since September 25, 1871. The Western Union Telegraph Company now occupy the handsome building at the corner of Pearl and Meridian streets, with ten branch offices in different parts of the city, and employment is furnished to 150 persons in the offices. Six linemen operate from this point. Many important improvements will be finished in the near future, notably the placing of all wires under ground that are now strung through the mile-square in the center of the city. This company has the largest telegraph system ever established. It has 21,000 offices and 750,000 miles of wire. The company leases the two cables of the American Telegraph & Cable Company from Nova Scotia to Penzance, England, which are extended to New York City by the company's own cable; it also connects with the four cables of the Anglo-American Telegraph Company, limited, from Valencia, Ireland, to Hearts Content, New Foundland, and from Brest, France, to St. Pierre, Miquelon; and with the cable of the Direct United States Cable Company from Ballinskelligs, Ireland, to Rye Beach, N. H. It has thus service of seven Atlantic cables as well as direct connection with the South American cable at Galveston, Texas, and messages may be sent from any of its offices to all parts of the world.

The Postal Telegraph Cable Company established its office in Indianapolis, November 1, 1885, with Mr. H. E. Kinney as manager, occupying a room in North Meridian street, in the Yohn Block. The following month Mr. Kinney resigned and Mr. F. W. Samuels was appointed to the position which he has since filled. The following year the office was moved to Nos. 9 and 11 South Meridian street, its present location. From an office with four wires and one operator, the business of the company has gradually in-

SOLDIERS' AND SAILORS' MONUMENT.

Y. M. C. A. BLOCK.

creased until it now has in its equipment thirty-one first class copper wires and twenty operators, with branches at the Stock-yards, Kingan's and West End, Board of Trade, Bates House, Fruit District, Indiana Trust Company, Indianapolis Hominy Mills, Parry Manufacturing Company, Nordyke & Marmon Company, Moore Packing Company, Atlas Engine Works and Indiana Bicycle Company. Their plant in this city is first class, their current being produced by dynomotors which are far in advance of the gravity battery. The postal Telegraph Cable Company also inaugurated copying telegrams direct from the wire on typewriters. Competition in the telegraph service, in some form or other, has existed ever since this most important artery of commerce was developed, and will probably continue to exist so long as the telegraph remains a private enterprise. Such keen rivalry for public favor as now exists is productive of many benefits to the public, inasmuch as it results in the best possible service at the least possible cost. It is the only telegraph company in America operating its own cable system. It owns three duplex cables which gives it the capacity of six cables of the other systems, by means of which a message can be sent and received over the same cable at the same instant.

The Central Union Telephone Company—The present telephone system is the outgrowth of the consolidation of the Bell and Edison Telephone The Exchange service has grown until at present there are more than 2,000 in the city, and connections through the United States over the lines owned by the Central Union Telephone Company, Long Distance Telephone and other allied systems. The Long Distance System was brought into Indianapolis in 1893. The telephone company has spent great sums of money in housing their wires in cables, preparatory to the inauguration of the underground system.

The Indianapolis District Telegraph Company was incorporated November 4, 1885, by E. G. Ohmer, John A. Holman, Thomas Taggart, John T. Brush and Charles Farnum. The present executive officer of the company is C. C. Hatfield, who became president of the company March, 1887. The general electrical construction and supply department of this company enjoys a large business locally and throughout the state. The officers of this department, as well as those of the messenger service department, which is under the management of Mr. J. E. Bombarger, are located at 15 South Meridian street. The messenger service, under the charge of Mr. Bombarger, has arrived at a state of great efficiency, and the night-watch system inaugurated by this company has become of invaluable service to business men and manufacturers generally. This company has a complete system of call-boxes for fire and police service distributed throughout the city. By a unique system in connection with the use of the company's call-boxes, its patrons are enabled to call the police or fire department, call a phsician or summons a carriage, by simply turning the indicator to a given number on the call-box. From twenty-five to forty-five messengers are employed, night and day, in the service of the company.

The Commercial Club was organized in January, 1890, by twenty-seven business and professional men of Indianapolis, the membership of which increased within a month to nearly a thousand. Its name does not fully indicate the Club's purpose, which is not commercial in a sense of devotion to trade interests, but is broadly stated to make the Indiana capital a better place to live in. Among the work to which the Club has given its attention

WESTERN UNION BUILDING

are the securing of a new city charter, the inauguration of a system of street improvements and of sewerage, the securing for Indianapolis of the twenty-seventh National Encampment of the G. A. R., and the promotion of a park system and of the University of Indianapolis. In a word, the Club's accomplishment is that no one's thought for the betterment of the community has had to be unrealized for lack of co-operation. With a view to permanence in this effort of public spirit, an eight-story stone-front building has been erected by the Club at the southwest corner of Meridian and Pearl streets as its home. During the first five years of the Club's history, its president and secretary were respectively Colonel Eli Lilly and William Fortune. The present officers are: William Fortune, president; D. M. Parry, first vice-president; A. C. Ayres, second vice-president; Evans Woollen, secretary; A. B. Gates, treasurer. The board of directors consists of A. C. Ayres, W. D. Bynum, J. P. Dunn, D. P. Erwin, J. A. Finch, William Fortune, C. C. Foster, J. H. Holliday, J. S. Lazarus, J. L. Keach, A. B. Gates, Albert Lieber, Eli Lilly, Albert E. Metzger, Nathan Morris, D. M. Parry and John M. Spann.

Indianapolis Water Company.—January 1, 1870, there was granted to the Water-Works Company of Indianapolis, a franchise to erect and maintain water-works in this city, there having been a law enacted by the legislature authorizing cities to grant such privileges to corporations organized for the purpose of supplying a city and citizens with water. That company built a substantial pumping station on White river below Washington street, and was to take water from wells along the river. The machinery consisted of pumps driven by water-power and steam, with a capacity of 6,500,000 gallons. The pumps were of the rotary character. The company laid one 24-inch supply main in Washington street and one 20-inch main in Pearl street, with branches 18 and 20 inches. This company continued in existence until '81. During that period it laid 52 miles of mains and added to its machinery one quadruplex engine of 7,500,000 gallons capacity. The present company has added pumps of 10,000,000 capacity to this station. To provide money to make the system and maintain it, that company issued a large amount of bonds and incurred a large floating indebtedness aggregating nearly $1,350,-000. The high rate of interest, with its small patronage, was too much for the company to carry, and in '81 the first mortgage bondholders brought suit to foreclose their mortgage, which resulted in the organization of the present company, called the Indianapolis Water Company. This company provided the means and began a reconstruction of the system, and erected a new station a mile and one-quarter north of the first station, and there constructed a filter gallery and laid a line from the first station, 30 inches in size, to the gallery and new station, which are located at the intersection of Fall creek and White river, and placed in the new building one Gaskill compound engine of 15,000,000 gallons capacity, and has added to the system more than 100 miles of mains. So there are now about 155 miles of mains in the system. It also supplies the towns of Haughville and West Indianapolis under contract with those towns. The company has erected another new building, which is said to be the handsomest station in the United States, and there is being erected in the station a 20,000,000 triple expansion engine with all the latest improvements by the Snow Steam Pump Works. The company is also putting in a large boiler plant of 1,300 horse-power. This is in addition to the present boiler plant. The water supplied is taken from a gallery of an average width of nearly 40 feet, and nearly 2,000 feet long. In addition to this supply, it has 6 artesian wells drilled 450 feet deep. These wells flow into the gallery. It also has a filtering bed under the river. So far this supply has proven to be a good quality and of sufficient quantity. The company has under consideration the erection of a filtering plant, as soon as experiments made by one or two other cities are determined by experience to be the best form of filtration. In all of its constructive work and plants the company has aimed to provide everything of ample capacity and of the best quality. In fact, the company does not consider anything too good for its purpose, as evidenced by the very handsome structure, which has heretofore been mentioned. This building is 77 feet by 45 feet interior. The foundations consist first of 3 feet of concrete laid under the entire building. On this are constructed the foundation walls which are 6 feet at the base, tapering wedge-shaped to 4 feet at the top. The building proper has a steel frame, and the walls are about 18 inches in thickness and 52 feet above the foundations. The outside and inside finish are white brick with bold terra cotta trimmings of the most beautiful designs. The walls of the inside are finished the same as the walls on the outside. The windows are 24 feet high and are plate glass. The gutters are copper and the roof cypress finish covered with Spanish tiles. On the outside of the walls is fine ashlar work of oolitic stone for 5 feet to the water table, which is also of stone. The inside wainscoting is white enamel brick. The foundations for the engine consist of brick piers 44 feet long, 21 feet high, 12 feet at the base and 7 feet on top. These, like the foundation walls, are laid with Portland cement. Surrounding these 2 stations, the company has about 150 acres of land which it intends to convert into a park. With the completion of this station, the company will have 3 pumping stations with a total capacity of 57,000,000 gallons in 24 hours. The building has been erected from plans furnished by consulting engineer L. K. Davis, of New York, who has supervised the erection of the building as well as the machinery.

The company furnishes water for the city for fire protection, and receives $50 a plug, which sum covers water for flushing sewers, park fountains and other uses, and lays pipe under the direction of the Board of Public Works. The domestic pressure is 65 pounds and fire pressure 125 pounds. It has 1,205 public fire hydrants in service. The rate to supply the consumers is comparatively low, being for a house of seven rooms, including water for bath, closet and laundry, and water in as many rooms as desired and sprinkling for 30-foot lot, including lawn, garden and street, $18 a year. The company has 7,000 attachments in service. The Water Company owns the Indiana Central canal, from which it supplies water to several manufacturing

INDIANAPOLIS WATER CO., NEW STATION.

establishments, and makes use of 475 H. P. for its water power Gasgill pumps. The capital stock of the company is $500,000; the bonded indebtedness is $1,000,000, which, in all probability, will be increased in the near future, as the company will expend this year about $300,000 upon its plant.

The officers are T. A. Morris, president; F. A. W. Davis, vice-president and treasurer; M. A. Morris, secretary. The directors are T. A. Morris, E. P. Kimball, V. T. Malott, C. Heckman, C. H. Payson, Edgar R. Payson, J. L. Ketcham, John K. Bates, Albert Baker, Edward Daniels, O. S. Andrews, John H. Langdon, F. A. W. Davis.

The Consumers' Gas Trust Company was organized November 5, 1887, and has demonstrated how a great enterprise may be conducted for the public good without the stimulus of private gain. Following the discovery of

PUBLIC LIBRARY, CHRIST CHURCH, COLUMBIA CLUB, WATER-WORKS OFFICE, JOURNAL BUILDING.

natural gas in this vicinity, it was apparent to every one that it would be of immense value to this city if natural gas could be piped into the city and used for manufacturing and domestic purposes. The Standard Oil Company, local corporations and speculators immediately attempted to secure control of this valuable resource, but it remained to A. A. McKain, a well-known citizen of our city, to put into motion the forces that resulted in the organization of the Consumers' Gas Trust Company. To him more than to all others must the credit be given that Indianapolis now has natural gas at a price less than one-third the cost of hard fuel. Over $1,000,000 annually are saved to the patrons of this company as compared with what they would have to pay for other fuel. About 15,000 homes are served by this company in the city and suburbs. The officers of the company are: Robert N. Lamb, president; Henry Coburn, vice-president; Bement Lyman, secretary and general manager; Julius F. Pratt, treasurer; Wm. H. Shackelton, superintendent.

University of Indianapolis.—Realizing the desirability of a union of the divers educational institutions of the city, conferences with that end in view were begun during the month of February, 1896. Representatives from Butler College, the Medical College of Indiana, the Indiana Law School, and the Indiana Dental College, together with others prominent in mercantile, educational and professional circles, constituted themselves an advisory committee for the furtherance of the project. Public sentiment was never more unanimous regarding a public work. Pulpit and press joined in commendation; men of all creeds and nationalities assisted in the organization, and in six weeks from the date of the first meeting held the University of Indianapolis was an accomplished fact. It is expected in the near future to purchase grounds for a centralization of buildings. Until this is done, the four existing departments will continue to occupy their present quarters. The university will open the session of 1896–97 with about 1,000 students. The mutual aid and support that each department will give the others can not fail to be a source of benefit to all. And the existing departments are but a nucleus. Departments of music, art, pharmacy, technology, engineering, pedagogy, etc., will follow as a natural sequence of what has gone before. The University of Indianapolis will eventually become one of the great centers of learning in the central states. The board of trustees are: Allen M. Fletcher, president; Addison C. Harris, vice-president; George E. Hunt, secretary; Herman Lieber, treasurer; Benjamin Harrison, Sterling R. Holt, Eli Lilly, W. P. Fishback, J. W. Marsee, Scot Butler, Thomas Taggart, Hilton U. Brown, M. J. Osgood, P. H. Jameson, E. H. Dean.

Butler College (Department of Liberal Arts, University of Indianapolis). In January, 1850, an institution under the name of the Northwestern Christian University began a corporate existence in the city of Indianapolis. Its charter was catholic and broad and had been obtained under the auspices of the Christian churches of the state. Its history has been in many respects a repetition of that of many predecessors in the educational field. Growth has been slow and disappointments have been not a few. At the same time it has been blessed with more than ordinary fortune and has had its friends loyal and generous. It was started in corporate capacity as a stock company with seventy-five thousand dollars as subscribed stock. During the nearly half century of its existence this has increased to two hundred and fifty thousand. Its work and its success have been more than commensurate with the support accorded it in benefactions. More than three hundred and fifty students have graduated from its halls. Probably six thousand others have pursued partial courses of study with its faculty. The financial resources of the institution, through fortuitous circumstances and the prudence of the management, have increased to nearly double the stock subscribed. In 1877, on account of the peculiar beneficence of Ovid Butler, the original title was changed and the corporate name since then has been "Butler University," until the recent organization of the University of Indianapolis, when it adopted the new title. The change of title does not betoken any change of

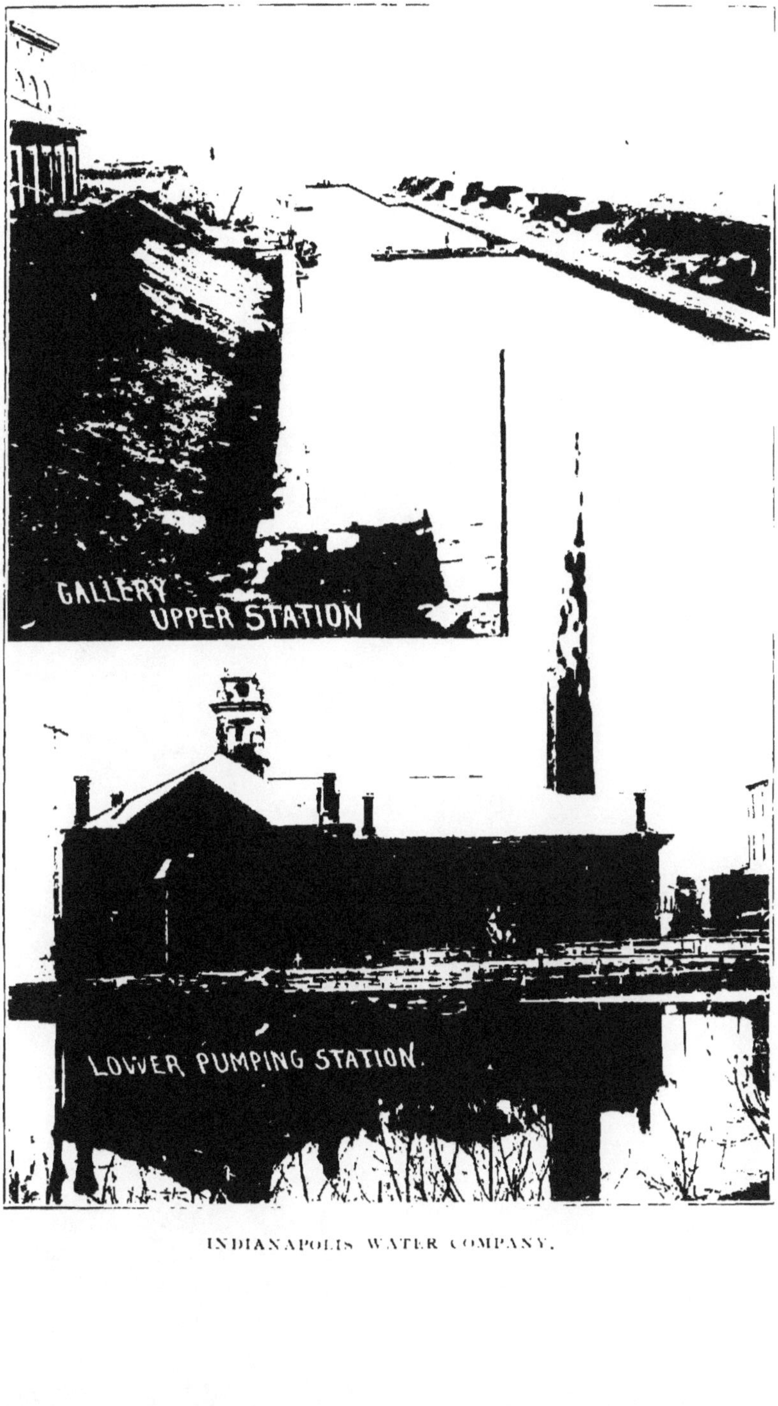

INDIANAPOLIS WATER COMPANY.

policy, rather does it emphasize the spirit which in all the past has dominated its work. The salient features of its educational policy may be summed up thus: It has stood from its inception for the broadest culture to all who have desired it. There has been no discrimination against any on account of sex or color. It has believed, it still believes, that the atmosphere in which the broadest culture is to be realized is one which is distinctly Christian. It was the first institution in the world of collegiate grade which opened its doors to women on exactly equal terms with those offered to men. It is bound by its charter "to teach and inculcate the Christian faith and Chris-

MAIN BUILDING BUTLER COLLEGE.

tian morality as taught in the sacred Scriptures." Lastly, in an age which has seen many institutions swept away by a desire for notoriety, which has seen schools, meagerly equipped, advertising their ability to develop specialists, it has not failed to realize the truth that 'specialization' in any true sense of the term must rest upon a substantial and broadly-laid basis of knowledge. It has never claimed ability to take students fresh from the graded schools or from the secondary schools and make specialists of them in a few brief years. It has discountenanced the idea that crude youth is best fitted for the battle of life by a sky-rocket course of 'specialized' study, self-selected and aimlessly pursued. Rather has it stood for that thorough laying of the basis of all culture which in all times has been the real foundation of true specialization and of genuine success. In point of equipment it is without a superior in the state, and with few rivals in the west. The buildings, five in all, situated on a beautiful campus of 25 acres, have been erected since 1874. The main college building (135 x 75 ft. and three stories high) itself furnishes extensive accommodations for college work. For some years it stood alone upon the campus. It contains sixteen large class rooms besides a chapel seating 500, and the offices, parlors and private studies of the

LIBRARY HALL BUTLER COLLEGE.

professors. At various times there have been added Library Hall, the College Residence for Women, the Gymnasium and Power Plant, and the Astronomical Observatory. Of these, the largest is Library Hall (100 x 55 ft.), three stories high, of brick and stone, which contains at present the library and reading room, the laboratories, the college museum and the recitation rooms of the Preparatory School. The Residence is a three-story brick structure of thirty rooms fully fitted, as is all the rest of the plant, with steam heat and electric light. The Gymnasium and Power Plant is a building of pleasing architectural design which offers the fullest facilities for its intended purposes. The battery of boilers with the accessories of deep well pumps and dynamo and engine leave nothing to be desired as to physical equipment in the great essentials of heat, light and water. The Gymnasium proper is a room 50 x 30 ft. and 20 ft. to the roof, thoroughly equipped with the essential apparatus for general gymnastics and with the bathing accessories demanded by hygienic law. The Astronomical Observatory, while not an imposing structure, is thoroughly built, and equipped with an instrument

RESIDENCE FOR WOMEN, BUTLER COLLEGE.

by the finest makers in the world. The telescope is of six inch aperture and eight feet focal distance, equatorially mounted and fitted with clockwork for rotation. The mechanism is the work of Fauth & Co., of Washington, D. C., and the lenses are the work of Alvin Clark & Sons, of Boston, Mass., who have made all the finest lenses in the world. With this equipment Butler College may feel that she is making no pretension in her claims for a place in the college world. She offers to the student facilities of high grade in an atmosphere of culture conducive to their best use. The president of the college is Scot Butler.

Indiana Dental College (Department of Dental Surgery of the University of Indianapolis). The Indiana Dental College was organized in 1878 by the members of the Indiana State Dental Association. The college occupied rooms in the Thorpe Block, on East Market street, until 1881. From 1881 to 1894 it was located in the Ætna Block, on N. Pennsylvania street. During the summer of '94, the present building of the college was erected on the corner of Ohio and Delaware streets. The growth of the college has been steady and constant. During the session of 1895–1896 there were 157 students enrolled. These came principally from the central, western and southern states. The increase in facilities for teaching has kept pace with this growth. The building at present occupied by the college was built for dental educational purposes. The arrangement of the floor space is designed to attain the very best results. Each department is amply large to accommodate a school of 200 students. The laboratories, lecture rooms and infirmary are completely equipped and appointed. Improvements in equipment and facilities for teaching are constantly being made. The faculty of the college is composed of fourteen members. The course is strictly a graded one; no two classes receive the same lectures. The practical work is required and a high standard is insisted upon. Careful attention to details in every department has placed the college on its present high plane. Its uniform increase in popularity and strength attests its value as an educational institution. The college course extends over six months, from the first week in October to the first week in April. At the session of 1895-96 there were 157 students in attendance. The officers are John N. Hurty, M. D., Ph. D., president; George E. Hunt, M. D., D. D. S., secretary; Harry S. Hicks, D. D. S., treasurer.

INDIANA DENTAL COLLEGE.

The Indiana Law School (Department of Law of the University of Indianapolis). The Indiana Law School, now entering upon its third year, has already taken high rank among the professional schools of the country. The results thus far have justified the opinion of the founders of the school that Indianapolis possesses exceptional advantages for such an institution. Being the capital city of the state, where the Supreme and Appellate State Courts, the Federal Courts, and the local, civil and criminal courts are in session throughout the year, the students have unusual opportunity for witnessing court procedure in all of its various forms, and the sessions of the legislature, which are held in the State House, quite near the school building, enable them to see how the business of law-making is transacted. For the young men who expect to practice law in Indiana this school is especially fitted. With the rapid growth of the state in wealth and population, the law of Indiana, while in its general and elementary features it is like that of the other states of the union, has developed a jurisprudence of its own. In its one hundred and sixty volumes of reports and its numerous statutes there is a body of law peculiar to Indiana, a knowledge of which is essential to the Indiana lawyer. This knowledge can not be acquired at law schools located in other states. While not neglecting the general principles of the law, which are alike in all states, the faculty and instructors of the Indiana Law School give especial attention to our state jurisprudence. William P. Fishback is dean, and among the instructors and lecturers are Hon. Byron K. Elliott, Hon. William A. Woods, Hon. Addison C. Harris, Hon. John R. Wilson, William F. Elliott, Charles W. Smith, Hon. George L. Reinhard, William E. Kappes, Evans Woollen, Thaddeus S. Rollins, Hon. John A. Finch and Hon. John L. Griffiths.

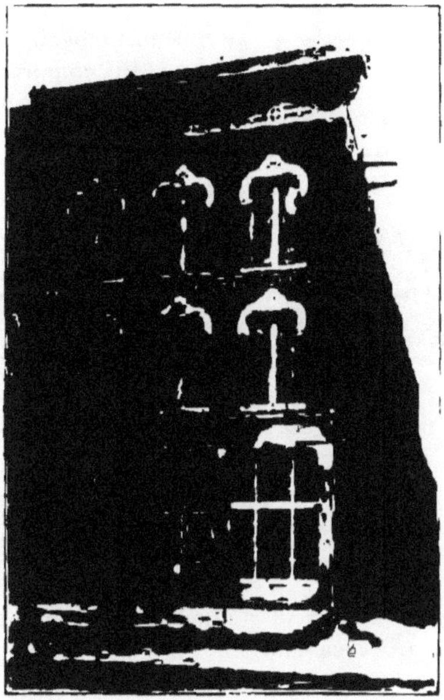

INDIANA LAW SCHOOL.

The Medical College of Indiana (Department of Medicine of the University of Indianapolis). This institution was organized in 1869 by a committee appointed by the Indianapolis Academy of Medicine, under the name of the Indiana Medical College. In 1878 it was consolidated with the College of Physicians and Surgeons, and the name changed to its present form. As a result of this union this college adopted the alumni of both the parent institutions. These alumni now number about twelve hundred. The college has been twice burned out while in session, in 1880 and 1894. No time was lost in either case, the lectures being immediately resumed in temporary quarters. As a result of the last fire, the faculty has erected a commodius and admirably arranged building on the corner of Market street and Senate avenue North, especially adapted to the constantly growing needs of advanced medical education. Without going into particulars, it is believed that the college equipment need not fear comparison with that of any competing institution. The faculty numbers twenty with sixteen assistants. Hospital facilities are excellent, and will be much improved by the erection, in time for its next session, of a thoroughly modern and comfortable clinic hall, at each hospital. Women are admitted on the same terms as men, and special efforts made to render their attendance pleasant and profitable. Although the fact of thirty-six years of prosperous and successful existence is a sufficient guarantee of the institution's permanence, yet its lately acquired relationship as a department of the University of Indianapolis is a still further proof of stability. A dispensary giving very fine opportunities for clinical instruction is located in the college building. Students remaining in the city during the summer are cordially welcomed. This college is a member of the Association of American Medical Colleges, and conforms strictly to the schedule of minimum requirements adopted by this association. The officers of the college are Joseph W. Marsee, M. D., dean; Alembert W. Brayton, M. S., vice-dean; John H. Oliver, M. D., treasurer, and Franklin W. Hays, M. D., secretary.

MEDICAL COLLEGE OF INDIANA.

Girls' Classical School. The school building, a three-story brick structure, at 426 North Pennsylvania street, completed and occupied in September, 1884, has proved to be perfectly adapted to the needs of the school. The location is central; the building is substantial, tasteful in appearance, commodious and conveniently arranged. The lighting, heating and ventilation are excellent. Each room has an abundant supply of pure warm air, and capacious ventilating flues. The building contains four session rooms, six class rooms, an office, a toilet room, ample hallways and a spacious gymnasium.

THE GIRLS' CLASSICAL SCHOOL.

The Girls' Classical School was opened in September, 1882. The design of the school is twofold. First, to give girls a thorough preparation for all colleges that admit women; second, to provide higher courses for the benefit of girls who, for any reason, are unable to take a college course, but still desire a more extended course than is usually given in schools, academies or seminaries. Pupils whose work is not definitely limited by the requirements of college examinations may take full courses in Modern Languages (English, French, German), in the Classics (Latin, Greek), in Science (Physiology, Zoology, Physical Geography, Botany, Geology, Physics, with Laboratory work), in History (Greece, Rome, Outlines of the World's History, English History, History of Modern Europe and Civil Government), and in Mathematics (Higher Algebra, Solid Geometry, Trigonometry). The regular course of study gives a good academic education. The courses in Mathematics, Science, Latin, Greek, French, German, History and English Literature are much more extended than the courses in these subjects usually given in preparatory and high schools, and graduates of such schools find it profitable to spend one or more years in this school. Graduates of the best high schools in Indiana and other states have entered the Classical School to pursue its higher courses and obtain its diploma. Graduates of the Girls' Classical School enter the Junior year of the Indiana University, the Sophomore year of the Leland Stanford, Jr., University, the Freshman year of Vassar, Smith and Wellesley Colleges, also of the University of Michigan, and the University of Chicago, on their school certificates. Twenty-one have passed examinations for admission to the Harvard Annex (Radcliffe College) and Bryn Mawr College. At this time (October, 1896) fifty-five pupils have been admitted to college from this school. The school is unsectarian. Simple religious exercises are held daily at the opening of the session.

The chief advantages of the school are the following: First, the classes are small, and the teachers are thus enabled to give a relatively large amount of time and instruction to individual pupils. Pupils who do not desire to give the time necessary to obtain the school diploma in the full course may select from the course of study those subjects which they prefer, and will receive a certificate stating the work done by them and the percentage attained. Latin, English Literature, History, French, German and Advanced Science, are especially adapted to the needs of such pupils; while superior opportunities are offered for the study of Vocal and Instrumental Music, Drawing and Painting. English Composition, Declamation, Drawing, Chorus Singing, Gymnastics and Oral French are regular exercises throughout the course in all departments.

The school is well equipped with reference library and apparatus; the faculty includes eighteen instructors, each a specialist in her or his department.

In the Lower Primary department boys and girls of six years are received and prepared for the Upper Primary department. Boys are not retained in this school above the Lower Primary department. The course includes reading, spelling, numbers, singing, drawing, writing, simple lessons in natural science, conversational French and gymnastics.

The experience of the school has clearly shown that pupils who pass through the lower departments have a completer and stronger preparation for the work of the advanced department than those who come from other schools. The lower work in the child's education is as important as the higher, and it is a great gain to a child to be identified at an early age with an institution in which the course of study is symmetrically developed from its very beginning through the full preparation for college. The course is arranged mainly with reference to the highest college requirements. For many colleges a shorter course will suffice. The school prepares girls for all colleges, and each pupil's course, as far as possible, is selected and continued with reference to her individual wants.

INTERIOR INDIANAPOLIS BUSINESS UNIVERSITY.

Pupils may graduate with diplomas (the full course) or with certificates (the shorter course). Special certificates, signed by the principal, are accepted in place of examinations in the subjects covered, by the following institutions: Smith College, Vassar College, Wellesley College, The Leland Stanford, Jr., University, Indiana University, Purdue University, DePauw University, Butler University, University of Michigan, and the University of Chicago.

English Literature is studied during the entire five years of the advanced department. The girls are divided into sections, according to their capacity for the work. Selections from the standard English authors are studied in the most thorough manner, with analysis of the thought and language, discussions upon the style, and investigations of biographical and historical allusions in the text. The drill in this subject is believed to be one of the most profitable features of the school work. The composition work is mainly based upon the works studied in the courses of literature; it gives a systematic and comprehensive course continuing through five years, including not only formal essays, but also analyses of plots, and of characters, critiques upon style, conversations upon literary themes, etc. The books read are made the basis of lessons in grammar, rhetoric and composition. The greatest care is taken in every department of the school to teach the pupils to pronounce English with correctness, and to read it with taste and expression; a systematic course of study in these branches is pursued.

French is begun in the lower primary department, where oral instruction is given daily by means of object lessons. These oral exercises, continued through the upper primary department, are a source of pleasure to the pupils, and are important in training the ear and tongue, thus preparing the way for text-book work, begun in the lowest intermediate grade. The courses in French and German in the advanced department are designed to give a good knowledge of the grammar, composition, translation and conversation. Recitations are conducted wholly in French or German, and the conversational method is freely employed. As an aid to proficiency in conversation, French and German soirées are occasionally given in the residence parlors; and selections in French and German are given as declamations before the school.

The pupils in all departments are divided into sections for declamations, which are given weekly before the instructor and the class. Declamations of unusual merit are selected for delivery before the school at stated intervals, usually at the first hour on Fridays. The preparation for these declamations is in charge of the teacher of reading; extravagance in gesture and stage effects are sedulously avoided. The exercise before the school is made available for literary culture by questions as to the author, the style and other matters suggested by the selection. The competitors for the annual prizes in declamation are chosen from the girls having the highest record during the year. Lectures, informal addresses by visitors of distinction, and discussions of topics of general or special interest, are substituted for the Friday declamations from time to time.

Beginning in the lower primary department with the simplest principles, the pupils are advanced to drawing from flats of the antique, to the making of designs in colors, and to the study of art in relation to historic ornament. When sufficiently advanced they enter the studio class, in which they are instructed in drawing from casts and natural objects, in perspective, in shading and in drawing from life.

Apparatus for illustrating the study of the physical sciences is provided. The classes in physics, botany, zoölogy and physiology devote much time to laboratory work.

A definite course of instruction is given in chorus singing, beginning in the Lower Primary department and progressing through all the classes. The school choir leads the daily morning singing, and the school chorus takes part in the exercises of commencement week.

A course of lectures on various themes is a permanent feature of the school. Some of them are given by the principals, and others by friends of the school, or visitors of note. These lectures, or familiar talks, are usually given on Friday mornings, following the opening exercises. Parents are always invited to be present. Among those who have addressed the school are many men and women of distinction.

The gymnasium has an unobstructed floor space of thirty-four hundred square feet and a height of eighteen feet. It is well supplied with Sargent's improved apparatus, and the apparatus used in the Swedish system, besides an outfit for Turner work. The director of the gymnasium devotes her entire time to the physical culture of the pupils. The teachers of music and reading work with the gymnasium director to secure correct breathing and standing. Soon after the opening of the school, in September of 1882, a simple school dress for the every day wear of the pupils was adopted; and all pupils, unless specially excused from the gymnasium work by medical certificate, are now required to wear the costume.

The school residence, at 343 and 345 North Pennsylvania street, contains two of the handsomest residences in the city, affording accommodations for twenty-eight pupils. A matron and a residence governess are in charge of the residence life. Mrs. Sewall has a general supervision of the home life of the pupils; she also spends Saturday evening of each week with them in reading and in general conversation on practical and literary themes; and on Sunday afternoon discusses with them topics suggested by the religious services attended by the pupils in the morning. The school residence has enrolled pupils from twenty-one states and territories in recent years.

The exhibit of the school at the Columbian Exposition received an award for excellence of careful and thorough training, and for its results in preparatory work. This exhibit, with the diploma and medal awarded, now adorns the school building.

Central College of Physicians and Surgeons was incorporated on July 8, 1879. The organizers of the college were Drs. Joseph Eastman, R. E. Hough-

CENTRAL COLLEGE OF PHYSICIANS AND SURGEONS.

ton, W. S. Haymond, Charles D. Pierson, Ira A. E. Lyons, J. R. Featherston and W. H. Thomas.

From its inception the growth of the college has been steady. Its faculty is honored with the names of some of the most eminent, progressive and skillful in the profession, and thoroughly qualified to impart to others a complete medical education.

The college building, which is owned by the stockholders, is a substantial brick and stone edifice four stories in height, with an aggregate floor space of 13,000 square feet for teaching and clinical purposes, situated but two squares from the Union Railway Station and one square from St. Vincent's Hospital, and is in the heart of the clinical district of the city. The college has adopted the four years' graded course, with four courses of lectures of six months each as a condition of graduation. The H. W. Clark library, one of the largest and most complete collections of medical books and literature in the state, is open to the students and the alumni of the college. To this collection have been added valuable contributions by Drs. L. D. Waterman and G. V. Woolen. The faculty is composed as follows: John Moffett, M. D., emeritus professor of obstetrics; W. B. Fletcher, M. D., emeritus professor of diseases of the mind and clinical medicine; Joseph Eastman, M. D., LL. D., president, professor of diseases of women and abdominal surgery; John A. Sutcliffe, A. M., M. D., professor of surgery, genito-urinary and rectal diseases; Samuel E. Earp, M. S., M. D., dean and secretary, professor of materia medica, therapeutics and clinical medicine; Allison Maxwell, A. M., M. D., professor of the principles and practice of medicine, physical diagnosis and sanitary science; E. J. Brennan, M. D., professor of obstetrics and clinical midwifery; John B. Long, M. D., professor of descriptive and surgical anatomy; John F. Barnhill, M. D., professor of physiology; William H. Thomas, M. D., professor of diseases of the nervous system; Green V. Woolen, A. M., M. D., professor of rhinology and laryngology; William V. Morgan, M. D., professor of fractures and dislocations, orthopedic and clinical surgery; Albert E. Sterne, A. M., M. D. (Univ. Berlin), professor of the anatomy, physiology and pathology of the nervous system and clinical medicine; Minor Morris, A. B., M. D., professor of pathology, dermatology and bacteriology; L. L. Tedd, M. D., professor of clinical medicine and lecturer on gastric and pulmonary diseases; John L. Masters, M. D., treasurer, professor of diseases of the eye and ear and of histology; John A. Lambert, Ph. G., M. D., professor of diseases of children and medical chemistry and toxicology; Joseph Rilus Eastman, B. S., M. D., adjunct professor of physiology; Thomas B. Eastman, A. B., M. D., assistant secretary, adjunct professor of anatomy and assistant to the chair of diseases of women; Charles O. Durham, M. D., demonstrator of anatomy; Thomas E. Courtney, M. D., assistant demonstrator of anatomy; Martin V. B. Newcomer, M. D., lecturer on railroad surgery; H. G. Gaylord, M. D., demonstrator of bacteriology; S. P. Scherer, M. D., assistant to the chair of practice of medicine; F. C. Tinsley, M. D., assistant to the chair of materia medica; Leonard Bell, M. D., assistant to the chair of pathology; John Kolmer, M. D., lecturer on physiology; Amelia R. Keller, M. D., clinical assistant to the chair of clinical gynecology; J. J. Booz, M. D., assistant to the chair of chemistry; Ralph Wilson, M. D., assistant to the chair of histology; Max Bahr, M. D., assistant to chair of operative and clinical midwifery. The board of trustees are: G. C. Smythe, M. D., Greencastle, Ind.; M. V. B. Newcomer, M. D., Tipton, Ind.; G. W. Burton, M. D., Mitchell, Ind.; M. H. Field, M. D., Indianapolis, Ind.; H. S. Herr, M. D., Bloomington, Ind.; William Wands, M. D., Indianapolis, Ind.; B. Wallace, M. D., Franklin, Ind.; Harrison Gable, M. D., Centerville, Ind.; E. G. Regennas, M. D., Hope, Ind.; George W. Burke, M. D., New Castle, Ind.; J. H. Ross, M. D., Kokomo, Ind.; L. T. Lowder, M. D., Bloomington, Ind.

The Indianapolis Business University, comprising Bryant & Stratton and Indianapolis Business College established in 1850 and incorporated in 1886 by the present management, is an institution for business training, for which definite purpose it is equipped in the most thorough and practical manner. It is recognized as one of the foremost educational institutions in this city. Thorough preparation is the demand, and it is upon this high plane that the Indianapolis Business University places its design and maintains its commanding position at the head of business schools. Not alone does the nniversity qualify its graduates to be competent bookkeepers, accountants, stenographers, secretaries, managers and clerks, but prepares its students to take positions so thoroughly qualified in the essentials of a business education, so disciplined in business habits, and so deserving of advancement that they rise to positions of trust and proprietorship, and finally reach the highest attainments in business life. To accomplish this end, the most judiciously arranged courses of study are provided, which, rejecting what is cumbersome, present what is most useful for thoroughness and efficiency in qualifying persons in the best way, in the shortest time, and at the least expense, for success in the actual duties of a business life. The university places at the head of its departments of study instructors who are experts in their specialties, who are conscientious and earnest in the discharge of their duty, and who have been connected with the institution many years, consequently make the advancement of the students their chief aim. The entire organization and work of the institution is under the immediate personal management of the president, ably assisted by a large faculty of experienced business educators. He devotes his time to directing the instruction and progress of students, to securing them home-like comforts and advantages and toward maintaining cordial fellowship between the business men who employ skilled help and the students of the university who are preparing to enter desirable positions in the commercial world. The president of the college is E. J. Heeb, an educator of recognized ability and mature experience under whose management the university has been brought to its present high state of efficiency.

The Industrial Training School, occupying the block bounded by South Meridian, Garden, Merrill streets and Madison avenue, is the largest and most thoroughly equipped institution of its kind in this country. The history of manual training in Indianapolis begins with the year 1889, when a course in wood-working and mechanical drawing was opened at High School No. 1. The numerous applications for admission to this department soon proved the popularity of a course of this nature in the High School curriculum, and the school board of '91 conceived the idea of the establishment of a school in which special attention should be paid to manual training. Due principally to the untiring efforts of Mr. John P. Frenzel, the idea soon materialized. The city council sanctioned the establishment of such an institution, and levied a special tax of five cents per hundred dollars for its erection and maintenance. Consequently ground was purchased in '92, and the building begun in March, '94. The school was opened February, 18, 1895, with 550 pupils. It has steadily grown until it now has an enrollment of 800 pupils. The curriculum of the Industrial Training School includes a regular high school course and a course in mechanic and domestic arts. The latter consists of wood-working, forging, foundry-work, pattern-making, machine-shop practice and mechanical drawing, for the boys; cooking, sewing, hygiene and home-nursing, for the girls. Further, courses in stenography, type-writing and book-keeping. The faculty consists of a corps of thirty teachers, besides a number of assistants and instructors, and the work in all departments is complete and thorough.

The Physio-Medical College of Indiana was organized in 1873. The first session consisted of a term of sixteen weeks and was conducted by five professors, and seven students were in attendance. The college has had a marked success and steady growth since its establishment, and the course now consists of four terms of six months each as a requisite to graduation. The present faculty is composed of sixteen professors and five special lecturers, and 71 students are in the class of 1895-6. The building now occupied at the corner of North and Alabama streets is the property of the faculty, and extended improvements by way of additional stories are contemplated. The Physio-Medical College conducts a free dispensary, where all deserving poor are treated free of charge. Clinics are held regularly on Tuesday and Friday of each week. The college has made a proposition to treat a large portion of the poor of the city who have heretofore been treated in the city dispensary, and thus by the co-operation of the Indiana Medical and the Central Colleges to dispense entirely with the need of the city dispensary. The officers and trustees of the college are: N. D. Woodard, M. D., president; C. T. Bedford, M. D., secretary; E. M. Outland, M. D., treasurer, and the

THE PHYSIO-MEDICAL COLLEGE OF INDIANA.

trustees are J. A. Stafford, W. H. Drapier, N. R. Elliott, B. F. Coffin, A. W. Fisher, Geo. Hasty.

The Indianapolis Propylæum was incorporated June 6, 1888, for the purpose of promoting and encouraging literary and scientific endeavors, also for erecting and maintaining a suitable building that would provide a center of higher culture for the public, and particularly for the women of Indianapolis. The organization of the Propylæum was due to the suggestion of Mrs. May Wright Sewall, who has from the beginning held the position of president of the association. The membership of the organization is composed exclusively of women. The leading organizations of the city, both those composed of women only, and those composed of both men and women, find in the Propylæum suitable quarters for their meetings. The building which is owned by

THE PROPYLÆUM.

GOVERNOR WHITCOMB STATUE.

the association is striking in appearance, of modern Romanesque architecture, and constructed of oolitic limestone, brick and iron. The location is beautiful, fronting upon the grounds of the Institution for the Blind. The building is handsomely furnished throughout with exceptional facilities and convenient accommodations for club meetings, banquets, lectures, public and private receptions, concerts, art exhibits, and, in general, for all social, literary, musical and other gatherings for which private houses are too small and public halls too large, too inconvenient or for various reasons unattractive. Officers: May Wright Sewall, president; Margaret D. Chislett and Carrie F. Robertson, vice-presidents; Eliza G. Wiley, secretary and Elizabeth Vinton Pierce, treasurer.

The Dramatic Club, which was incorporated in 1891, is the outgrowth of an organization of young ladies formed to give dramatic performances. The first play given by the club was at the Propylæum, where it still continues to hold its meetings. While the prime object of the club is to entertain its members and friends, it has been instrumental in arousing thought and intellectual interest in the art of acting. Plays of remarkable dramatic power as well as of fine literary merit have been written by some of its members, notable among which are the productions of Mrs. Margaret Butler Snow, Miss Louise Garrard, Miss Susan Van Valkenburg and Newton Booth Tarkington. In the seven years of its existence the club has more than fulfilled the expectations of its founders, and has proved to be a public benefactor. Its plays have often been repeated for charity.

Art Association of Indianapolis was organized at the home of Mr. and Mrs. T. L. Sewall, May 7, 1883, and incorporated on October 11, 1883. The object of the organization is the cultivation and advancement of art, and the establishment of a permanent art museum in this city. To this end it gives exhibitions, provides lectures and purchases works of art; only one year since its organization has it failed to hold an annual exhibition. The assembly hall of the Propylæum has been used as the art gallery of the association since 1891, with the exception of one season. In May, 1895, the Art Association received substantial recognition in the will of John Herron, who bequeathed to it $200,000 to be used in the erection of a museum. Owing to a contest of the will by the relatives of Mr. Herron, no progress

GIRLS' CLASSICAL SCHOOL RESIDENCE.

has been made in this direction. The association possesses the nucleus of an art gallery in sixteen paintings by eminent artists. The present officers are: May Wright Sewall, president; Charles E. Coffin, Amelia B. Mansur, Theodore C. Steele, vice-presidents; India C. Harris, recording secretary; Laura Fletcher Hodges, corresponding secretary, and Lillian Wright Dean, treasurer.

The Indianapolis Local Council of Women.—This organization is a result of a suggestion made by Mrs. May Wright Sewall at a meeting of the stockholders of the Indianapolis Propylæum, May 11, 1891. A permanent organization, however, was not effected until February 1, 1892. There are now over fifty affiliated societies represented in the Council. The pur-

DAS DEUTSCHE HAUS.

pose of the organization is to bring together women engaged in various lines of work, and to give their united influence to general lines upon which all can agree. The Council has demonstrated that it can accomplish enterprises far beyond the power of any single society. It has impressed its influence on the political as well as the social life of the city and state to such a degree that some of the most wholesome laws now on our statute books are the results of its efforts. The meetings of the Council are held monthly when papers are read by some notable person on subjects of general interest followed by general discussion. Officers: Flora Wulschner, president; Mrs. S. E. Perkins, recording secretary; Hester M. McClung, corresponding secretary; Mrs. Roscoe O. Hawkins, treasurer.

Matinee Musicale, was organized in November, 1877, with a charter membership of nine music loving women. To their zeal the society owes its permanent organization. The club meets at the Propylæum where it receives its members and guests on alternate Wednesdays, from October to May inclusive. The plan of work of the Musicale has been solicited and copied by many sister societies in and beyond the state, and the programs have increased in breadth and interest with each succeeding year. It is the second oldest women's musical club in the United States, and was one of five amateur societies to receive a special diploma of honor from the Columbian Exposition of 1893. From two to four recitals are given each year by artists of renown free to all members, active, associate and student. The membership, in 1897, numbers 275. The following are the officers: Carrie F. Robertson, president, to whose executive ability and untiring energy the present high standing of the club is due, has been president for thirteen years. Other officers are: Mary W. Whittier, vice-president; Harriett K. Lynn, secretary; Mary I. Jenckes, corresponding secretary; Adaline N. Branham, treasurer; Sarah T. Meigs, librarian; Gertrude C. Jameson, chairman of reception committee.

The Contemporary Club, one of the leading literary societies of the city, was organized at the home of Mr. and Mrs. Sewall June 27, 1890. Its membership is open to men and women on equal terms, and its object is to consider and discuss philosophical, religious, social, political, economical, æsthetic, scientific, literary, or other questions, in a catholic spirit, and in general to take advantage of all opportunities for information and culture that may from time to time come within its reach. The meetings of the club are of a social character, and are held in the Propylæum. The membership, numbering some two hundred, is drawn from among citizens of known social qualities and intellectual interests. Among those who have addressed the club during the last five years are many of the most brilliant thinkers in the fields of science, philosophy and literature. Much is due to the valuable suggestions of Mr. Sewall, in his four years' service as secretary, for the exceptional success of the club. Officers: John L. Griffiths, president; Noble C. Butler, Demarcus C. Brown and Edward Daniels, vice-presidents; George T. Porter, secretary; Dr. Charles E. Ferguson, treasurer.

Indianapolis Woman's Club (Literary), was founded in 1875, with seven charter members. Its membership is limited to 100. The regular meetings are held in the east parlor of the Propylæum on the first and third Fridays of each month, except the third Friday of June, the Fridays of July, August, and September. The president is Mrs. H. D. Pierce.

Indiana School of Art was established in 1889 and reorganized May, 1891. The school has an adequate collection of casts, and also a collection of drawings from old masters. It is prepared to offer excellent facilities in drawing and painting from life and the antique. The course of study in the school is aimed to be as near that of the best academies of the old world as circumstances will allow, and the training such as thoroughly to ground the pupils in drawing and painting, and to fit them to carry on their work either at home or abroad. Students may enter at any time, and will be assigned to classes according to their experience and accomplishments.

BRENNEKE ACADEMY.

The Brenneke Academy, corner of North and Illinois streets, was built in 1895, by professor D. B. Brenneke. The building is a three story brick and stone structure, 60 by 105 feet. It is especially designed and devoted to the art of dancing, and no city in the country has a building better adapted for the purposes for which it has been specially erected. It also affords special facilities for social gatherings, having an assembly hall 57 by 76, with a gallery sufficiently commodious to accommodate 300 spectators, and a banquet hall 37 by 57 feet. The building is also equipped with a well furnished kitchen, and all accessories necessary for banquets and other social functions. Professor Brenneke came to this city in 1882, and has maintained the foremost position as an instructor of dancing during that period.

Indianapolis Mænnerchor was organized in 1854 by Gottfried Recker, Nicholaus Jose and several other German citizens. It has given in concerts and in courses of instruction that have great influence the best works of German composers, and it has been potent in developing the love for music in this community. Its membership is composed of active members who are musicians or students, and others to whom the social features of the organization appeal. The present musical director is Alexander Ernestinoff. There are other musical organizations, prominent among which are the Indianapolis Liederkranz and the Indianapolis Choral Union and several glee clubs.

Indianapolis Literary Club is the foremost organization of its character, and its membership embraces many of the most prominent citizens of the city. Rev. M. L. Haines is president; Louis Howland, secretary, and John N. Hurty, treasurer of the club. Meetings are held every week in Plymouth Church building.

THE INDUSTRIAL TRAINING SCHOOL.

Fortnightly Club (Literary), meets every other Tuesday at the Propylæum. Elizabeth Dye is president.

Century Club is one of the important literary organizations of our city. Meetings are held every Tuesday in the Denison Hotel. Ernest P. Bicknell is president, and Herbert W. Foltz, secretary.

Over the Tea Cups, a social club of importance, meets weekly at 828 N. Pennsylvania street. Mrs. D. W. Marmon is president.

The Portfolio Club is devoted to the cultivation of art, music and literature, meets every other week at the School of Music. Herbert W. Foltz is secretary.

The Indianapolis Press Club is an organization whose membership embraces many bright men and women engaged in newspaper and other literary work. Arthur C. White is president, and Laura A. Smith secretary of the club.

Political Clubs and Debating Societies are numerous, prominent among which are the Columbia and Marion Clubs (Republican), and Hendricks Club (Democratic.)

The Joseph Eastman Sanitarium, the first to be established in the State, and one of the most complete institutions in the country for the treatment of the diseases of women and abdominal surgery, was established by Dr. Joseph Eastman in 1885.

The present model edifice, which is solely and entirely devoted to the uses of the sanitarium, was erected in 1894, at a cost of nearly $50,000. It is equipped throughout with every modern convenience, and all the necessary appliances and apparatus for the successful treatment of the diseases of women. The sanitarium has accommodation for the treatment of 60 patients,

DR. JOSEPH EASTMAN'S SANITARIUM.

and is reputed to have one of the finest private operating rooms in the country. Additional buildings will be erected during the coming year.

Dr. Joseph Eastman, the founder and present head of the sanitarium, is recognized as one of the leading American gynecologists. He was born in Fulton county, New York, January 29, 1842. His early education was confined to the limited advantages of winter schools and night study, and before the age of eighteen became a proficient blacksmith, working three years at that trade.

On the outbreak of the civil war he enlisted as private in the Seventy-

FIRST PRESBYTERIAN CHURCH

CHRIST'S CHURCH

seventh New York volunteers, went to the front and took part in four battles. Stricken with typhoid-malarial fever after the battle of Williamsburg, he was sent to the Mt. Pleasant Hospital, Washington, D. C. After his recovery he was placed on light duty, and afterward discharged from the regiment and appointed hospital steward in the U. S. army. While thus engaged for three years he attended three courses of lectures at the University of Georgetown, where he was graduated M. D. in 1865. He then passed the army examination and was commissioned assistant surgeon U. S. volunteers, and served in this capacity until mustered out at Nashville, Tenn., in May, 1866. Soon after this he located at Brownsburg, Ind., where he engaged in general practice for seven years. His medical education was supplemented by attending Bellevue Hospital Medical College, where he was again graduated in 1871. He became demonstrator of anatomy in the College of Physicians and Surgeons at Indianapolis in 1875, and was soon after appointed consulting surgeon to the City Hospital, which position he held for nine years, delivering lectures on clinical surgery during that time. He was the assistant of Dr. Parvin, the distinguished obstetrician and gynecologist, for eight years.

In 1879 he was one of the original organizers of the Central College of Physicians and Surgeons of Indianapolis, and accepted the chair of anatomy and clinical surgery. After having taught anatomy in the two colleges for seven years, a special chair was established in the last-named institution—that of diseases of women and abdominal surgery—which he has held ever since.

For the past six years he has been president of this college. Since 1886, Dr. Eastman has limited his practice to the diseases of women and abdominal surgery. During this practice he has opened the abdominal cavity more than thirteen hundred times, and is the only American surgeon who has ever operated for extra-uterine pregnancy by dissecting out the sack which contained the child, saving both the life of the infant and the mother. His operations are referred to in many of the standard text books, and have been described and discussed in all the leading European and American medical and surgical journals. He has been a liberal contributor to the literature on medical and surgical science, which has been widely translated in Germany and France. Dr. Eastman has originated and perfected many instruments for use in abdominal surgery and diseases of women, which are used by the more advanced gynecologists of Berlin, Vienna, and the great hospitals throughout Europe. In 1891, as recognition of his eminent skill and professional merit, the degree of LL. D. was conferred upon him by Wabash College. He was elected president of the Western Surgical and Gynecological Association, December 29, 1896. Associated with Dr. Eastman are his two sons, Thomas B. Eastman, graduate of the Central College of Physicians and Surgeons, of Indianapolis, and the Post-Graduate Medical Schools of New York and Chicago, who is now in London, Eng., and Joseph R. Eastman, a student in the University of Berlin, Germany.

Fletcher's Sanitarium, was established by Dr. W. B. Fletcher in 1888, for the treatment of mental and nervous diseases of women and was first located in North Pennsylvania street. The present institution is located at 124 North Alabama street and is equipped with the latest and most improved electrical and other appliances for the treatment of all nervous disorders of women.

Since establishing a private sanatarium Dr. Fletcher has had associated with him in the business, Mary A. Spink, M. D., who has full control of the female patients. Dr. Spink has had 12 years' experience in the treat-

DR. W. B. FLETCHER'S SANITARIUM.

ment of insane women, and has shown by her works what a woman of courage and possessed of a gentle and refining influence can accomplish toward soothing and restoring her sex from its greatest affliction. Dr. Spink is a member of the Board of State Charities and the state and local medical societies. It is a rule of the sanitarium to accept acute cases only in rare instances. The percentage of cures from this institution have been notably greater than that of any similar sanitarium in the country. Each patient is furnished with a separate room and special attendant, with meals served in the room. The fee is from $60 to $150 per month. Special arrangements are made with guardians for the treatment of chronic cases supposed to be incurable, at low rates by the year.

Dr. Fletcher was born in Indianapolis, August 18, 1837. His father, Calvin Fletcher, was one of the earliest settlers, locating here in 1821, before the settlement had become dignified by a place on the map. He was a lawyer and at once became prominent, not only in his profession, but foremost also in the work to advance civilizing influences, notably, in establishing a public school system and the introduction of the law establishing township libraries in every township in Indiana.

Dr. Fletcher's school career began in a little log school house that was located at the spot now marked by the intersection of South and New Jersey streets; afterwards in the old seminary then located in the University Park. In 1855 he studied under Agassiz and Tenny, botany, zoology and other natural sciences and the study of medicine in the College of Physicians and Surgeons in New York from 1856–9, graduating in 1859. He returned to Indianapolis and remained until 1861 when he was first among those to respond to the call for troops. His company was the Sixth Indiana, and he was detailed for duty on the staff of General T. A. Morris, and later transferred to the staff of General J. J. Reynolds. His war experience was of a brief but thrilling order and before his first year's service he was captured, brought in irons before General Robert E. Lee, confined in prison, made two attempts at escape, was wounded in October, 1861, was tried, court-martialed, condemned to death and ordered to execution. He was fortunately reprieved by order of General Lee pending an investigation, and by a providential occurence and through the blunder of the notorius Captain Wirtz, his identity was lost to the confederates as a special prisoner. He was paroled and placed in charge of the gangrene hospital in Richmond, and in March, 1862, was paroled from the service, but during the entire war gave his best services to the Sanitary Commission, the State or the general government. In 1866–7 Dr. Fletcher visited Europe and studied in the hospitals of London, Paris, Glasgow and Dublin. For many years he has been professor of various departments of the Indiana Medical College and is now professor of mental diseases in the Central College of Physicians and Surgeons. He is a member of the American Medical Association, of the State Medical Society, the New York Medico-Legal Society and of the State Microscopical Society of which he was the first president. He established the City Dispensary in 1870, and was for many years consulting physician of the City and St. Vincent hospitals. In 1882 he was elected State Senator from this county and in 1883 was made superintendent of the Indiana Hospital for the Insane. During his administration the institution witnessed great progress, the most notable innovation being the abolishment of restraint as a means of treating insanity. He was the first superintendent to appoint a woman physician to have charge of the female patients. He has been a liberal contributor to the literature on the treatment of the insane and other branches of medical science.

Runnels's Private Hospital was established in 1890 by O. S. Runnels, A. M., M. D., 276 North Illinois street, to meet the requirements of the best services attainable in surgical and gynecological practice. After an extensive surgical experience of twenty years under the most favorable conditions possible in the various public hospitals, hotels and homes, Dr. Runnels recognized the need of better service than could be thus commanded. Finding it impossible to secure the best results in the unfavorable environment of the old order, the service was transferred to the private hospital where everything has been specialized to the highest degree.

DR. O. S. RUNNELS'S SANITARIUM.

The building itself, very commodious, pleasantly situated, and easily accessible, has been made to conform in all its appointments to the demands of absolute asepsis. It is surgically clean and entirely free from the odors and hospital suggestions incident to large institutions, especial care being taken to combine home comforts and enjoyments with the requirements of science.

All the nurses are graduates of the best training schools and selected because of their special adaptation to the work of nursing. They have not the acquirements of the schools merely, but that intuitive touch and tenderness given to the true nurse at birth, and which is such an essential feature of acceptable service. Special attention is paid to the abundant provision of the best food; to good cooking and a liberal table as the patient becomes able to enjoy it: The starvation diet of most hospitals is condemned. The "building up" policy adopted by Dr. Runnels is believed to be one of the chief reasons for the quick and thorough recovery of his patients. Every effort is made to restore the patient without resort to surgery. Homœopathic medi-

PLYMOUTH CHURCH.

cation, massage, electricity, the "rest cure" and every means for recuperation are employed to their full extent, thus making conservative work a specialty. Dr. Runnels avoids the knife if possible, believing that all other reasonable means should be exhausted first. But his natural aptitude, extensive observation and long experience in surgical practice have placed him in the front rank of the best surgeons. He does all the operating himself and is in daily attendance. All abdominal, pelvic, rectal and nutritional diseases are honestly and skillfully treated by the most approved methods.

The hospital has a capacity for twenty patients, and plans are perfected for its enlargement. Visiting physicians are always welcome and correspondence receives prompt attention.

Dr. O. S. Runnels was born at Fredonia, Ohio, in 1847; was educated at Oberlin College, Ohio, and at the Cleveland Homœopathic College—his doctor's degree bearing date 1871. He immediately engaged in general practice in Indianapolis, where he speedily attained distinction, and has since been surpassed by none in the extent and high character of his work. Excelling as an obstetrician he at once entered upon the practice of gynecology, which he has now followed as a specialty for over twenty years. He has practiced pelvic and abdominal surgery extensively, and has a percentage of successful cures unsurpassed by the best operators. He has from the first kept in touch with the best professional minds of the world, having the largest and choicest physician's library in Indiana, and taking regularly twenty-five of the best medical journals published. In addition so this he has supplemented his education by special courses of post-graduate work in Chicago, Philadelphia, New York and Boston, and in Edinburgh, Birmingham, London, Paris, Vienna and Berlin. He has been a voluminous contributor to the medical societies and periodicals, and is at the present time writing a book entitled "Surgical Diseases of the Uterus, Tubes and Ovaries." He is a member and ex-president of the American Institute of Homœopathy; president of the American Association of Orificial Surgeons; member and ex-president of the Indiana Institute of Homœopathy; American Association for the Advancement of Science; American Public Health Association; American Society of Electro-Therapeutists; honorary member of the Massachusetts Surgical and Gynecological Society, member honorary and vice-president of the World's Homœopathic Congress, Basel, Switzer land; and member of the Indianapolis Literary Club. Oberlin College in 1894 conferred upon Dr. Runnels the honorary degree of Master of Arts.

The Fox & Garhart Specialty Company, manufacturers of dentists' specialties, was incorporated in May, 1893. The offices and laboratory are located in the old library building, in Pennsylvania street. The principal product is the manufacture of High Standard Gold White Alloy.

Dr. A. R. White, manufacturer of proprietary medicines, began business in 1876. He manufactures White's Pulmonaria and Dandelion Alterative, which have a large sale throughout the country. The laboratory and offices are located in his building, in South Meridian street.

Dr. L. H. Dunning's Sanitarium was established in May, 1892, for the treatment of diseases of women and the practice of abdominal surgery. It is located at the corner of Alabama and Michigan streets, in the handsome and commodius residence which the doctor purchased and fitted with all the necessary requirements for the proper treatment of the classes of cases to which it is limited. In this respect its appointments are the equal of the best sanitariums in the land. It is the aim of the management to make the surroundings as homelike as possible with the proper adherence at all times to sanitary laws and antiseptic requirements. The sanitarium can now accommodate about twenty patients, but improvements are in contemplation to increase its facilities. Since its establishment, Dr. Dunning has found it necessary to remodel and enlarge the sanitarium to meet the demands made upon it

DR. L. H. DUNNING'S SANITARIUM.

Dr. Leham H. Dunning is a native of Michigan and was born at Edwardsburgh in that state in 1850. He was educated in the Edwardsburgh high school, studied medicine in the University of Buffalo, and completed his course in the Rush Medical College, of Chicago, where he graduated with honor in January, 1872. He began his practice in Troy, Michigan, where he was for a time District Superintendent of Instruction. He was appointed correspondent of the Michigan Board of Health, and while filling these duties acquired his first experience as a writer on medical and surgical subjects which have since proven of great value to the profession and himself. In 1878 he moved to South Bend, Ind., where he enjoyed a wide and lucrative practice. His contributions to medical literature began in Troy, Michigan, were continued here and soon gained for him a national reputation. He took several special courses in the Post Graduate Medical School and Polyclinic of New York and supplemented these courses by studying in the hospitals of London and Vienna during his trip abroad. On his return to this country, at the request of the faculty of The Medical College of Indiana, he moved to this city, accepted the position of Adjunct Professor of Diseases of Women and practiced his profession here with a special reference to gynecological and abdominal surgery. On the death of Dr. T. B. Harvey, who had filled the chair of Diseases of Women in The Medical College of Indiana for twenty years, Dr. Dunning was elected as his successor. He is consulting gynecologist in the City Hospital and the City Dispensary and Deaconess' Home. He is a member of the Marion County Medical Society, Indiana State Medical Society, and fellow of the American Association of Obstetricians and Gynecologists.

DR. LOUIS BURCKHARDT'S LYING-IN HOSPITAL.

Indianapolis Lying-In Hospital was established in October, 1894, by Dr. Louis Burckhardt for the convenience and accommodation of women who wished to be confined away from home, and requiring the care of a skillful physician and trained nurses. The hospital is located at the corner of Alabama and McCarty streets, and is admirably equipped for the particular purpose for which it is designed. The hospital has accommodation for eight patients, with a corps of trained nurses.

Dr. Louis Burckhardt came to this city in May, 1893, and is a graduate of the University of Zurich, Switzerland, where he received his medical education. He studied in the hospitals of Freiburg, Strassburg, Zurich, Leipzig,

Berlin, Vienna and Paris. He was physician in the Children's Hospital and the Maternity Hospital at Basel, Germany, occupied the chair of operative and clinical midwifery at the Central College of Physicians and Surgeons, and is consulting obstetrician to the City Dispensary and the Protestant Deaconess' Home.

DR. H. O. PANTZER'S SANITARIUM.

Dr. H. O. Pantzer's Sanitarium was established in 1892. It is located at the intersection of Massachusetts avenue, New Jersey and Michigan streets, in a handsome residence building that has been remodeled and specially equipped as a private hospital by Dr. Pantzer for the treatment of the diseases of women.

Dr. Pantzer graduated from the Medical College of Indiana in 1881, and engaged in the general practice of medicine until 1892, during which period he devoted nearly four years to study in several European universities, perfecting his general knowledge in medicine and surgery under some of the most eminent professors in those colleges. He is a member of the American Medical Association and other well-known medical societies, and occupied the chair of clinical gynecology in Central College of Physicians and Surgeons.

Other Private Sanitariums have been established in the city, prominent among which are Dr. John Randolph Brown's for the treatment of mental diseases of men, and Dr. Frank Ferguson's Sanitarium for the treatment of diseases of women.

FIRST BAPTIST CHURCH.
MERIDIAN STREET M E. CHURCH.
SECOND PRESBYTERIAN CHURCH.
ST. JOHN'S CHURCH.

Fletcher's Bank was founded by Stoughton A. Fletcher, Sr., in 1839. It is the oldest and largest banking institution in the state and has been in continuous operation since its establishment. Its present capital is $1,000,000. Surplus $100,000. It is owned and controlled by the now existing partners, S. J. and A. M. Fletcher. The firm owns more government bonds and securities than any other financial institution in the state of Indiana. The bank is commodiously housed in its building at 30–34 East Washington street, the site originally occupied fifty-seven years ago.

The Indiana National Bank, one of the oldest financial corporations in this city, began business as the branch of the Bank of the State of Indiana in 1857 in a building where the Claypool block now stands, at the corner of Washington and Illinois streets. George Tousey was president, Columbus Stevenson cashier, and Volney T. Malott teller. The conditions immediately following the war not being favorable to banks of this character, the major portion of the business was transferred to a national bank, and on March 14, 1865, the Indiana National Bank opened its doors on North Meridian street, with Oliver Tousey as president and D. E. Snyder, cashier. Later on the branch of the Bank of the State of Indiana was merged into the Indiana National, and George Tousey and D. M. Taylor were president and cashier, respectively. William Coughlin, who succeeded Mr. Tousey, was president until 1882, when he retired to become vice-president, and Volney T. Malott, who had for a period left the bank to engage in railroading and other enterprises, returned, purchased a large portion of the stock and was elected president. Mr. Snyder, cashier, was succeeded by Mr. D. M. Taylor. He was followed by William E. Coffin, and when the bank charter was renewed Edward B. Porter was appointed to the position, and has filled it ever since. Under the management of Volney T. Malott the bank has been exceptionally prosperous, and has taken a high place among the foremost financial institutions of the country. The paid up capital of the bank is $300,000; surplus $720,000 and a line of deposits aggregating more than $3,000,000. It is also the government depository.

The destruction of the bank's building by fire September 18, 1895, necessitated the removal to temporary quarters in the Indiana Trust building, awaiting the erection of a permanent home is undoubtedly one of the finest and most complete bank structures in the country. The building is located on the ground formerly occupied by the Bank of Commerce and other buildings at the corner of Virginia avenue and Pennsylvania street, and is used by the bank exclusively.

The Merchants' National Bank began business January 18, 1865, with $100,000 capital, its officers being Henry Schnull, president, and V. T. Malott, cashier. Its first charter expired January 19, 1885. An extension was secured from this date for twenty years. During the period of the first charter $279,000 in dividends were paid to its stockholders and $20,000 set aside as a surplus fund with which the bank started on its new lease. Its capital is now

MERCHANTS' NATIONAL BANK.

$1,000,000, and surplus fund $90,000. The present officers of the bank are J. P. Frenzel, president; O. N. Frenzel, vice-president and cashier; Frederick Fahnley, second vice-president, and O. F. Frenzel, assistant cashier.

The Merchants' National Bank has always been a distinctively home institution. Its business has been strictly local and devoted almost exclusively to our own merchants and manufacturers. One of the features of the bank is its foreign department, organized in 1870 by Frenzel Brothers, where drafts and letters of credit are issued on all parts of the world. The bank has been uniformly prosperous, and is considered one of the strongest and most conservative financial institutions in our state. It occupies very handsome and commodious quarters at the corner of Washington and Meridian streets.

The Capital National Bank was chartered November 13, 1889, and commenced business December 8, of the same year, in the Western Union building, with a capital of $300,000. The officers and directors were M. B. Wilson president, John S. Spann, S. P. Sheerin, M. O'Connor, J. A. Lemcke, Edward Hawkins, W. D. Ewing, cashier, N. F. Dalton, Josephus Collett vice-president, N. S. Byram, Noble C. Butler and P. H. Blue. This organization continued until the spring of 1891. Immediately upon the completion of the Commercial Club building the bank was removed to its present quarters, which were specially designed for its uses. The bank has enjoyed a profitable and steady growth since its organization. It has added $45,000 to its surplus fund and has $12,000 in its undivided profits account. The present officers and directors are M. B. Wilson, president; William F. Churchman, cashier; N. S. Byram, C. F. Smith, E. S. Wilson, N. F. Dalton and A. A. McKain.

FITZGERALD BUILDING.

The State Bank of Indiana was organized in December, 1892, but did not begin business formally until January 3, 1893. It was incorporated with a capital stock of $200,000, and has enjoyed a marked prosperity from its inception. The officers are Hiram W. Miller, president; Daniel A. Coulter, vice-president; James R. Henry, cashier.

The Indiana Trust Company was incorporated May 1, 1893, with a capital stock of $1,000,000. It was the first company in the state to be organized under the act of March 4, 1893, of the General Assembly of Indiana, authorizing the organization of loan and trust and safe deposit companies. Its heavy capitalization, and the character of its incorporators and stockholders endowed it with the ability to discharge the manifold functions that a trust company is called upon to fill, and from its inception has been successful to a large degree. The officers of the company are, J. P. Frenzel, president; Frederick Fahnley, first vice-president; E. G. Cornelius, second vice-president; John A. Butler, secretary. The directors are, Frederick Fahnley, of Fahnley & McCrea, wholesale milliners; Albert Lieber, president Indianapolis Brewing Company; James F. Failey, capitalist; O. N. Frenzel, vice-president and cashier Merchants' National Bank; F. G. Darlington, superintendent Indianapolis division P. C. C. & St. L. Railway Company; E. G. Cornelius, president Indiananaplis Chair Mfg. Company; Edward Hawkins, manager Indiana School Book Company; H. W. Lawrence, proprietor Spencer House; Charles

B. Stuart, attorney at law, Lafayette, Ind.; William F. Piel., Sr., manager National Starch Mfg. Company, and J. P. Frenzel.

The company is authorized by law to act as executor, administrator, guardian, assignee, receiver, trustee and agent. It assumes the management of estates, real and personal, attending to the investment of funds, the collection of rents, the payment of taxes and the general administration of property. It is a legal depository for courts and trust funds as well as for building associations. It buys and sells municipal and county bonds, and loans money on first mortgages and collateral security. It acts as surety on the bonds of executors, administrators, and guardians throughout the state. It accepts deposits, which may be withdrawn on notice, or at a fixed date previously agreed on, and allows interest on them. The liability of the stockholders of the company, added to its capital makes a sum of $2,000,000, pledged for the faithful discharge of its trusts.

An important feature of the company's business is its Safety Vault Department, where nearly 2,000 safety deposit boxes are at the disposal of the public at rental ranging from $5 yearly, and upwards. The vaults are without doubt the handsomest and most complete in the west, and furnish absolute protection against burglary and destruction of valuables by either fire or water. Commodiously arranged in the rear of the vaults are the offices, where the patrons can retire and arrange and transact their business in utmost capacity. P. S. Cornelius is manager of this department, and Mrs. Mary McKenzie, manager of the woman's department.

The Union Trust Company of Indianapolis, Ind.—To no other custodians are such important interests confided as to the trust companies which exert such a power in the financial affairs of all our leading and most progressive cities. The scope and aim of these institutions is, primarily, the safe keeping and management of funds for heirs, absentees, non-residents and all those whose circumstances do not permit their own personal administration of their affairs. The moral, as well as the material obligations, assumed by a trust company are, therefore, more weighty than those imposed upon any other manner of financial institutions, and it is manifest that their operations should be distinguished by the utmost conservatism and guided by a management qualified by long and active experience and a broad and comprehensive knowledge of all matters embraced in the realm of legitimate financiering. An institution which is managed upon the principles above expressed is The Union Trust Company of Indianapolis, Indiana. Although this company dates its incorporation back only to 1893, the well understood resources, experience in financial affairs and high standing of those to whose enterprise its inception was due, at once placed it among the strongest and most influential institutions of its kind in the West, in fact, in the country. Its stock is held by leading capitalists and business men to be an investment of the soundest and most remunerative character, while its presiding officers and its directors are men whose names are synonymous with all that guarantees financial stability, and an energetic, yet conservative management.

FLETCHER'S BANK.

The officers are: John H. Holliday, president; Addison C. Harris, vice-president; Henry Eitel, second vice-president; H. C. G. Bals, secretary. The directors are: Charles H. Brownell, Peru; S. A. Culbertson, New Albany; Thomas C. Day; I. C. Elston, Crawfordsville; John H. Holliday, Addison C. Harris, Sterling R. Holt, George Kothe, Henry C. Long, Volney T. Malott, Edward L. McKee, and Samuel E. Rauh. The company has a paid up capital of $600,000, and a surplus of $60,000, and the stockholders' additional liability is $600,000.

If the volume of deposits and the magnitude of the interests confided to its care in the varied relations which it holds with its patrons in its capacity as a trust company, are any criterion of the confidence reposed in the management of the Union Trust Company by the surrounding community and non-resident clients, there are no similar organizations anywhere which can make a better showing. As a matter of fact, this company's services are held in the same high estimation by the people of Indianapolis as are those of the old established and influential Eastern trust companies by the people of New York, Philadelphia and Boston.

The operations of the company cover a very wide field; they give special attention to the settlement of estates, acting as executor, administrator, guardian, assignee, trustee and agent. They assume entire charge of property and estates for heirs and absentees, paying taxes, collecting rents, interest, dividends, etc., writing insurance, etc., and they also make a feature of the investment of funds for individuals and corporations.

A general financial business is transacted in negotiating first mortgage loans on farm and city property in the best counties in Indiana, and in buying and selling high grade investment securities, such as municipal, county and school bonds, etc., and in this connection their services are invaluable to non-residents seeking investments combining as high a rate of interest as is consistent with absolute safety. The company have their offices at 68 East Market street, Indianapolis, Ind., and correspondence thus addressed always receives prompt and careful attention.

The Marion Trust Company was incorporated December 10, 1895, with a capital of $300,000, and has all the powers granted to trust companies. Is authorized by law to act as executor, administrator, guardian, assignee, receiver, depository of money, trustee under wills or by appointment of court, and agent for individuals and corporations. It acts as trustee in cases as designated by court and in deeds, mortgages, or trusts given by persons or corporations; as agent for the management of property of corporations or persons; as a financial depository for corporations; as agent in issuing, registering, transferring or countersigning stocks, bonds and debentures; as custodian of wills, and consults as to them and other trust matters, and receives money in small or large sums as time deposits and pays interest thereon. It thus offers a profitable and secure investment for savings, inheritances and other funds.

A special department of the Marion Trust Company is its savings department, in which savings deposits of one dollar and upwards are received and on which interest is allowed on all sums remaining on deposit for six months

MANSUR BLOCK, EAST WASHINGTON STREET.

or longer. Demand and time certificates of deposit are also issued on which special rates of interest are allowed. The advantages possessed by the savings department of the Marion Trust Company over the ordinary savings bank is that it has safely invested a large capital that stands as security to its depositors and interest is paid at a fixed rate and not dependent on the earnings of the institution.

The officers and directors are as follows: Frank A. Maus, president; Ferdinand Winter, vice-president; Henry Kothe, second vice-president and treasurer; Byron K. Elliott, Allen M. Fletcher, Herman Lieber, Charles Mayer, Albert E. Metzger, Michael O'Connor, Samuel O. Pickens, George G. Tanner and Chas. N. Thompson. The offices of the company are located in the Franklin Building, southeast corner of Market street and Monument Place.

The Mutual Life Insurance Company of Indiana was incorporated under the insurance laws of 1865, in the name of "The Mutual Life and Endowment Association of Indiana," February 17, 1882, by Henry Malpas, Dr. H. F. Barnes, Charles Oliver, and other parties. Soon after its organization, J. C. Green, Deloss Root and W. R. Myers became interested in the organization.

In 1893 the legislature confirmed the charter under the Acts of 1865, and in 1895, the name was changed by legislative enactment to "The Mutual Life Insurance Company of Indiana."

For the past 5 years the company has issued none but level premium and investment policies, and is the only level premium company chartered by the state. It is now carrying over $4,000,000 life insurance, and has since its organization paid out over $600,000 to its policy holders. It has at the present time $350,000, loaned on first mortgage securities in the state, and has gross assets of $394,313.97. Its home office was for over 14 years located on the corner of Delaware and Court streets in this city.

MARION TRUST CO.—FRANKLIN BUILDING.

In March, 1896, it took quarters on the third floor of the Lemcke building, corner of Market and Pennsylvania streets. It has branch offices in Fort Wayne, Terre Haute, Lafayette, and numerous other cities in the state. It is also doing business in Pennsylvania, with headquarters at Pittsburgh.

The growth of this company has not been of the mushroom order, but slow and healthy. It has, by its conservativeness, secured a firm hold on its patrons, and is recognized as one of the strongest and safest financial institutions in the state. Its present officers are W. R. Myers, president; Henry Malpas, secretary and treasurer, and J. C. Green, attorney.

The Industrial Life Association was incorporated August 28, 1877. It is a purely mutual company. The officers and directors of the company are: J. O. Cooper, president; J. W. Morris, secretary and treasurer; I. S. Gordon, Alonzo Hendrickson, George E. Townley, and Dr. Henry Jameson. It is the oldest life insurance organization in the state, and during its existence has issued over 45,000 policies, in the industrial department, and has paid to its policy-holders over $300,000. The company is doing a large and constantly increasing business in Indiana, and many other desirable states. The offices of the company are located in the Hartford block, in East Market street.

The State Life Insurance Company.—The organization of this company was the outgrowth of a popular demand in Indiana for a home insurance company that would meet all modern requirements as to the scientific soundness of its basis, and the equity of its plans; accordingly, the company has adopted the standard scientific premiums and reserves of the American Experience Table of Mortality and 4 per cent. interest in all its policies; it is consequently above criticism as to soundness and permanency.

So well has the company and its plans met the approval of the best and most conservative business and professional men of the state that they have, in the exercise of an intelligent self-interest and state pride, given it a support unparalleled in the history of life insurance. It has made the greatest first year record ever made by any company in the world, measured by the very large premium income, the high character of the business, the low expense ratio and the large reserve accumulated.

The company is now issuing a full line of policies, including ten-year term and whole life policies, with annual and deferred dividends, and 10, 15 and 20 payment policies, with all modern features. It is now doing business in four states, and is meeting with great success in all of them, and expects to enter two more in the near future. From its sworn statement filed with the auditor of state it is shown that the total of insurance written and in force December 31, 1895, amounted to $3,548,500; premium income, $70,661.48; losses paid, $7,500; disbursements (aside from losses including dividends to policy holders, commission to agents, $39,548.90; net assets, $23,612.58; losses unpaid, none; liabilities, none.

The amount of business secured by this company during its first year from the best known and most conservative business men in Indiana must be credited not only to a desire to support a home institution, but also to the confidence inspired by the high standing and recognized ability of its management. The officers are as follows: Andrew M. Sweeney, president; Samuel Quinn, vice-president and superintendent of agents; Wilbur S. Wynn, secretary and actuary; Allison Maxwell, M. D., medical director; Charles F. Coffin, general counsel; Union Trust Company (capital $600,000) treasurer. The home office of the company is located at 515 to 520 Lemcke building.

Indiana Insurance Company.—This company was organized by a special act granting the company a special charter on February 13, 1851, to some of our best known citizens of that date. Among the number were included Wm. H. Morrison, Benjamin I. Blythe, Oliver H. Smith, Timothy R. Fletcher, Royal Mathews, Robert B. Duncan and John W. Hamilton, all of the city of Indianapolis, Ind., continuing them in office perpetually, and making the charter of the company a perpetual charter, and by that name made capable and able in law to have, purchase, receive, possess, enjoy and retain to themselves and their successors lands, tenements, rents, goods, chattels and effects to any amount not exceeding in the whole $300,000, as capital stock; to transact the business of fire, life, accident, tornado, inland, marine insurance and annuity and also banking and trust company business.

INDIANA INSURANCE COMPANY.

The organization was completed and the charter was accepted in March, 1851. On March 5, 1875, the legislature amended the charter continuing it as a perpetual charter under special act and adding and retaining the following names as members of the corporation, to wit: Wm. H. Morrison, Robert B. Duncan, Abraham W. Hendricks, Elijah S. Alford, James A. Wildman,

Addison L. Roach, Thomas D. Kingan, Richard J. Bright, John Love, Robert L. McKee, George Clark, A. F. Armstrong, Wm. R. McKeen, by the name and style of the Indiana Insurance Company, to re-organize the company and subscribe for the capital stock of the same, and elected their officers and directors according to the terms of the charter.

It was continued under their administration until the year 1880, when the present management of the company purchased a controling interest in the stock of the company, and have been operating it successfully ever since. The present officers and directors are as follows: M. V. McGilliard, president; Otto Stechhan, vice-president; E. G. Cornelius, treasurer; J. Kirk Wright, secretary; Charles Schurman, assistant secretary; W. A. Wildhack, A. A. Young, James S. Cruse, George C. Pearson, C. G. Dodge and W. F. Browder. The company confines its business entirely to fire insurance upon dwellings and contents, mercantile buildings and contents, churches, school houses, colleges, brick warehouses, hotels and office buildings and their contents. They do not write upon special hazard property of any kind. The capital stock has been placed at $300,000, of which $200,000 has been taken and the balance of the capital stock is being placed at the present time. The McGilliard Agency Company are general agents of this leading company, which is the largest insurance company organized in the state of Indiana. The McGilliard Agency Company consists of M. V. McGilliard, Edwin Hill, Albert W. Hall and J. Kirk Wright. It is the oldest fire insurance agency in the state of Indiana, with one exception.

The German Fire Insurance Company of Indiana is the outgrowth of the German Mutual Insurance Company, organized April 1, 1854, and which, during the long period that has since intervened, gained a foremost position among the leading mutual fire associations of the country. After conducting business for over forty years on the mutual system, it was decided to incorporate as a joint stock company, and this change was effected March 11, 1896, under the title of The German Fire Insurance Co., of Indiana. The last statement submitted by the old company to the Auditor of State showed actual resources of $353,078.54, and insurance in force of $5,733,362.50, with no valid claims outstanding. Incorporated with a capital of $100,000, the company begins business under the new system with actual assets of nearly half a million dollars, thus making it the strongest fire company in the State, over all of which it does business. The new management comprises Theodore Stein, president; Frederick Schrader, first vice-president; John W Schmidt, second vice-president; Lorenz Schmidt, secretary, and Theodore Reyer, treasurer. These five gentlemen, together with Messrs. Ferd A. Mueller, Wm. F. Kuhn, Wm. Wilkins and Wm. Kohlstaedt, compose the directory. The management comprises some of the best-known business men in Indianapolis.

The Fidelity Building and Savings Union was chartered in December, 1889, and in 1891, Nos. 2, 3, 4 and 5 of the "Fidelity" were chartered with a capital stock of $1,000,000 each. This is the largest and among the oldest building and loan associations doing a general business in Indiana. The oldest stock is now being paid off at a net profit of 12 per cent. to the members. In addition to this profit the stock is exempt from taxation, which makes it equivalent to a 20 per cent. investment to the stockholders. The total dividends apportioned to members since the organization has been $377,400. The amount of loans in force exceed $1,000,000, and 38,722 shares of stock were issued up to December 31, 1895. The officers of the company are J. B. Patton, president; A. M. Sweeney, vice-president; E. J. Robison, secretary; H. H. Mosier, treasurer; O. Z. Hubbell, attorney, and J. H. Slater, actuary.

The Indiana Society for Savings was incorporated on April 6, 1893. It is recognized as one of the most solid and substantial institutions of the kind in Indiana, and has at this time assets exceeding $450,000. The policy of this association has been to confine its loaning operations almost entirely to the city of Indianapolis, and it has at the present time in excess of 97 per cent. of its loans on Marion county real estate. It has earned for its stockholders, since its organization, an annual dividend of 10 per cent. compound, and has paid during its existence over $50,000 in cash dividends to its stockholders. This association was a pioneer in the movement toward the abolishment of the expense fund. It was organized without this feature, and as a result its officers have exercised the strictest economy in its management, with the result that its expense rate during the past year has been one and nine-tenths per cent. as compared with twelve and one-half to sixteen per cent. on the part of its competitors. It issues stock at any time without the payment of an entrance fee, while its stockholders at any time have the privilege to withdraw without the payment of a penalty. It pays 8 per cent. cash dividends on its investment stock, and allows interest on such stock up to the date of its withdrawal. It has been the policy of the association to pay such withdrawals practically on demand, not taking advantage of the legal right to 90 days. The capital stock of the association is $1,500,000, of which $1,200,000 has been subscribed. The officers of the association are: Charles E. Thornton, president; John A. Finch, vice-president; Charles A. Bookwalter, secretary and treasurer, and Charles N. Thompson, attorney. The directors are: Charles E. Thornton, J. Augustus Lemcke, Thomas C. Day, John A. Finch, Guilford A. Dietch, J. W. Sawyer, M. D., and Charles A. Bookwalter. Fletcher's Bank is depository.

The Monument Savings and Loan Association of Indianapolis, Indiana, U. S. A., is a corporation duly organized under the provisions and acts of the General Assembly of the State of Indiana, providing for the incorporation of building and loan associations, and placing them under the supervision of the Auditor of State. The authorized capital of this association is one million dollars ($1,000,000), and at the time of the last report to the Auditor of State, on the 30th day of June, 1895, the association had a subscribed capital of $523,000, and 1,352 individual shareholders, the shares being issued in four classes, viz.: installment, fully paid, prepaid and debenture shares.

The officers and directors of the association are Walter T. Cox, president (attorney C. C. C. & St. L. R. R.); R. French Stone, M. D., vice-president (author of Biographical Sketches of American Physicians); William

F. Churchman, treasurer (cashier of Capital National Bank); (Henry F. Stevenson, secretary and general manager (lawyer); W. E. Stevenson (real estate and loan broker); and L. L. Burr (capitalist and broker), New Castle, Ind. These gentlemen are identified with the highest business element in the city, and Mr. Henry F. Stevenson, the secretary, is especially qualified by virtue of his past experience and record as a successful lawyer and loan agent for his present responsible position. The methods employed by this association, which operates what is known as the "definite contract plan," are bound to be very popular. This "definite contract" is issued to every applicant for shares. There are no "estimates" or "believe we can mature" figures given. All is definite. You get a certificate in which the withdrawal value of your shares for each month is printed. You do not have to go to the secretary or any one else to find out the value of your shares. It is set down in the certificate, and you KNOW exactly at any time what your money has earned you. A look at the certificate of shares of a definite contract association, will at any time reveal to its holders that he can withdraw not only all he has invested, but a definite amount of interest besides. These amounts are fixed, and the investor or the borrower can determine precise results before any money is paid on shares. In the larger cities such definite contract associations have operated for several years, and are some of the most prosperous associations. The figures of the Monument are based on careful experience and due consideration of all that it involves, $7,000 having been expended in the preparation of tables, and in the gathering of data; hence it is no experiment, but a fact, and an attractive one at that, for the investor. In addition to the definite contract plan, the Lawyers' Loan & Trust Co., a strong financial concern, after having carefully examined the plans and methods of the Monument Savings and Loan Association, have consented to issue, in connection with every certificate, an Indemnity Contract guaranteeing interest, maturity and withdrawal of each and every share of the association, thus making all doubly sure.

The Monument can be pronounced as safe and solid as its name indicates, and its unique features are especially attractive to all those preferring a certainty to an estimate.

I. N. Richie, real estate and loan agent at 60 East Market street, in the Lemcke Building, began business in 1892. His business is exclusively devoted to real estate and mortgages loans, and receives his personal attention. He is recognized as one of the most prominent and enterprising men in his business in the city. In 1891 he platted Richie's Clifford avenue addition, and in 1893 Capital Park addition in the western portion of the city, and is also interested in Ardmore addition at Central avenue and 30th street. Mr. Richie was instrumental in purchasing the property and securing the terminal facilities for the Louisville, New Albany and Chicago Railroad Company at this point. This was the most important real estate transaction during 1895.

John S. Spann & Company, established in 1857, have had a longer continued existence and identification with the real estate and insurance business in Indianapolis than any other firm. They have participated in many of the most important real estate transactions recorded during their long and successful career, and some of the attractive portions of the city of to-day are the results of their far-sightedness and good judgment, having been platted and sold by them. Notable among these are the Wm. H. Morrison addition, platted in 1873; Gen. T. A. Morris' addition and the larger portion of the northeast section of the city; Spann & Company's Woodlawn addition and other well-known additions. The members of the firm are John S., Thomas H., John M. and Henry J. Spann. The firm also represents some of the most noted and substantial foreign and American fire insurance companies and are the financial agents for the Connecticut Mutual Life Insurance Company of Hartford, Conn., and the United States Mortgage and Trust Company of New York. The offices of the firm are located in the Hartford Block, 89 East Market street.

JOHN S. SPANN & CO.

W. E. Mick & Co., real estate, rental and loan agents, have been established since 1868, and is one of the oldest and best known firms in this line of business in Indianapolis. The members of the firm are W. E. and E. L. Mick. The main offices are located at 68 East Market street, with a branch office in their handsome modern three-story brick building, at the corner of Illinois and Twenty-second streets. The business of this firm has kept pace with the growth of the city, and many of the principal additions to Indianapolis are the results of its enterprise. Among the properties that Mick & Co. either owned directly or were instrumental in adding to the city are: King's Arsenal Heights addition in 1871; King's subdivision of Highland Park, 1872; T. A. Lewis & Co.'s Arsenal Heights addition, 1872; Shoemaker & Lippincott's Brookside addition, and Ramsey's Brookside addition, 1871. They subdivided Clark's addition to Haughville in 1885, Clark's second addition to Haughville in 1886; Clark's third addition to West Indianapolis in 1888. Mick & Clark's Haughville Park addition in 1893, Jameson's 1st Belmont West Indianapolis addition in 1890, Hyde Park in 1891, and many other valuable and important properties. Among the notable real estate transactions made by this firm was the sale of the Denison Hotel property to D. P. Erwin.

W. E. MICK & COMPANY BUILDING, ILLINOIS AND 22D STREETS.

The A. Metzger Agency was organized in 1863 by Alexander Metzger, who at that time sold out a flourishing steam bakery to Parrott & Nickum. From its very inception this agency has taken a very prominent part in the development of the city. After the death of Alexander Metzger in 1890, he was succeeded by his sons, Harry A. Metzger and Albert E. Metzger.

In every branch of its extensive business this firm has steadily grown, and holds its place in the foremost rank of the city's like enterprises.

The loan and rental departments are under the supervision of Albert E. Metzger. The loan department has become one of the important centers of distributing money. From a small beginning it has grown until now large sums of money are intrusted to its care for investment, both by residents and non-residents. The rental department has the care of properties in the city and surroundings, comprising a list of over eleven hundred (1,100) tenants.

The real estate department, under the supervision of Benjamin F. Goodhart, has in the past years consummated some of the most important sales of business and suburban properties. Many of the largest additions, such as Kenwood Park, Metzger's East Michigan street addition, Marion Park, Beaty addition, several additions on Prospect street, and many other additions, comprising thousands of lots, have been platted and sold by this firm. Among the larger transactions consummated by this agency may be mentioned the sale of the old Exposition grounds to the state, the sale of the Work House grounds to the county, and the sale of the Industrial Training School site to the city.

The insurance department, under the management of Harry A. Metzger, has grown with equal pace, and comprises a number of the very strongest and most reliable companies.

The steamship, foreign exchange and draft department, under the management of Henry Grummann, has for many years been the recognized exchange for tourists, in securing passage to and from Europe, or in taking advantage of its facilities to issue money orders and drafts. The collection of claims in Europe also receives attention in this department, and many estates have been collected by means of the large number of reliable correspondents in Europe which this agency has at its disposal.

The firm has now in contemplation, plans for an extensive building to be erected on its own ground between the Scottish Rite and the Indiana National Bank buildings, on South Pennsylvania street, that will furnish the necessary accommodation for its growing business.

Dyer & Rassmann.—The substantial progress that a city makes during any given period is perhaps due more to that class of real estate dealers who have identified themselves closely with the welfare of the place, and prefer to see and aid her steady growth, rather than to assist in those unnatural inflations so aptly termed "booms." In the front rank in this class, who have done much to place Indianapolis in her present prosperous condition, are the firm of Dyer & Rassmann, whose offices are located at 31 Circle street. These gentlemen began business in 1882, and have gradually formed the most influential connections and are now conducting the largest renting business in the city. They conduct a general real estate business, in buying, selling, renting and exchanging reality, loaning money up to sums of $20,000, upon first-class real estate security, the placing of insurance in companies of known stability, and the management of estates for non-resident owners. They represent the following well-known insurance companies: National of Hartford, Conn.; America of New York; Phœnix of London, England, and Reading of Pennsylvania. Mr. S. M. Dyer is a native of Indiana, and a member of the Board of Trade and the Commercial and Columbia Clubs. Mr. E. C. Rassmann was born in this state, and belongs to the Commercial Club, and held the position of vice-president of the City Council.

Robert Zener & Company, whose offices are located in the Talbott building at the corner of Market and Pennsylvania streets, are the successors to the fire insurance business that was established by Cleavland & Company in 1868. Robert Zener & Company have been in business since July 1, 1886. The firm is composed of Robert Zener and his son Clarence M. Zener. Beside being general agents for Indiana and Kentucky for the Employers' Liability Assurance Corporation, Limited, of London, England, they are the representatives of some of the best known fire and marine insurance companies

UNION RAILWAY STATION.

C. E. Coffin & Company, investment bankers and brokers, 90 East Market street, was founded by C. E. Coffin. He came to Indianapolis in 1867 and secured employment in the office of Captain William Y. Wiley, one of the first real estate agents in the city. He remained with him six years, during which time he took a law course at a night school, and was admitted to the bar of Marion county in 1871. Finding the real estate business more promising, he decided to continue in that line, and on the death of Captain Wiley, in January, 1873, he opened up an office of his own, and by a close attention to business and strict integrity has built up a very large trade. In January, 1880, he associated with him in business his brother-in-law, Charles E. Holloway, under the firm name of C. E. Coffin & Company, investment bankers and brokers. The firm buys and sells real estate, takes charge of rental property, makes mortgage loans in which it handles large amounts of eastern capital, and represents a number of first-class fire insurance companies. In 1883 the firm moved into Mr. Coffin's new block, in East Market street, where it has one of the most complete and handsomely furnished offices in the west. Of this firm it can be said, that there is none other that has taken a greater interest in the development of the city. It has at all times figured prominently in all movements looking to this end.

C. E. COFFIN & CO.

McGilliard Agency Company; Insurance; Nos. 83 and 85 East Market street.—The business was originally established in 1866, and the present company was incorporated January 2, 1896. It has a capital of $10,000, and is officered as follows: M. V. McGilliard, president; Albert W. Hall, vice-president; J. Kirk Wright, treasurer; Edwin Hill, secretary. This company is especially prominent as general agents for the Indiana Insurance Company, the Fort Wayne Insurance Company, the Vernon Insurance and Trust Company, and the Citizens' Insurance Company, Girard Insurance Company, Fireman's Fund, Allemania Insurance Company, Western Underwriters Association, Rockford Insurance Company and the Central Accident Insurance Company, of Pittsburg, Pa.

Elliott & Butler, Abstracters, are located in Hartford Block. The business was established by Mr. Elliott in 1866. The firm is recognized as one of the leading and most reliable engaged in this line in the city. The members of the firm are Joseph T. Elliott and Ovid D. Butler.

THE INDIANA, DECATUR AND WESTERN FREIGHT DEPOT.

The Indiana, Decatur and Western, with its 153 miles of road connecting Indianapolis with the rich agricultural lands of central Illinois, is one of the more recent additions to the splendid railway facilities of this city. It is the only direct route from Indianapolis to Decatur, Illinois, operating four trains daily between these points, and two local trains between this city and Tuscola, also through reclining chair and sleeping car service to Jacksonville and Springfield, Illinois, and St. Louis. At Roachdale it connects with the "Monon" for Chicago with a daily through car service between Cincinnati, Indianapolis and Chicago. On this railway are located the celebrated Bloomingdale Glens, one of the most picturesque spots in the country, and the famous Sulphur Springs at Montezuma, with the largest bathing pool in the Union. This sulphur water is of great value in certain diseases, and a number of marvelous cures have been effected by its use. The company's extensive shops are located near Haughville, a suburb of Indianapolis, where several hundred men are employed. The general offices are located in the Commercial Club building. R. B. F. Peirce is general manager, John S. Lazarus, general freight and passenger agent, and George H. Graves, superintendent.

Lake Erie & Western Railroad, "The Natural Gas Route," connects this city directly with all the important cities and towns situated in the famous gas and oil belt of Indiana and Ohio, and with its numerous divisions make it an important and popular line. The main line of the road extends from Peoria, Ill., to Sandusky, Ohio, and from this city the road runs to Michigan City, crossing the main line at Tipton, connecting with all trains and furnishing a quick and popular route to all points east, west and north. The different divisions embrace 890 miles, as follows: Main line, 420 miles; Indianapolis and Michigan City division, 162 miles; Ft. Wayne and Cincinnati division, 109 miles; Louisville division, 24 miles; Minster branch, 10

miles, and Northern Ohio Railway, 165 miles. It is the popular line between Peoria, Sandusky, Michigan City, Indianapolis, Connersville, Rushville and Ft. Wayne, making direct connections at these cities for all points in the country. At Bloomington it makes union depot connections with solid vestibuled limited trains for St. Louis, and at Peoria with the Burlington and Rock Island Routes for Council Bluffs, Omaha and Denver, also for St. Paul, Minneapolis and the Northwestern Territory. The general offices are located in the company's building on East Washington street, where the affairs of the road are directed. George L. Bradbury is vice-president and general manager, and Chas. F. Daly, general passenger agent.

LOUISVILLE, NEW ALBANY AND CHICAGO RAILWAY FREIGHT DEPOT.

The Louisville, New Albany and Chicago Railway Company operated what is familiarly known as the "Monon route." This is the favorite short line to Chicago running three solid vestibule trains daily consisting of parlor cars and elegant coaches on day trains and Pullman and compartment cars, the finest in the land, on night trains. These trains are heated by steam and lighted by Pintsch gas, and the speed with which they are run is the highest consistent with safety. They are marvels of elegance. Two trains daily except Sunday furnish the service between Indianapolis and Michigan City, connecting at Monon with the main line of the L., N. A. & C. Ry., which is the direct route from Louisville to Chicago. On this division of the "Monon" the famous health resorts, West Baden and French Lick Springs, the "Carlsbad of America," are located. This division also taps the inexhaustible quarries around Bedford, Ind., from which the world-famed oolitic limestone is taken. The summer tourist also finds an inviting spot on the main line between Monon and Chicago in the attractive resort "Cedar Lake," with its beautiful expanse of water. This is one of the finest of the numerous lakes that dot northern Indiana, furnishing delightful boating and excellent fishing. From Indianapolis to Chicago the "Monon" connects with all the roads crossing the state, and at Chicago with all the great trunk lines, making it one of the most desirable and direct routes for reaching all points in the west, north and northwest. The offices in this city are located at the northwest corner of Washington and Meridian streets. Frank J. Reed, general passenger agent, is located at Chicago, and George W. Hayler, district passenger agent, has charge of the passenger traffic at this point.

The Cincinnati, Hamilton and Dayton Railway has, since its opening on August 9, 1867, taken an important part in the development of this city, and of all the roads centering at this point none show more forcibly the great improvements that have taken place in American railroads. In point of equipment there is none that surpasses it; in fact, it was the first road leading into this city (in connection with the "Monon" with which for a number of years it has been closely associated), to introduce safety vestibuled trains, and it has aggressively maintained its position to give the traveling public the very best in service, high speed and regularity with which it operates. The main line from this city extends to Cincinnati, a distance of 121 miles; six trains are operated daily each way. It makes direct connection at Hamilton for Dayton, Toledo and Detroit, and at Dayton connects with the "Erie" for all points in New York state. At Cincinnati it connects with the Baltimore and Ohio and the Chesapeake and Ohio railroads, forming one of the most popular and delightful routes to all eastern points, and the "Queen and Crescent" for all southern points. It also runs a parlor car and sleeper over the Indiana, Decatur and Western railroad, connecting at this point for Jacksonville, Illinois, making a desirable route to western and southwestern points, and in conjunction with the "Vandalia" furnishes through car service to St. Louis from this city. Its train service from Cincinnati to Chicago through this city in conjunction with the "Monon" can not be surpassed if equaled, affording a popular line to all points in the north and northwest. The offices in this city are located at the northwest corner of Meridian and Washington streets. D. G. Edwards is passenger traffic manager at Cincinnati. The road is represented in this city by George W. Hayler, district passenger agent, and Henry G. Stiles, general agent.

The Cleveland, Cincinnati, Chicago and St. Louis Railway, popularly known as the "Big Four Route," operates seven distinct lines from this city, furnishing direct service to all the important points in the central west, and to every point in the country by close connection with the leading trunk lines. From St. Louis it runs its famous "Knickerbocker Special" *via* Cleveland to New York and Boston through this city, and the "Southwestern Limited" from New York and Boston to Indianapolis and St. Louis. At Columbus, connection is made with the trunk lines for Washington, Baltimore and all eastern points. Magnificent service is maintained by the line between Chicago and Cincinnati over which runs the famous "White City Special," connecting at Cincinnati with the C. & O. Railway for the East, and with all lines for the South and South-east, and at Chicago for all points in the North-

BIG FOUR FREIGHT DEPOT.

west. By an alliance with the Toledo & Ohio Central, a through car line to Toledo and Detroit has been formed, giving connection for Michigan and Lake points. The outlet for Iowa, Nebraska and the North-west is over their Peoria division, formerly the I. B. & W. Route, the old original line to the West. One of the most valuable lines on the system is the line from this city to Benton Harbor, Michigan, running through the gas belt of Indiana and the fruit district of Michigan. This is the favorite route for Michigan tourist resorts. One of the valuable acquisitions to the railway facilities of this city is the new route to Louisville, this company having invested nearly $3,000,000 in terminal facilities at that point, which includes the new Louisville and Jeffersonville bridge, one of the largest that spans the Ohio river. This company also operates branch lines to Cairo, Ill., and Sandusky, Ohio, having 2,345 miles of road in Indiana, Illinois and Ohio. There is no railway system in America that is operated with greater regularity, and the equipment generally is kept up to the very highest standard. The service throughout the system is excellent. The local representatives are H. M. Bronson, assistant general passenger agent; Benj. C. Kelsey, city ticket agent, and S. M. Hise, city passenger agent. Henry S. Fraser, general agent, and W. A. Sullivan, commercial agent, have charge of the local freight business. E. O. McCormick, passenger traffic manager, and D. B. Martin, general passenger and ticket agent of the system, are located at Cincinnati.

The Belt Railroad and Stock Yard Company of Indianapolis was organized in 1877. The many advantages that Indianapolis possessed for the proper administration of a business of its character impressed those engaged in the live stock trade so forcibly that from the date of its organization the business conducted here has been exceedingly large and constantly growing. The geographical location of the yards has made this the most important point in the country for the unloading, watering and marketing of stock destined for New England and export slaughter. From November 12, 1877, to January 1, 1897, there have been received at the yards over 20,000,000 hogs, 2,000,000 cattle, 2,500,000 sheep and 250,000 horses. The total receipts for 1896 were 1,255,405 hogs, 135,253 cattle, 120,890 sheep, and 22,546 horses.

The system of railroads centering at Indianapolis makes it the most accessible point in the country for live stock shippers. The great capacity of the yards and the facilities for unloading, resting and reshipping are unequaled by any other yards in the country, east or west.

The Belt Railroad, having been built and owned by the Stock Yard Company, gives this market a decided advantage over others in the respect that *no terminal charge is ever imposed on its shippers:* besides, the shipper is assured of a prompt service in the handling of his shipments into the yards.

Shippers and owners are furnished with separate pens for feeding, watering and resting their stock. All pens are entirely covered with composition gravel roofs, furnishing protection to stock from the storms of winter and the hot suns of summer, which is a very great saving to the shipper in the way of shrinkages in weights, and a great protection in all sorts of weather to buyers and sellers in their daily trade operations.

This is a strictly cash market, and is noted the country over for its steady prices and the limited range of its fluctuations as compared with other markets.

This company makes but one yardage charge during the entire time stock remains on the market. The only other source of revenue is the charge for feed, from which sources the revenue is derived to cover all expenses incident to the operation and maintenance of the yards, comprising construction and betterments, maintenance of property, cost of hay, corn, oats, weighing of live stock, water-works system, taxes, insurance, fuel, gas, electric lighting, tools lost, stock yards cleaning, labor of a vast number of employes; current expenses, such as attorneys' fees, books, stationery, printing, salaries of officers, agents and clerical force and of police and fire departments, interest on bonds and capital invested, all of which expenditure is incurred for the maintenance of this market, and accrues to the direct benefit of its patrons and shippers of live stock. The charges at these yards are lower than at any other yards in the west, there being no yardage charge on live stock in transit unloaded here and destined for other points. The unloading, yarding, watering, feeding and weighing of live stock is done by the

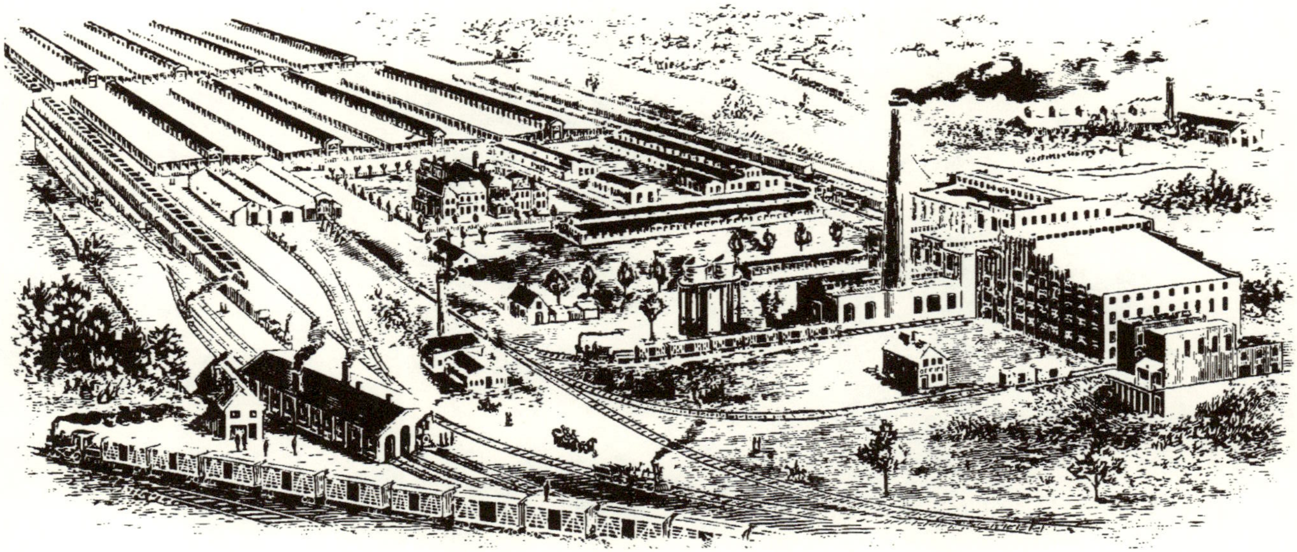

THE BELT RAILROAD AND STOCK YARD COMPANY.

company's employes, relieving the shipper from all such responsibility and care.

The beef and pork packing interests are showing a steady and substantial growth at this point, three different firms having at present under process of construction additions to their plants for the manufacture of dressed and canned meats. The buying interest for eastern slaughter and export is also more fully represented than ever before, all packing houses at New England and seaboard points being represented by buyers on our market for all classes of cattle, hogs, sheep, lambs and calves.

The commission salesmen and buyers of live stock on this market enjoy the reputation of being thoroughly reliable and energetic, and at all times alive to the interests of their patrons.

HORSE AND MULE AUCTION BARNS.—The horse and mule market at this point has shown a phenomenal growth since the auction and sale barns were built a little over two years ago, over 75,000 horses have changed hands on this market in that short time. Addi-

HORSE AND MULE AUCTION BARN, UNION STOCK YARDS.

tional barns were built to meet the demands of this rapidly increasing branch of the business. Private and auction sales of fancy drivers, coachers, cobs and park horses, and all other grades, are being conducted all through the week by the reliable and energetic firms, Messrs. Blair, Baker & Walter, and Warman, Chamberlain, Black & Co., who have brought to the support of this market large numbers of European, eastern and southern buyers for all grades of horses, all of whom concede that this is the coming horse market of the country. The facilities for stabling, moving and showing horses at this very attractive market are unsurpassed by any market in the world. Shippers or others having horses to sell will find it to their advantage to bring them to this market.

Stock Yard Hotel.—The Exchange Hotel, connected with the Exchange building, under its able management, offers every accommodation looking to the convenience and comfort of its patrons at the very low rate of

EXCHANGE BUILDING—STOCK YARDS.

$1 per day. This rate was made and is held at this nominal figure for the benefit of stock men and shippers to this market. The hotel is kept thoroughly renovated, and is heated by both steam and natural gas. It has also a first-class lunch room in connection with it, which is kept open day and night for the benefit of shippers arriving during the night.

The officers of this company are: Sam E. Rauh, president; Julius A. Hanson, vice-president; H. C. Graybill, traffic manager; Jno. H. Holliday, secretary, and H. D. Lane, auditor.

The following reliable firms of commission salesmen are located at the Union Stock Yards: M. Sells & Co., Middlesworth, Benson, Nave & Co., A. Baber & Co., Stockton, Gillespie & Co., Tolin, Totten, Tibbs & Co., Capital Commission Co., Clark, Wysong & Voris, Dye, Valodin & Co., Jeffery, Fuller & Co.

Among the list of buyers at Union Stock Yards are the following well-known firms: Kingan & Co., Moore & Co., Coffin, Fletcher & Co., Indianapolis Abbatoir Co., Chas. J. Gardner, Geo. C. Beck & Son, R. R. Shiel & Co., A. Kahn & Son, Joseph Corwin, John Powell & Sons, P. Sindlinger, Coburn & Weelburg, Chas. Kramer, Chas. Woldt, John Meuser, H. Temperley, D. Bryan & Sons, S. K. Barrett, Schwarzchild & Sulzberger Co., Eastmans Company, Nelson Morris & Co., Myers & Hausman, Swift & Co., and other large western buyers.

M. Sells & Company enjoy the honor and distinction of selling the first consignment of stock that arrived at the new Union Stock Yards, in November, 1877, and they have been continuously at it ever since, conducting business under the same style of firm name, and without a single change in membership during the past 18 years, the present firm at that time succeeding Sells & McKee, the original firm. Mr. Sells was engaged in this line for 12 years prior to the opening of the yards.

For many years past the firm has been recognized as one of the largest handlers of cattle, sheep and hogs at the stock yards, and their business annually reaches a large magnitude. The house owes its prominence and valuable clientage to a career of strict business integrity. Sales of consignments of any magnitude are conducted by them with the utmost promptness, and buyers of the choicest grades of cattle, hogs and sheep, have naturally come to depend upon the firm for the best offerings in the market. In either respect they render the best service to buyers and shippers. Of the two members of the firm, Mr. Sells gives his exclusive attention to cattle, while Mr. T. S. Graves takes care of the consignments of hogs. There is no firm of live stock salesmen in the country which stands higher than this, and its long and honorable business history is the best recommendation that can be offered shippers of live stock to this market.

Jeffery, Fuller & Company, of which Mr. Thomas A. Jeffery, the head of the firm, has been actively and prominently identified with the live stock interests of this market prior to, and ever since, the opening of the Union Stock Yards in 1877, having been the principal business head of one of the earliest firms to engage in this business. The new firm was organized and began business in October, 1895, and has rapidly taken rank among the largest handlers and firms doing business at the yards. Mr. George W. Fuller, of the firm, has had many years experience in the handling and sale of hogs; enjoys an intimate acquaintance among the leading buyers for both local packing and shipment; he is assisted by W. J. Shinn, who has been actively connected with the stock yards for the past eighteen years. Mr. F. F. Churchman is the financial man of the house. Mr. Wm. E. Deer looks after the sale of sheep, and Mr. Will Stanton handles the hogs which arrive by wagon, both being well qualified for the transaction of business in their departments. Messrs. Jeffery, Fuller & Company, have at their command every possible facility for the prompt sale of all lots entrusted to them or consigned to them direct, and are always ready to take immediate charge of shipments, and through their knowledge of the local market, and acquaintance with heavy buyers, are enabled to effect satisfactory sales without delay.

Warman, Black, Chamberlain & Company, who conduct the large commission sale stables at the Union Stock Yards, began business in Indianapolis in 1894. The business has always ranked as one of the largest of its kind in the West, and in order to secure the facilities afforded at the Union Stock Yards, moved to their present location October 13, 1896. Their barns were built especially for their purposes and they have a capacity for over one thousand head of horses and mules. The principal stables are 66 by 340 feet and the mule barn 72 by 172. Sales are conducted every Tuesday. The members of the firm are Enoch Warman, one of the oldest and best known men in the trade in Indiana, who was born in this city, nearly sixty years ago; George W. Black, J. H. Chamberlain and J. C. Davis. The business of the concern extends throughout this and foreign countries.

D. Bryan & Sons, Wholesale Beef and Pork Butchers, with offices at the Indianapolis Abattoir, is one of the representative firms engaged in this line of business in this city. The trade is devoted entirely to local jobbing and are extensive dealers in lard and fresh and smoked meats, etc. The business was originally established by Dennis Bryan, in 1877, and has materially helped in the growth of the packing trade here.

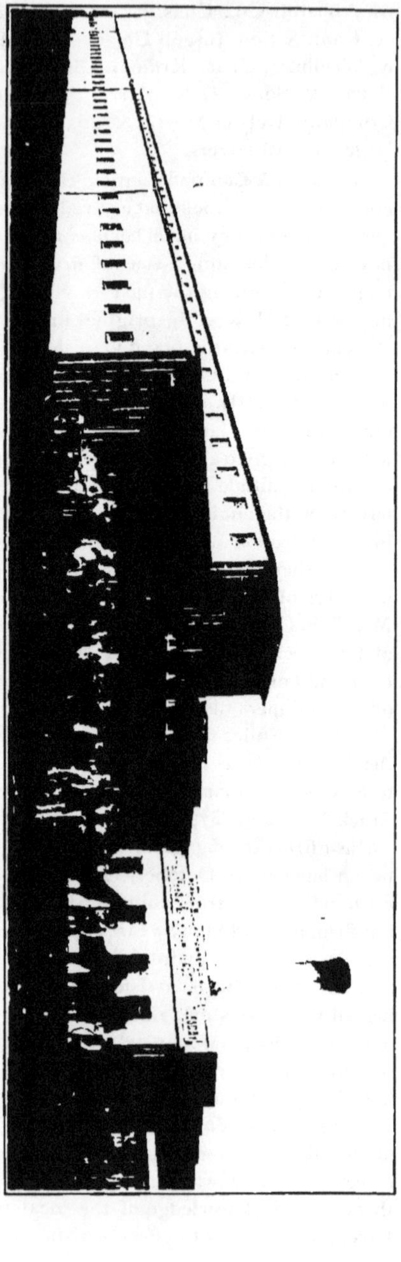

WARMAN, BLACK, CHAMBERLAIN & COMPANY, UNION STOCK YARDS.

A. Baber & Company, live stock commission salesmen, a firm of great financial strength, was established here shortly after the opening of the stock yards. There has never been a business change in the history of the firm, but an unbroken and continuous record of complete and honored identification with the sale of live stock on commission in this market.

With the annual growth and expansion of receipts and shipments at the yards, the business proportionately increased in volume, and during several years past they have been credited with doing as large a business as is done in the Indianapolis market. Mr. A. Baber, of the firm, is an extensive land owner, and a resident of Illinois, the business of the firm being ably and successfully managed by the other members. Mr. J. B. Sedwick gives his attention to sales of cattle exclusively, and in this respect he has no superior in this market.

Mr. E. Nichols and Mr. Chas. W. Sedwick handle the hogs, and of which the firm handle an enormous number annually, while Mr. J. R. Wilhite looks after the selling of sheep.

Stockton, Gillespie & Company began business in 1889. The firm is composed of young men, all of whom have practically grown up in the business. They are alert, active and quick to take advantage of every opportunity which can in any way further the interests of their patrons. The sale of cattle is directed by Mr. W. W. Stockton and Mr. J. F. Clay, the latter gentleman having only recently become a member of the firm. Both are thoroughly expert cattle men, and capable of promptly disposing of the largest offerings. Mr. B. W. Gillespie, with the assistance of Mr. S. J. Acklen, give their exclusive attention to consignments of hogs, and are thoroughly well-posted and experienced salesmen. Mr. James Tolly handles the sheep, while the office is capably managed by Mr. C. H. Clark. The heads of this now well-known firm are among the best known and respected members of live stock salesmen who do business at the Union Stock Yards. They are known among shippers as successful salesmen, to whose good judgment it is always safe to trust. Consignments of any magnitude may, therefore, be entrusted to their care, with the full confidence that sales will be made promptly, and that returns will be satisfactory. The firm keep their customers constantly posted as to the condition of the market, the offerings and opportunities, and give all matters relating to the sale of live stock the closest and most careful attention.

Clark, Wysong & Voris was established seven or eight years ago, as C. J. Clark & Company and continued, with the usual minor business changes, until a year ago, when the present firm was formed. Under past and present management the firm has always occupied a significantly leading position in the live stock commission circles of the country, and enjoys a wide and valuable patronage among the largest shippers of cattle, hogs and sheep to the Indianapolis market. It has been the rule of the firm during its entire existence to be prompt in all its business transactions, to guard carefully the interest of consignors, and to be perfectly accurate in the character of reports rendered the trade, so that large and small shippers alike have come to place implicit confidence in the judgment of the firm. The firm is composed of C. J. Clark, B. F. Wysong and W. C. Voris, all experienced and well-posted salesmen, who enjoy the confidence of a large list of buyers, and who are capable of handling all business entrusted to them to the best advantage and to the complete satisfaction of consignors.

Tolin, Totten, Tibbs & Company, the well organized firm of live stock salesmen, is a consolidation of the business of A. B. Tolin & Co. and Fesler, Totten & Co., and has enjoyed a uniformly successful business since their establishment. As now constituted the firm comprises in its management that long experience in the trade and knowledge of the market so essential in effecting prompt sales at prices satisfactory to shippers. Mr. A. B. Tolin, J. J. Totten and J. B. Harrell, who give their personal attention to consignments of cattle exclusively, are thoroughly experienced salesmen, who keep fully posted as to the needs of buyers, for both local consumption and re-shipment, consequently they are enabled to dispose of all lots offered through their hands with out delay. D. W Tibbs, who looks after the receipts of hogs, is equally well posted in this branch of the business, and enjoying, as he does, the confidence of every shipper who has ever entrusted his sales to him, naturally secures his full share of the shipments to this market. E. C. Rockwood, a capable and energetic business man, will give his attention to the office and the general business of the firm. With its present excellent facilities, well established reputation for promptness and large business, the firm of Tolin, Totten, Tibbs & Co. is prominent among the live stock commission salesmen of Indianapolis. The firm is very conveniently situated for business in Rooms 15 and 17 of the Exchange Building, and makes it a rule to keep its customers in constant touch with the market.

R. R. Shiel & Co., live stock purchasing agents, located in the Exchange Building, Union Stock Yards, is one of the representative concerns in this line of business in Indianapolis. The business was established in 1884 by the present proprietors, Messrs R. R. Shiel and R. R. Reeves, and since that time has grown to large proportions. The firm purchase on orders for Eastern markets, purchasing annually to the enormous amount of between three and four millions of dollars. They handle mostly hogs and cattle, and are everwhere recognized as expert buyers, whose judgment can be implicitly relied on. The firm have developed unlimited facilities in their special line, and this business is rapidly increasing in their hands.

A. Kahn & Son, live stock purchasing agents, began business with the opening of the stock yards in 1877. The specialty of the firm is to buy on order only, and they have enjoyed the confidence to the fullest degree of all those they have served in the capacity of buyers throughout their long business career. Prior to 1877, and running back to 1868, Mr. A. Kahn, the senior member of the firm, was engaged at different times in the live stock trade, and in the wholesale butchering business. Associated with him in the business is his son, H. A. Kahn, an energetic young business man. There is no firm of buyers at the yards that is more deserving of confidence and the large business transacted by them has been earned by straightforward and upright methods, good judgment, and a strict and prompt attention to business.

The Capital Live Stock Commission Company, which was chartered under the laws of Indiana about the first of March of the present year, is a very strong enterprise in point of capital and management. The new enterprise, which has a full-paid capital of $30,000, is really the incorporation of the business of the old and well-known firm of Fort, Johnston & Helm, which, with its predecessor, Fort & Johnston, dates back to 1877, to the opening of the Union Stock Yards. The members of the old firm, who stand deservedly high in Indianapolis live stock circles, for probity, enterprise and honorable business methods, continue with this new organization, Mr. John W. Fort being president; T. B. Wilkinson, vice-presdent; H. B. Lewis, secretary; R. F. Helm, treasurer, and W. M. Johnston, manager.

As now organized and directed, the Capital Live Stock Commission Company is one of the best equipped at the Stock Yards, and offers the most superior advantages to shippers who desire the highest ruling quotations, immediate sales and prompt settlements. The long experience of the management of this substantial company, their knowledge of the market, acquaintance with resident and visiting buyers, gives them superior facilities for handling all grades of cattle, hogs and sheep, realizing for their owners the best possible sales and affording the most satisfactory business relations. Under the new style of firm name and organization the company enjoys largely increased facilities for the transaction of a general live stock commission business.

Blair, Baker & Walter are the headquarters for the sale of horses in Indiana, at the commission, auction and sales stables at the Union Stock Yards, and it is beyond question one of the largest, best arranged and finest establishments of the kind in this country. The stable covers a ground area of 62 x 340 feet, and is constructed on the latest and most approved plan for the care, comfort and handling of horses and mules, there being accommodations for 1,000 animals. The stables are provided with all modern conveniences, there being padded stalls, private compartments and complete veterinary hospital, where animals which require it, receive attention from thoroughly skilled veterinarians. There are also ample exhibition facilities, where the good points of horses offered for sale are shown by expert horsemen to the best advantage. Messrs. Blair, Baker & Walter are recognized as among the most expert horsemen in the western country. They enjoy the intimate acquaintance of the leading owners, trainers, and stock men in all sections, and have earned for themselves the reputation of being thoroughly honorable and reliable business men. The finest animals may be entrusted to their care with absolute confidence, that the interests of both sellers and buyers will be fully protected. They hold auction sales of horses and mules every Wednesday throughout the year, and these sales are always attended by horsemen from all parts of the United States. There are also permanent resident buyers at the stables for Glasgow and Paris, who each ship a car-load weekly.

E. Rauh & Sons, manufacturers of high-grade pure bone fertilizers and dealers in hides, pelts, tallow, grease, etc., rank among the oldest and most prominent manufacturing concerns in this city. The business was established in 1864, at Dayton, Ohio, by Elias Rauh, father of the gentlemen who are now conducting the business. The firm is now operating two large manufacturing plants in this city, one located at the intersection of the Belt railroad and South East street, and another at the Union Stock Yards. Both plants are well supplied with the latest improved machinery, and employment is furnished to more than fifty hands. The product, which consists of ammoniates, phosphates and bone fertilizers, have a large market throughout the

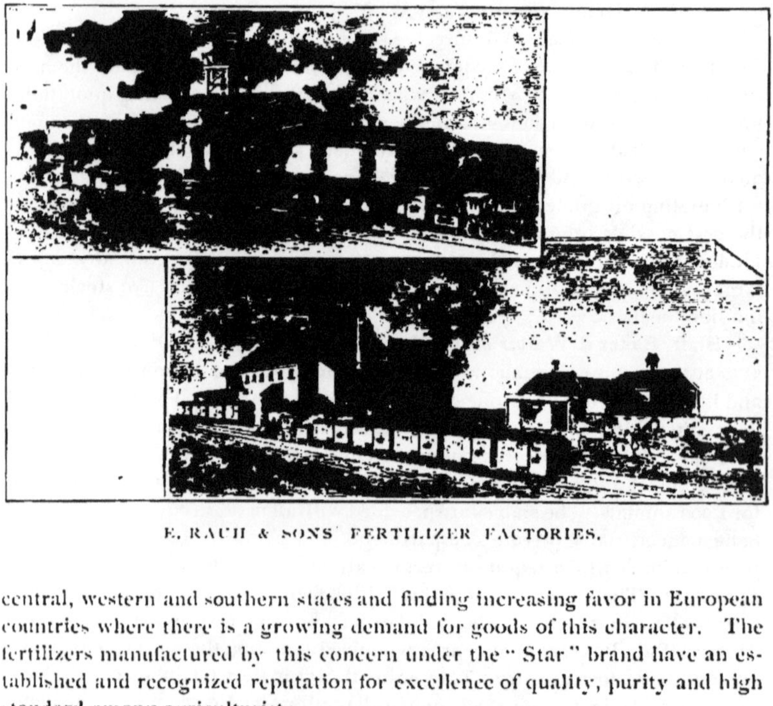

E. RAUH & SONS' FERTILIZER FACTORIES.

central, western and southern states and finding increasing favor in European countries where there is a growing demand for goods of this character. The fertilizers manufactured by this concern under the "Star" brand have an established and recognized reputation for excellence of quality, purity and high standard among agriculturists.

Besides the fertilizer factories, the firm have a large hide warehouse, at 219 South Pennsylvania street, where the offices are located. Employment is furnished to 12 men in this branch of the business. In this particular line the firm ranks among the heaviest in the west. The members of the firm are Leopold Rauh, who conducts the business of the Dayton branch, and Henry and Samuel E. Rauh of the city. Both of the latter named gentlemen have

KINGAN & COMPANY, LIMITED.

been prominently identified with many of the progressive movements of the city, and are closely associated in many growing enterprises of Indianapolis. Mr. Henry Rauh was a member of the Board of Aldermen of this city during 1893–4. Sam E. Rauh is president of the Belt Railroad and Stock Yards Co.

Joseph Allerdice & Company, 128 Kentucky avenue, has been prominently identified in the hide, pelts, tallow and wool trade, and is one of the largest firms in this line in the state. The business was established by Joseph Allerdice, the present head of the firm, in 1877. The trade of the house extends throughout Indiana, Illinois and points west of the Mississippi river. The firm furnishes employment to twenty-five people.

Coffin, Fletcher & Company, pork packers, rank among the first in the country to engage in this line of trade. The business was originally estab-

COFFIN, FLETCHER & CO.

lished by Barnabas Coffin in 1840, and there have been minor changes in the personnel of the firm since its establishment. The firm kills during the winter period about 50,000 hogs, the trade supplied being throughout the eastern, southern and central western states. The present plant, which was erected in 1873, is as substantial as it is extensive, covering a ground area of about five acres, and is well supplied with modern appliances. Over 200 hands are employed during the winter season. The present members of the firm are A. W. Coffin, L. W. Fletcher and S. H. Fletcher. Mr. L. W. Fletcher is the oldest living pork packer in America to-day, beginning his career in the trade when it was in its infancy. The Primrose brand of hams, breakfast bacon and lard, put up by this firm, have earned a reputation for excellence and high standard of quality second to no other in the country.

Kingan & Company, Limited, pork packers, by far the most important and extensive in Indianapolis, was established in 1863. The first plant was destroyed by fire in 1865, and was immediately rebuilt. This was the first house in America to prepare meat for the English market. In point of completeness and amplitude of facilities for every process of this vast and extended business, it is second to no other. The extent and magnitude of its business can be judged from a few facts. Fifteen acres of ground are occupied by the extensive plant with its new buildings; all the buildings are from three to five stories high, with cellars, and generally sub-cellars. Over $3,000,000 are invested in the business, and from 800 to 1,250 hands employed, according to the season of the year, and from 600,000 to 700,000 hogs are slaughtered annually. The warehouses have a storage capacity of 30,000,000 pounds of cured and smoked meats. To cure the meats it requires nearly 14,000,000 pounds of salt, 500,000 pounds of saltpeter, 1,000,000 pounds of sugar, and over 20,000 tons of ice. To ship, it requires 175,000 boxes and crates, and 100,000 tierces for lard and hams. The hogs, when killed and scalded, are scraped by machinery invented in the house. In addition to the above come numberless bi-products, made from the materials that but a few years ago the packers paid to have taken away as entirely useless. So thorough and rigid is the process of utilization, that absolutely nothing is wasted. The trade of the house, as its operations will indicate, is of vast proportions, and the celebrated Kingan's hams have an enviable reputation that extends beyond the bounds of this country.

The export branch of this business is constantly growing. The location of the premises occupied by the firm is at the west end of Maryland street, is central and convenient, with railroad facilities of superior character. The officers of the company are: Robert S. Sinclair, John M. Shaw and Samuel Reid.

Moore & Company, pork packers, are located at the Uniòn Stock Yards. The business was established December 1, 1892, and the facilities for all purposes of the business are unsurpassed. Ten acres of ground are owned and occupied by the company, opposite the Union Stock Yards, on the line of the Belt Line Railroad. Four hundred to five hundred hands are employed, besides many teams and wagons, with a capacity of 2,000 to 3,000 hogs slaughtered, cured and packed daily. The buildings are all substantial structures, erected expressly for the purpose, designed and equipped throughout with new machinery and all necessary vats, tanks and a powerful steam engine. The main building is four stories high, 200x200 feet in area, built of brick. There are also store-houses, an abattoir, smoke-houses, packing-houses, etc. Western Union and Postal Telegraph wires connect with the office, and, taken altogether, the establishment is one of the most complete of its kind in the United States. The trade of the house aggregates hundreds of thousands of dollars a year, and a substantial business has been built up in all the great commercial centers in this country, and an immense quantity of pork, beef, etc., is shipped to Europe. The company packs pork on an extensive scale, and also makes a specialty of smoked ham, bacon, shoulders, etc. It carries a very heavy stock of pork, beef and smoked meats, lard, casings, etc., and also manufactures fertilizers. Only the finest and best meats are handled by the company, and it can always offer special inducements to the trade. J. M. Shaw, president; Sam Reid, vice-president; Robert Reid, treasurer; John Chestnutt, secretary.

Swift & Company, branch of their packing establishment, Chicago, was established in this city in October, 1895. The business is located at 123 to 127 Kentucky avenue, is a model of completeness, and is the finest one of the 400 branches operated by this firm in the United States. It was built under the direct supervision of the company's own architect and is complete in every detail. It has ice storage of 300 tons capacity. 1,000 tons of ice are used annually in their cold storage department, and 1,000 cars of the finest grades of beef. The building is a handsome brick structure supplied with ample switching and railroad facilities. The firm only sells wholesale, and supplies the local butchers and those in adjacent towns. Mr. C. H. Simons is manager.

Parrott & Taggart, branch of the U. S. Baking Company, is the outgrowth of the business established by Parrott & Nickum, in 1860, and that of

PARROTT & TAGGART.

Taggart Brothers in 1869. The houses were consolidated in 1883, forming the firm of Parrott & Taggart. The present firm became members of the U. S. Baking Company, in 1890. It is the largest business of its character in the state, and its business operations extend throughout Indiana and Illinois. The product, which consists of crackers, bread and fancy biscuits, sustains a reputation second to none for uniform excellence. The company employs over 150 people, and more than 30,000 barrels of flour are consumed annually in the manufacture of the product. The plant is a model one and is equipped throughout with the very latest and improved machinery. It is located at the corner of Georgia and Pennsylvania, in a substantial three-story and basement brick building, 72x200 feet. The managers of the business are Alexander Taggart and Burton E. Parrott.

Peter F. Bryce began the manufacture of bread, crackers, and cakes, in 1870, in the present location, at the corner of Meridian and South streets. The capacity of the bakery is 25,000 loaves of bread daily, which find a ready market in the city and the surrounding towns. Mr. Bryce's plant is equipped with a bread-making machine of his own invention, that has a capacity of 70 loaves of bread a minute. Over 50 hands are employed, and the business ranks as the second largest of its kind in the country. Mr. Bryce also operates an extensive baking plant in Chicago. In 1879–84. Mr. Bryce served as a member of the city council.

Home Cracker Company, located at 192 and 194, South Meridian street was established in 1893. It is one of the most important concerns in the city engaged in the manufacture of crackers, cakes, and other sweet goods. The firm employs over 30 hands in the bakery, and three travelers, who cover the territory throughout Indiana, Ohio, and Illinois. The plant is modern in every detail, and as well equipped for the purposes as any similar institution in the country. The "Dove" Brand, under which the goods of this house are manufactured and sold, are recognized for their excellence, and have an established reputation for quality second to no other in the market. Mr. J. H. Plum is manager of the company.

The Indianapolis Board of Trade is the outgrowth of the Chamber of Commerce, organized in 1864, for the purpose of promoting the commercial, financial, industrial and other interests of the city of Indianapolis; to secure uniformity in commercial usages and customs; to facilitate business intercourse; to promote commercial ethics and to adjust differences and disputes. Among those who were instrumental in its organization, were Dr. T. B. Elliott, the first president, Fred P. Rush, and J. Barnard, the first secretary. The present handsome building, which is owned and occupied by the Board of Trade, was erected by the Chamber of Commerce Company, in 1873. The present membership consists of more than 500 of the most prominent and enterprising business and professional men of Indianapolis. It is in every sense of the word, strictly a business organization, and it has wielded a powerful influence in shaping the material growth of the city It was through the instrumentality of the Board of Trade that the new city charter was obtained, the board having originated the resolutions petitioning the legislature to grant the same. It is the headquarters of the grain trade of this locality, and the secretary of the board keeps a record of all local receipts and shipments which are received daily through the courtesy of the agents of the various railroads centering here. Jacob W. Smith, the present secretary, elected in 1891, has served continuously ever since, is a capable, efficient, and painstaking officer. Justus C. Adams was elected president June 8, 1896.

Fred P. Rush & Company was organized January 1, 1865. This is the oldest firm engaged in the grain business in this city. The business was established by Fred P. Rush, in 1857, who was the first person in Indianapolis to buy and sell grain on his own account. On Christmas of 1865 he presented an interest in his business to Edward F. Gall and George E. Townley, and from its incorporation to the present time the firm has maintained the foremost position in the grain trade at this point. The members of the firm are Fred P. Rush and George E. Townley.

Bassett & Company.—Notwithstanding the fact that the interstate commerce bill all but paralyzed the grain business of Indianapolis, still it easily maintains the position of being the best market in the country for white corn, and millions of bushels are consumed here annually, which, in connection with the large consumption incident to the demands of a city of nearly 200,000 population, the grain trade gives active business to several enterprising and solid concerns on the Board of Trade. Prominent among these is the firm of Bassett & Company, which was established April 2, 1895. The head of the firm is E. W. Bassett. His business is devoted to the wholesale purchase and sale of grain, grain products, hay and seeds for the local as well as export trade. The operations of the firm extend throughout Indiana and other central western states.

B. B. Minor, commission merchant and dealer in grain, hay and mill feed, room 18, Board of Trade, began business here in 1885. Prior to that time he had a continued identification in the grain business in Illinois, dating back to 1867, from which point he came to this city. Up to 1891, he was associated in business with Mr. W. H. Cooper, under the firm name of Minor & Cooper, at which time he retired, leaving the city, but returned again in a few months and re-embarked in business. Mr. Minor is regarded as one of the most prominent grain men doing business on the Board of Trade, qualified in every way to give satisfaction to those making transactions in the Indianapolis market.

W. B. Hixon, grain dealer and commission merchant, room 49, Board of Trade, has been a prominent dealer in this line for the past eight years. He is recognized as the largest and most extensive dealer in hay at this point. He is a large shipper of this product to Pittsburg, Baltimore and other eastern markets, and does a large business throughout the principal western points and the Union Stock Yards of this city His trade correspondents extend throughout the western states and Indian Territory and Oklahoma. He is also a heavy dealer in grain and mill feed. He is thoroughly equipped to serve all those who desire to trade in the Indianapolis market in the most satisfactory manner.

Osterman & Cooper, grain dealers, room 17 Board of Trade, are among the largest and most prominent dealers in grain, seeds, hay and mill feed, in this city. The firm is composed of J. Osterman and W. H. Cooper, and both gentleman have been actively engaged in the grain trade for the past 30 years. Mr. Osterman served as treasurer of Marion county during 1890–1, and was a member of the board of public works of Indianapolis, during 1895. He has been an active member of the Board of Trade since its organization, and was elected to the office of treasurer of this body, June 8, 1896. Mr. Cooper has also been prominently associated on the Board of Trade for a number of years. He was elected a member of the city council in 1888, serving continuously since that time. In 1894–5, he was elected president of the city council, and has always been one of its most useful and prominent members.

H. E. Kinney, grain merchant on The Board of Trade since 1887, is practically the successor to the business established by J. A. Closser & Co., in 1875. Mr. Kinney's business is devoted to the purchase of grain, hay, flour, and mill feed. His trade correspondents are located throught Indiana, Illinois, Ohio, and territory west of the Mississippi, and he is recognized as one of the leading dealers in the grain business engaged at this point. At the election held June 8, 1896, he was elected vice-president of the Board of Trade, and has been actively connected with it for a long time.

Foster & Company, wholesale commission merchants, are among the very oldest and most prominent firms doing business in this city. The firm was organized in 1866, as Foster, Holloway & Company, who then conducted a wholesale grocery and commission business. There have been numerous changes in the firm, and in 1870 the wholesale grocery business was sold, and the firm confined its operations to the wholesale commission of grain, hay, mill feed, field seeds, imported Portland and domestic cements. The firm at present consists of General Robert S. Foster and Ellis Y. Shartle.

General Foster, prior to the breaking out of the war, was engaged in the wholesale grocery trade in this city. Immediately upon the breaking out of the war he volunteered as a private, helped organize a company and was elected and commissioned captain in the 11th Indiana Zauaves. Soon after he was appointed major and assigned to the 13th Indiana regiment, and was subsequently promoted to lieutenant-colonel. On June 12, 1863, he was promoted to brigadier-general and breveted major-general on June 5, 1865, for gallant conduct on the field. He was in the army until and participated in the close of the war. In 1868 and 1872 he was elected city treasurer. He was elected president of the Board of Trade in 1894–5, and is still a member.

Mr. Ellis Y. Shartle, the junior member of the firm, was connected with the Vandalia Railroad in the capacity of passenger conductor, during 1861. He left the company in 1872 to become a member of the firm of R. S. Foster Company.

The Indianapolis Brewing Company, which was organized in May, 1889, is an amalgamation of the breweries that were originally founded by Peter Lieber, C. F. Schmidt, and Casper Maus, over forty years ago. Tracing the history of this institution backward, we find it contemporaneous with that period which has marked the city's development from a rough western vil-

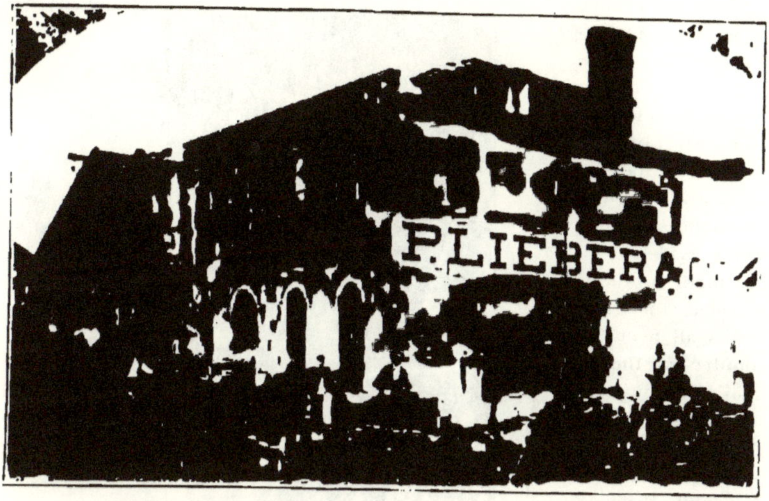

PLANT OF INDIANAPOLIS BREWING COMPANY, 1871.

lage to a magnificent metropolis, second to no other city, in the character and solidity of its growth. Side by side with its development, beginning in the humblest and most unpretentious manner, this business has grown until to-day it has expanded to such proportions as to be classed among the ten of the largest enterprises in America. When it is remembered that there are but two other lines of industries in the country aggregating a greater amount of invested capital, it becomes a matter of justifiable pride to refer to it in this connection.

To recount the many changes that have taken place in building the magnificent business of the Indianapolis Brewing Company, would almost be to write a book on the growth and development of the brewing industry and its collateral branches. A remembrance of what was one of the industries is the appended illustration of the original Peter Lieber's City Brewery as it appeared in 1871. The contrast of this crude establishment, as compared with the magnificent modern plant that has replaced it, is no greater than a comparison of the methods that have supplanted these old methods, when the malt was mashed by hand and brewed in a kettle. What was then determined by instinct, has come to be an exact science, and the old-time brew-master who "guessed by practice," has given place to the modern brew-master, the skilled chemist, who not only brings to his aid years of practice, but has the many advantages that ingenuity has brought with the use of modern appliances. Thus, the beer of to-day, is the combined result of years of practical experience and chemical skill. How well the public have appreciated the efforts of those engaged in the manufacture of this popular beverage to bring it to its very highest standard of excellence and purity, is evidenced in the many millions invested in great plants all over the country and the annually growing consumption.

Regarding the product of the Indianapolis Brewing Company its fame has become international, second to none, and from Maine to California, and from Canada to Cuba, is the demand for it increasing. The total output of the Company for 1895, was in excess of 200,000 barrels, and the total brewing capacity of the combined plants will aggregate over 600,000 barrels per annum. The united plants cover an immense space, and are models of perfect equipment, with their great store-houses, brew-houses, offices, boil-

PLANT OF THE INDIANAPOLIS BREWING COMPANY, 1896.

HOME BREWING COMPANY PLANT.

er-houses, ice machines, and refrigerator houses, warehouses, malt houses, wash and bottling houses, elevators, stables, cooper shops, shipping and packing departments, etc.

When it is taken into consideration that it employs directly and indirectly about 1,200 men, with wages ranging from $60 per month up to the high salary brew-master who receives $10,000 per annum, and the vast sums of money that are annually spent in building and equipments, all of which go into local circulation, beside paying into the city treasury by far more taxes than any other institution, the benefits derived from it by the community can not be overestimated.

The present manager and president of the Indianapolis Brewing Company is Albert Lieber, under whose control the business has been more than doubled and widely extended. J. P. Frenzel, the secretary, Otto N. Frenzel, the treasurer, and Frederick Francke, Albert Baker and Edward Daniels, are associated with the above-mentioned, as directors.

Richard Lieber & Company.—One of the latest and most important additions to the manufacturing facilities of this city is the bottling works recently established by Richard Lieber & Company, at the west end of New York street. When it is taken into consideration that the health of the entire community is affected by the degree of purity of its water supply, the importance of the industry just established can best be appreciated. One of the important and vital purposes of this new business will be the production of water of absolute purity, entirely free from organic or inorganic pollution. To make this, the plant is equipped with distilling apparatus having a capacity of producing one hundred gallons of perfectly pure water every hour. This will be supplied to consumers in sterilized packages, syphons, etc. A number of the most eminent physicians and chemists of this city have examined the plant and have, without exception, expressed their highest approval regarding the product and give it their unqualified indorsement. The members of the firm are Richard Lieber and Gustav Oberlaender. Mr. Lieber is a well-known journalist, who has been and still is associated with the *Indiana Tribune*, an influential German daily newspaper. Mr. Oberlaender has but recently come to Indianapolis from New York, where he was engaged in business for the past eight years. The plant covers an area of about two acres and will furnish employment to fifty people. Besides the distillation of water, the firm will manufacture a full line of carbonated beverages. Trade will be supplied throughout Indiana, Illinois and Ohio. The firm is especially desirous that the plant be visited and is open to the public at all times.

The Home Brewing Company was organized in 1891, and its officers and stockholders, nearly ninety in number, are all residents of Indianapolis. The brewery, bottling house, offices and outbuildings, are handsome and complete in all their appointments. The brewery is of the most modern construction, and the best equipped plant of its character in the state. The company has an incorporated capital of $200,000, and its investment now exceeds $300,000. The officers are all well-known citizens: President, Wm. P. Junclaus; vice-president, secretary and treasurer, Andrew Hagen. The quality of the output is of the best, and continually growing in favor. Fifteen wagons are required to make distribution to the city trade. Over 50 men are employed. The sales now amount to between 30,000 and 40,000 barrels yearly. This great business has been created within four years, and the trade in Indiana is rapidly increasing, showing that the trade appreciates a good article. The brands are, "Home Brew," "Columbia," "Pale Select," "Extract of Malt," Ale and Porter. In connection with the brewery is their large bottling house, with a capacity of 20 barrels daily, used entirely for home consumption.

The Anheuser-Busch Brewing Association, of St. Louis, Mo., opened a branch in this city, in 1891, which is under the efficient management of Mr. J. L. Bieler. The merits of the lager beer manufactured by this

ANHEUSER-BUSCH BREWING ASSOCIATION BRANCH.

great brewing association, one of the most prominent in the country, are well known, and the demand always active and brisk. The brewery plant is one of the largest in the world, and the brewing capacity is 1,800,000 barrels of beer, 3,600,000 bushels of malt, and 2,250,000 pounds of hops are consumed annually. The annual shipping capacity is 100,000,000 bottles, and 5,000,000 kegs. No corn or corn preparations are used in the manufacture of the Anheuser-Busch beer, it is therefore the finest, best, most wholesome, and of superior quality. The Anheuser-Busch beer has been brought into direct competition with the finest lager beer made in the world, and in every instance awarded the highest prizes. The premises utilized by Mr. Bieler, in this city, 450 to 460 East Ohio street, are three acres in extent. The main building, in which is located the bottling works, is two stories high, and 40 x

160 feet in dimensions. It is equipped with refrigerators having a total capacity for the storage of sixteen car-loads of beer, and also the best and most modern bottling machinery and appliances. There are also storage houses, stables, and carriage house on the premises. The beer is received direct from the brewery, in car loads, and to supply the city demand very many cars annually are required for bottling, besides hundreds of barrels for daily consumption. Mr. Bieler handles and bottles all the famous beers manufactured by the Association. All these popular beers are well aged, and never drawn from the vaults until fully seasoned. Twenty-five hands are employed in the bottling works, and six wagons kept in service. The trade is steadily growing in importance and magnitude. Mr. Bieler is a native of Baden, Germany, and has resided in this country since 1856, and in Indianapolis since 1861. From 1878 to 1880, he was a capable and efficient member of the city council, and subsequently, from 1880 to 1884, recorder of Marion county. Mr. Bieler has under his control sub-agencies in all parts of the state of Indiana.

The Terre Haute Brewing Company.—The Indianapolis branch of the Terre Haute Brewing Company, managed by Maurice Donnelly, than whom

TERRE HAUTE BREWING COMPANY BRANCH.

there are few of greater local popularity, is located at No. 148 South West street. The fact that this branch was established here shows the confidence the company has in its brew. In August, 1891, the plant was established here. The first year 8,000 barrels of beer were sold; the second year 11,000 barrels; the present year the sale will reach 16,000 barrels. This does not include the sale of bottled beer, which would bring this year's sales up to 26,000 barrels. The beer made by this concern is of the choicest flavor, absolute purity, and unexcelled by any in the world. The Terre Haute Brewing Company, at Terre Haute, Crawford Fairbanks, president; Edward P. Fairbanks, general manager; George, Maier, secretary and treasurer, makes over 100,000 barrels of beer annually. The success of the Indianapolis branch of the Terre Haute Brewing Company has been unexampled in the history of business enterprises in this city, but while it has been great, it has been deserved. Notwithstanding the strongest local competition, the product of this brewery has come to the front, and steadily maintained its place. The company has found especial favoritism in the homes of this city for their bottle goods, which are put up by the C. Habich Company.

The C. Habich Company, mineral water manufacturers and bottlers of the Terre Haute Brewing Company's prodnct, are located in their new plant at

THE C. HABICH COMPANY.

Nos. 187, 189 and 191 West Ohio street. The building is a solid brick structure, 60 x 50. The plant was recently equipped throughout with the latest and most improved machinery, and ample cold storage facilities. About twenty men are employed and seven wagons used for city delivery. Over 3,000 barrels of beer are bottled annually besides immense quantities of all kinds of spring and mineral waters. The business was originally established, nearly twenty years' ago, by Carl Habich, Sr., one of the most prominent and influential pioneer citizens, who settled here nearly forty-six years ago. The officers are: C. Habich, Jr., president; Frank A. Maus, vice-president; J. C. Schaf, secretary and treasurer; and Crawford Fairbanks associated with the above as director.

Klee & Coleman, located at 227–229 South Delaware street, are devoted to the production of high-class mineral waters. The business was established in 1881, and has grown in magnitude and importance under the able management of Mr. W. H. Miller. The plant consists of a three-story and basement building, having dimensions of 44½ by 120 feet, which is completely equipped with all the latest machinery and plans known to the trade. The firm has enjoyed great success, and achieved a high reputation for the excellence of their productions. They manufacture large quantities of soda water and all the ordinary mineral drinks. In the manufacture of their product only the purest water from deep driven wells is used. City water is not used even for cleansing the bottles, thus insuring freedom from bacterial pollution. The bottling department is at the rear of the building. Steady employment is given to a force of 20 skilled hands, while experienced traveling salesmen are kept upon the road. Eight delivery wagons are kept busy delivering orders in the city. Beside this establishment, the firm has a large bottling works at Dayton, Ohio, and also at Louisville, Ky., and it has a large business throughout the Central States. It is perhaps due largely to the energy and wide acquaintance of Mr. Miller, whose personal popularity has done much to extend the interest of the house in this city.

Jacob Metzger & Company.—The largest, finest and most complete bottling establishment in the state of Indiana is that of Messrs. Jacob Metzger & Co., at 30 and 32 East Maryland street.

Mr. Metzger began the business in 1877 and in 1884 the trade had expanded to such proportions as to render increased facilities absolutely necessary. Accordingly, with his usual enterprise, he erected his present handsome and spacious building, four stories with basement in height, 34 x 118 feet, and L attachment in rear, 23 x 34 feet, and put in a complete equipment of all machinery driven by a 25-horse-power steam engine and all modern appliances known to the business. Many of the best known brands of imported and domestic beers and wines are bottled by this house and the stock is unsurpassed for variety, purity and excellence. An extensive equipment is employed for the distillation of water that is used in the manufacture of the carbonated beverages. The trade extends over Ohio, Indiana and Illinois. Mr. Metzger came to this city in 1850, and is prominent in business circles and enjoys the esteem of the community and all with whom he has business relations. On January 1, 1896, the business was purchased by Frederick C. Wellmann, who has been identified with the house since 1882. He conducts the business under the old firm name, and the policy of the house will be continued in the same liberal manner as heretofore.

Municipal Engineering, published by Municipal Engineering Co., the best and most important magazine devoted to the particular field which it fills, was established in 1890. It is recognized as the foremost representative of the interests connected with the improvement of cities, embracing the field of paving, sewerage, waterworks, parks, etc. It circulates throughout the United States, Canada and foreign countries, and at the World's Fair was awarded a medal and diploma for excellence. From an unpretentious pamphlet of 16 pages it has grown to a magazine of nearly 150 pages. Its editorial policy has been to rely on men whose technical education and experience have distinguished them as best qualified to discuss questions treated in the magazine, and civil engineers, analytical chemists, contractors and others who have achieved the distinction of being foremost in their class, are among its contributors. William Fortune is president, Charles C. Brown associate editor, and Charles O. Roemler advertising manager. A branch office is conducted in New York City.

Indianapolis Sentinel, Democratic, was established in 1822, is published by the Indianapolis Sentinel Company, daily, weekly and Sunday.

Indianapolis Journal, Republican, was established in 1824. Issued daily and Sunday, by the Indianapolis Journal Newspaper Company.

The Indianapolis News, an independent evening newspaper, was established in 1869, by John H. Holliday. It is published every afternoon except Sunday. Charles R. Williams is editor and Wm. J. Richards manager.

The Sun, an independent evening paper, is published every afternoon except Sunday, by the Sun Publishing Company.

Indiana Tribune, German, is published daily and Sunday.

The Daily Reporter, published by the Reporter Publishing Company, makes a specialty of court news, etc.

The Indianapolis Daily Live Stock Journal is devoted to the interests of shippers and is published at the Stock Yards.

The Daily Telegraph, established in 1864, is the only German newspaper published in this city that is a member of the associated press. It is the oldest German paper in the city and is published by the Gutenberg Company, and is Independent-Democratic in politics. The directors are H. O. Thudium, president; J. B. Jeup and F. Striebeck.

Indiana Volksblatt, established in 1847 and published by the Gutenberg

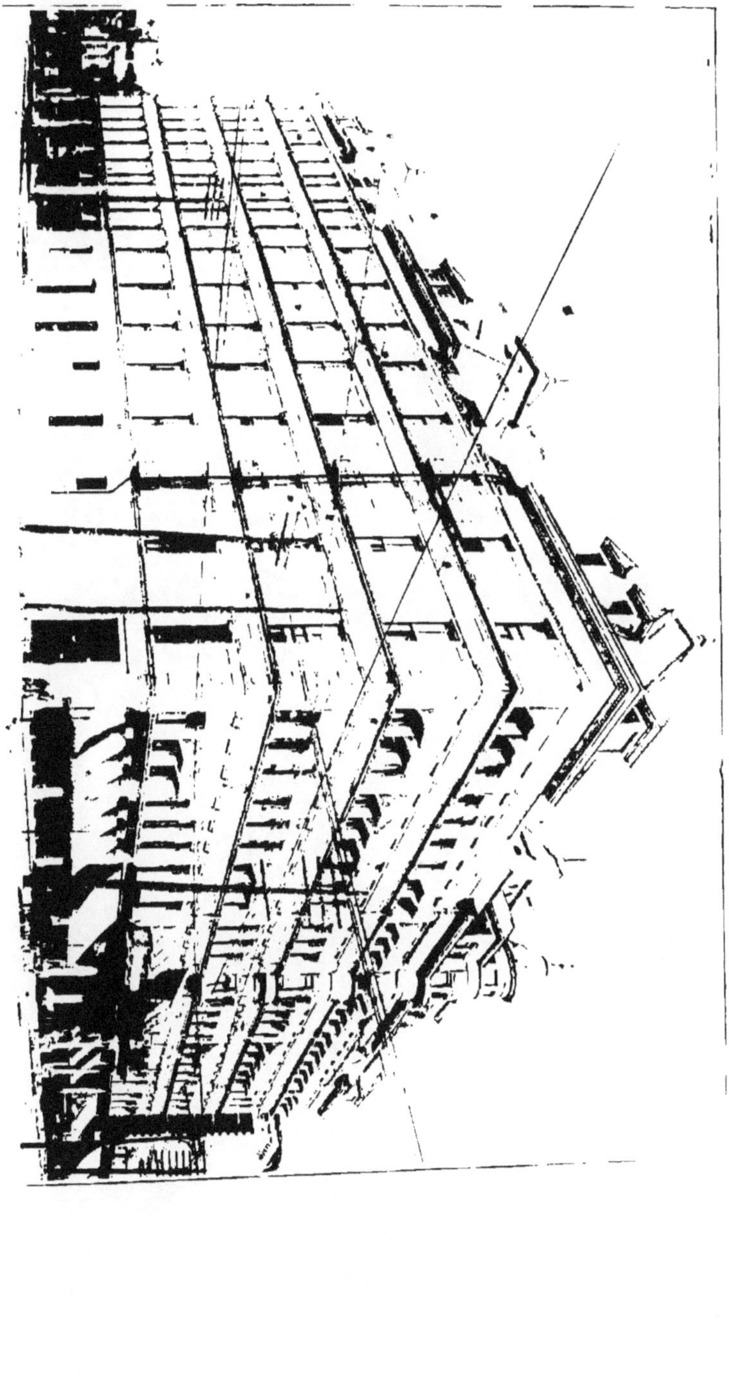

Company, is the oldest German weekly paper in the state. It is Independent-Democratic in politics. **Die Spottsvogel,** a humorous and literary family paper, established in 1864, is also published by this company.

Other publications are numerous, embracing weekly, semi-monthly and monthly issues, among which are a number of the most influential trade journals in America.

The Denison, erected in 1879, is one of the leading hotels, and occupies the finest building in the city designed exclusively for hotel purposes. In character of its appointments and management it ranks with the very best in America. It is a modern hotel in every detail. The building is an imposing six-story and basement structure, with a front of dressed stone, on Pennsylvania street, covers a quarter of a block of ground, and is a solid building, 200 x 202 feet in dimension. It is located in the heart of the city, and reached by the principal street railway lines passing the Union Railway Station. It is heated by steam and natural gas, and lighted by its own electric lighting plant. It contains 310 rooms, and can comfortably care for 800 guests. The rates are $3 and upward per day. The hotel is operated on the American plan. D. P. Erwin is the proprietor, and T. J. Cullen, one of the best-known and most popular hotel men in the country, is manager.

ENGLISH'S HOTEL.

The Commercial Club Restaurant is conducted on the top floor of the Commercial Club building, and is the most attractive and popular café in the city. It is first class in every respect, the rates are moderate, and the service is of a very high order. George H. Bryce is proprietor.

The Normandie, which is located at the southeast corner of Illinois and Georgia streets, one block north of the Union railway station, is the best

CHARLES MAYER & COMPANY.

strictly European hotel in the city. It was opened in September, 1894, by George W. Koehne, the present proprietor. The rooms are well furnished, and the rate is from 50 cents upwards. In connection with the house is one of the finest appointed cafés in the city, where the very best the market affords is sold at extremely moderate rates.

Hotel English was erected in 1884, and occupies a four story and basement stone front building, in the northwest quarter of Monument Place. The house has just been remodeled, with a lofty and spacious rotunda, elegantly appointed offices and reading rooms, dining room, etc., on the ground floor, and over 100 guests' rooms newly furnished throughout. The house is brilliantly lighted by electricity from an independent electric light plant. Everything in connection with the hotel is strictly first class, and it is undoubtedly the best and cosiest hotel in the west operated at its rate ($2 per day and upward). Jerry S. Hall is the proprietor of the hotel.

Peter Sindlinger, wholesale and retail pork and beef packer, 207 West Michigan street, Indianapolis, Ind. Supplying the population of a city such as

NORMANDIE HOTEL AND CAFE.

.ndianapolis with necessary meat products is a business of ever-expanding dimensions, which is well represented by a number of active, progressive men of enterprise, ability and capital. Among these is Mr. Peter Sindlinger, wholesale and retail pork and beef packer, whose packing house stores are at 207 West Michigan street. He is one of the oldest established dealers in this line, and his house has always commanded a prominent position in the foremost rank. He founded this business over a quarter of a century ago. He .s well equipped with every convenience, and provided with every facility for conducting and managing his business on a large scale, and besides supplying a substantial, permanent family custom, fills orders at wholesale for the trade. Mr. Sindlinger does all his own curing and packing, and makes a specialty of sugar cured hams, breakfast bacon, shoulders, kettle lard, dried beef, bologna and other sausages.

John Wimmer, optician, 14 N. Pennsylvania street, began business in 1878. His specialty is the manufacturing of optical goods, lenses for spectacles and lense grinding of every description. He carries in stock a full line of optical goods and artificial eyes. Mr. Wimmer brings to his business a thorough and practical knowledge of its science and requirements. He is a graduate of the Chicago Opthalmic College, the Cleveland School of Optics and the Eclectic School of Physicians and Surgeons of Indianapolis, and is president of the Indiana Optical Society.

The C. B. Cones & Son Manufacturing Company, manufacturers of "Cones Boss" overalls, coats, pants and shirts, is one of the largest manufacturing establishments of its kind in the United States. The factory con-

INTERIOR OF COMMERCIAL CLUB RESTAURANT.

sists of a three story and basement building on North Senate avenue, 50 by 200 feet. The business was established in 1879 by C. B. Cones, Sr., and from a very small and modest beginning, it has extended its operations until at the present time the output is sold throughout all of the central, western, and southern states, furnishing employment to more than 400 hands and requiring ten traveling salesmen to visit the trade. The range of manufacture includes "Cones Boss" overalls, pants, shirts, hunting suits, boys' shirts and waists, and ducking clothing generally, in great variety. The business was incorporated in 1888. The present officers of the company are: C. B. Cones, president; H. B. Hibben, vice-president; John W. Murphy, treasurer, and H. L. Browning, secretary.

John L. Moore, Wholesale Grocer, 124 and 126 South Meridian street, has been established since 1880. His house does an extensive business throughout Indiana and Illinois, employing six traveling men. The business is commodiously housed in a three story and basement brick building, in which a very complete stock of staple and fancy groceries are at all times carried.

Ward Brothers Drug Company, 22 South Meridian street, was incorporated in 1896. This company is one of the large concerns representing the wholesale drug trade in this city. The business was begun in 1866 by Dr. Boswell Ward, who established himself in a retail way at the corner of New Jersey and St. Clair streets. In 1869, his brother Marion Ward joined him in the business, and continued with him at this point until 1871, when a branch establishment was opened in the Buschman Block on Fort Wayne

PEMBROKE ARCADE.

avenue, which he conducted until the consolidation of both stores in 1872. In 1879, the firm entered the wholesale trade by sending out a representative in the person of H. D. Porterfield to visit the retail trade of Indianapolis, and inaugurated a system of delivering goods directly to the purchasers. This concern, therefore, while not the first to engage in the wholesale jobbing trade in Indianapolis, is the first, however, to have a local representative to drum the local retail drug trade. In 1881 the firm moved to 40 East Washington street, where they conducted a wholesale and retail business on a much more extensive scale. In 1890, they again moved to 22 South Meridian street, devoting themselves entirely to the wholesale drug business. The concern now employs six men, and the trade extends throughout Indiana, and parts of Illinois. The officers of the company are: Boswell Ward, president; Marion Ward, treasurer; C. S. Dearborn, secretary, and H. D. Porterfield.

Sheridan Brick Works, office 88 North Pennsylvania street. The works of this company are located at Sheridan, Indiana, on the Monon railroad. The business was incorporated in 1891. The officers of the company are: M. J. Osgood, president, and Oliver H. Root, secretary and treasurer. The plant at Sheridan is equipped with the very latest improved machinery, and is one of the finest plants in the state, with a capacity for manufacturing 75,-000 sand red brick per day.

The Indiana Manufacturing Company, offices 401–405 Indiana Trust Building. This company was organized and incorporated in 1891. The officers and directors of the company are A. A. McKain, president; T. King, vice-president; J. K. Sharpe, Jr., secretary and treasurer, E. C. Nichols and B. T. Skinner. The company acquired the patents owned by James Buchanan on pneumatic straw stackers and forty-seven other patents, and after introducing their machine licensed every manufacturer of threshing machines in the United States and Canada to build them on a royalty in connection with their machinery. The first license was granted in 1892 and the first machine was built under license in 1893. It is now estimated that over three-fourths of all the threshing machines in the United States are equipped with these stackers.

Indiana Cigar Company was established in this city during the year of 1885, by the present proprietors, D. C. Hitt and J. B. Hitt, who are now located at No. 32 South Meridian street. The premises comprise a ground floor 20 x 120 feet in area, and are well equipped with all conveniences for conducting the large trade established. The factory of the Indiana Cigar Company is located at Urbana, Ohio, and is under the management of Mr. J. B. Hitt, while the Indianapolis house is in charge of Mr. D. C. Hitt. They employ a full force of assistants in the house and six traveling salesmen, this branch supplying the trade in Indiana and eastern Illinois, the trade being both wholesale and retail. The specialty and leading brand sold by the branch house, is the "Pathfinder," for which a large demand has been created; and they also deal in the best makes of fine grade five and ten cent domestic goods.

Charles Mayer & Co., importers and jobbers in toys, fancy goods, druggists' and stationers' sundries, etc., Nos. 29 and 31 West Washington street.—This business was established by the late Mr. Charles Mayer, Sr., in 1840. He was a pioneer citizen who contributed, while living, much to this city's advancement. In 1865 Mr. William Haueisen was admitted to an interest. In 1880 the latter named gentleman retired and in 1888 four new members were taken into partnership, the firm thus continued, consisting of Charles Mayer, Sr., his two sons Messrs. Charles Mayer, Jr., and F. L. Mayer, Fred. Berger and Louis Muir. In 1891, the worthy founder of the house died, and in January of the current year, Messrs. Berger and Muir retiring, the business has since been conducted by Messrs. F. L. and Charles Mayer under the original firm style. The premises occupied consist of a spacious and commodious five story and basement building, having a frontage and depth of 34 x 195 feet, also a warehouse in rear of the above, on Pearl street, five stories and basement, 34 x 80 feet, and one on Senate Avenue South, three stories and basement and having lineal frontage and depth of 60 x 120 feet. The system that prevails in this immense establishment indicates the most careful supervision, while the judgment and taste displayed in the character of the stock proclaim the management to be thoroughly experienced in the business and keenly acquainted with the wants of a highly critical trade. The assortment embraces a full line of fancy china and cut glass, sterling silverware. sporting goods, bicycle supplies, fishing tackle, stationery, fine perfumes, soaps, toilet goods, toys, druggists' sundries, cutlery, games, fancy goods and a vast array of small wares and notions far too numerous for particularization in these pages; importations of novelties being made direct from England, France, Germany, Switzerland, Austria, Bohemia and continental Europe generally. An average force of from ninety to one hundred and ten experienced assistants are employed in various capacities in the home headquarters, while the interests of the house on the road are ably looked after by a corps of nine traveling salesmen, a large and steadily growing trade being enjoyed, which radiates broadly throughout Indiana, Ohio, Illinois, Kentucky, Missouri, Iowa, Tennessee, Kansas and Nebraska. Messrs. Mayer are both natives of this city, and are prominent and popular members of the Board of Trade, Commercial and Country Clubs and German House.

CHARLES MAYER, 1840.

JACKSON PLACE.
Showing Main Entrance to Griffith Brothers, Wholesale Milliners.

Griffith Brothers, importers and wholesale dealers in millinery, began business at Dayton, Ohio, in 1863, and established themselves in this city in 1876. The market in millinery from this point at that time was very limited and did not extend beyond a radius of one hundred miles. Their enterprise and ability has contributed to make Indianapolis one of the most conspicuous millinery markets in the country to-day. The growth of this business has demonstrated that this city is specially favored in its location, for the firm finds it natural and easy to do business with all the trade in the central, western and southern states. The stock carried by this firm comprehends everything in millinery and no concern in the country has a better understanding of the wants of the trade nor has better facilities to meet them. Griffith Brothers' storerooms, which comprise six floors, a solid block in length, over 200 feet, supplied with two power elevators and handsomely appointed throughout for the accommodation of their large business, are located in the center of the wholesale district. The building has two fronts of imposing architecture, one being directly opposite the main exit from the Union Station in Jackson Place, as shown in illustration on preceding page, and the other on Meridian street, which is shown in accompanying engraving.

GRIFFITH BROTHERS.

D. P. Erwin & Co., Dry Goods, Notions, etc., No. 106 to 114 South Meridian street.—The dry goods trade in its various departments has no more able and enterprising exponent in this section of the country than the old established house of Messrs. D. P. Erwin & Co. This house dates its commercial existence back to 1859, when it was founded by Messrs. Webb, Kennedy & Co., to whom in 1880 succeeded Messrs. Johnston & Erwin. Four years later D. P. Erwin & Co. was organized, D. P. Erwin and Charles O. Lockerd as special, constituting the firm. In 1887 the scope of operations was further extended by the purchase of the interest of Messrs. Byram, Cornelius & Co., Charles H. Erwin and Alvin S. Lockerd becoming partners. The present structure was erected and taken possession of in 1890. The building rises six stories in height, is equipped with elevators, and is located on the corner of South Meridian and McCrea streets with an L on Georgia street. The stock is an immense one and the trade exclusively wholesale. The departments are eleven in number, covering every branch of the trade in dry goods, notions and woolens, the handling of carpets being made a feature in 1894. The firm is one of the most active and extensive importing

D. P. ERWIN & COMPANY.

houses in the state, and likewise controls the entire output of several of the largest cotton, woolen and carpet mills in the country. The interests of the house on the road are ably looked after by a corps of eighteen traveling salesmen. Mr. D. P. Erwin has lived here since 1880. He is also, apart from this interest, owner of the Hotel Denison, is now serving his second term as president of the Commercial Club, is ex-president of the Board of Trade. C. H. Erwin lives in New York city. Alvin S. Lockerd is an active, energetic young man of the highest standing. Mr. Louis P. Goeble, for 20 years with the firm, is in charge of the credits and several other departments.

Meyer Brothers, controlling agents throughout Indiana, Illinois, Iowa, Missouri, Kansas and Nebraska for the sale of the product of the Kis-Me Gum Company of Louisville, Ky., began business in this city in 1892. During their early connection with the concern their business was confined to Indiana and they were represented by four traveling men. The energy with which they applied themselves to their business, together with the merit of the goods they represented, attracted recognition, and the field of their labors was widened until the several states which they now control were added. To cover this territory requires fourteen travelers, and tons of advertising matter, reaching nearly $125,000, are used annually in advertising Kis-Me chewing gum in this field. During the year 1895 Meyer Brothers have sold over one hundred and thirty million cakes of Kis-Me gum, or on an average of two cakes to every man, woman and child in the country. Considering that their first year's business resulted in selling seventeen million cakes of gum it will be observed that their trade in three years has increased nearly eight-fold, a truly remarkable showing, in the face of the strongest kind of competition. Kis-Me Gum is made up in six flavors and is one of the most popular articles of its kind in the market, and the demand is constantly increasing. The offices are located in the Pembroke Arcade, and the members of the firm are Leo and Louis Meyer.

Wyckoff, Seamans & Benedict, sole manufacturers of the Remington Standard Typewriter, with a capital of $3,000,000, have become one of the gigantic and pre-eminent manufacturing establishments of America. There is nothing in the history of commercial enterprises more strikingly suggestive than the growth of this business. From very small beginnings about the year 1873, the growth has been unprecedented. The local office was opened in this city in 1885 by the present manager, Mr. G. E. Field, and several thousands of their well-known and popular machines are now in use in this state. The surprising success of the Remington is due to the fact that the manufacturers have kept up a constant march of improvements in order to keep pace with demands of the users. The result of this with the firm's enterprise in making known the merits of their machine has contributed to procure for the Remington Standard Typewriter its universal recognition as the standard writing machine of the world. The local office is located at 34 East Market street.

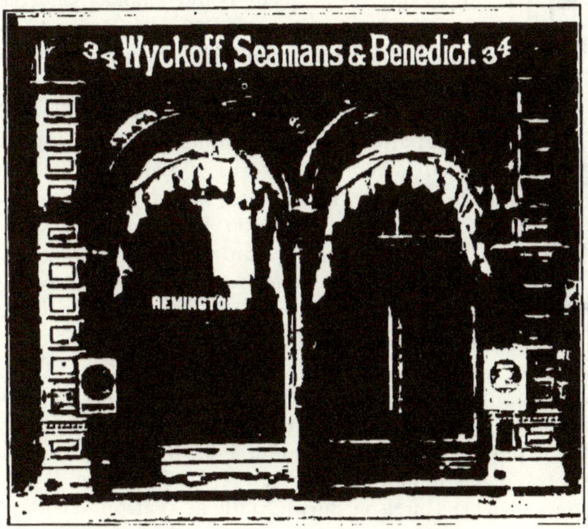

WYCKOFF, SEAMANS & BENEDICT.

The Bowen-Merrill Company, Publishers, Book-sellers, Stationers and Paper Dealers, has been in existence for more than half a century, tracing its establishment back to the house founded in 1838 by Samuel Merrill, Sr., grandfather of the present treasurer of the firm. In January, 1885, Bowen-Stewart & Co. and Merrill, Meigs & Co. were consolidated and the present house incorporated. The business is located at Nos. 9 and 11 W. Washington street, and occupies five floors, running clear through to Pearl street. A branch house is operated in Kansas City. The Indianapolis establishment is one of the largest, most complete and best equipped book stores in the country, and there are only two houses in the United States from which more books are distributed annually. It has been said that Cincinnati is the musical center, St. Louis the art center and Indianapolis the literary center of the west. True it is that Indianapolis buys more books than any other city of four times its size in the United States. In recent years The Bowen-Merrill Co. has directed special attention to publishing, building up a list which includes the works of James Whitcomb Riley, Edgar Wilson Nye ("Bill Nye"), Sarah T. Bolton, Richard Malcolm Johnston, Col. Richard W. Thompson, Hon. William H. English, Thomas L. Harris and many others of the prominent authors of this country. As law publishers, this house ranks among the very largest in the country. Its publications include some of the most successful law works that have been issued within the last ten years, and its list of authors contains the names of the most prominent legal writers in America, including Judge Byron K. Elliott, Charles Fisk Beach, Jr., Judge John M. Van Fleet, R. M. Benjamin, W. P. Fishback, Roswell Shinn, Judge Harrison Burns, William Watson Woollen. The publications from this department go into every nation in the world where the English language is spoken. Silas T. Bowen, one of the founders of the Bowen-Stewart Co. house, retired from active participation in the business in January, 1885, and died in December, 1895. Samuel Merrill, for many years at the head of the house, retired in 1890. The business is now under the management of William H. Elvin, William C. Bobbs, Charles W. Merrill and John J. Curtis. The history of the house is one which reflects credit upon the city and state, because to maintain and develop a large book establishment requires a community of culture and a population of book readers.

THE BOWEN-MERRILL CO.

MURPHY, HIBBEN & CO.

Murphy, Hibben & Co., Importers and Jobbers of Dry Goods, Notions, Woolens, etc. (wholesale exclusively), 93 to 99 South Meridian street, and 26 to 36 East Georgia street (annexed). This, the oldest and largest Jobbing Dry Goods and Notion house in the State, rightfully occupies a most important position in any review or history of Indianapolis as a jobbing center. The firm of Murphy, Hibben & Co., through all the various changes of title and interests occurring in the past twenty-five years, has maintained the highest position in the esteem and confidence of the trade, and steadily retained its early acquired supremacy, surviving the decline or retirement of many competitors in this and adjoining markets. Concentrating their energy in the prosecution of the business, and limiting the employment of their resources to its constantly widening field, their present ample capital and assured financial position have been acquired by no doubtful methods, but are the direct result of prudent and attentive business methods, combined with a broad spirit of commercial enterprise. As noted above, Messrs. Murphy, Hibben & Co., occupy the building at the corner of Meridian and Georgia streets, in the heart of the wholesale district, comprising Nos. 93, 95, 97 and 99, a frontage of 80 feet on Meridian street by 205 feet on Georgia, four stories in hight, to which is annexed by bridges and tunnels, the premises Nos. 26 to 36 East Georgia street, three floors of which are used as salesrooms and the balance for storage; these afford, in their entirety, 150,000 square feet of floor space, more than double that employed by any similar business in the State. The merchandise offered in the various departments includes all desirable lines required in a first-class modern store, covering a wide range of foreign and domestic dry goods, notions, hosiery, white goods, linens, woolens, floor oil-cloth, and linoleum, curtains, draperies, window-shades; also of their own manufacture a very large line of overalls, working-shirts, laundered and soft shirts, jeans, cottonade and cassimere pants. Liberal use has been made by this firm of the facilities of direct importation offered by the Indianapolis Custom-House, through which much merchandise is received in bond direct from all foreign markets. Special attention has been given to the products of Western and Southern mills with most encouraging results, as both the trade and the consumer hold this class of goods in constantly increasing favor, and many of the larger mills have found it advantageous to make Messrs. Murphy, Hibben & Co., their agents for general and special lines manufactured by them. In conclusion, it may be said that the wide acquaintance of the house, and its well-known reputation for solidity and fair-dealing, place it as a representative of the best element of commercial character and activity, and the firm is conceded to stand at the head in its own line, and among the best of the strictly jobbing interests of the State. The members of the firm are J. W. Murphy, H. B. Hibben and Louis Hollweg, and they are always prominently identified with all movements that tend to further the city's interest.

Fahnley & McCrea began business in 1865, and were the first firm to engage in the wholesale millinery trade in this city. Since their establishment this branch of trade has become one of the most important and largest in the wholesale business of Indianapolis, and the prestige secured by them as pioneers has been maintained and they are recognized to-day as one of the leading and most important millinery jobbing concerns in the west. The buildings occupied are the property of the firm and are located at 140–142 South Meridian, 39–41 McCrea and 8 West Louisiana streets. The stock is one of the heaviest and most complete in this line that is to be found between New York and Chicago, and is excelled by none in either of the above cities. A staff of fifteen travelers are required upon the road, covering Indiana, Illinois, Iowa, Ohio, Kentucky, Tennessee and Georgia. Upwards of fifty hands are employed in the store. The members of the firm are Frederick Fahnley and Rollin H. McCrea.

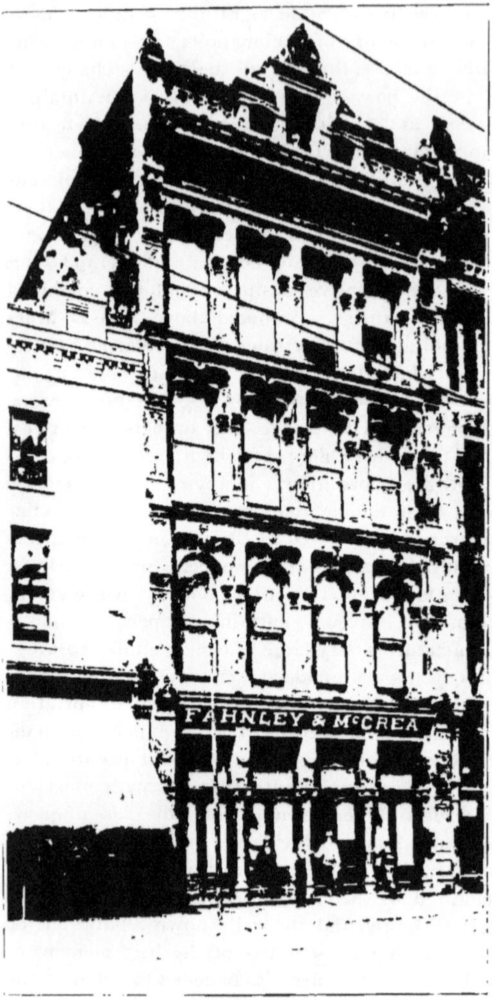

FAHNLEY & M'CREA.

McKee & Company, wholesale dealers in boots, shoes and rubbers, are located in one of the handsomest and most substantial buildings located in the jobbing district; has a frontage on Meridian street, at Nos. 136 and 138, and runs back and faces Jackson Place. The building employed consists of four floors and a basement. The house, which is one of the oldest in the wholesale trade of this city, was established in 1861 by Vinnedge, Jones & Co. It has changed its personnel twice, becoming McKee & Company in 1888. From its inception the house has maintained a foremost position in the jobbing trade of the city, and is recognized to-day as the largest in its line in the state, and one of the strongest in the west. The warerooms are exceptionally well appointed and provided with every convenience for the proper display, sale and shipment of the immense stock carried at all times. The trade of the house is heavy, and extends throughout Indiana, Ohio and Illinois, which is covered by their traveling men. The members of the firm are Edward L. and Robert S. McKee.

M'KEE & COMPANY.

Weinberger's European Hotel, 10–14 West Louisiana street, is one of the landmarks and will always be pleasantly remembered by many who have visited this city for nearly half a century. Mr. Herman Weinberger, the proprietor, is one of our pioneer citizens. He came to this city in 1855, engaging in business where he is still located. His son, Edwin Weinberger, is in charge of the hotel and restaurant. It is operated on the European plan, and furnishes the very best accommodation to the traveler and transient visitor at moderate rates. It is located opposite the Union Station and in the heart of the wholesale district. The rooms are comfortably appointed and, owing to its location, makes it one of the most convenient and desirable places for the accommodation of travelers in the city. The rates for rooms are 50 cents per day and upward.

William Wiegel, manufacturer of show cases, 6 West Louisiana street, began business in this city in 1877, and is the largest and only exclusive show case manufacturer in the state. He occupies a four-story and basement building 28x100 feet in dimensions, equipped with all requisite machinery and appliances for speedy and finished production, also containing ample accommodations for storage and display purposes, in addition to very available shipping facilities. His range of production embraces plain, square, round front, upright, circle, mansard, single and double monitor cases for ordinary use, also for special purposes, such as prescription, cigars, perfumeries, fancy articles, nick-nacks, etc., for counter, side wall and center of stores. No cheap or shoddy work is turned out by Mr. Wiegel, who is himself a practical mechanic and personally attends to the business, employing none but experienced workmen famillliar with their trade. He carries large stocks of cases, iron showcase stands, spring hinges, alarm money tills, etc., giving employment to from eight to ten hands, and does a large trade throughout Indiana, Ohio, and Illinois. He also manufactures adjustable show-case and wall-brackets, which have a large sale among show-case manufacturers and others throughout the country.

WILLIAM WIEGEL.
FAHNLEY & M'CREA.
WEINBERGER HOTEL.

Indianapolis Gas Company.—It might be said that few cities in the Union furnish a better exemplification of thoroughly systematized gas lighting than does Indianapolis, a fact due to the efforts of such progressive corporations as the Indianapolis Gas Company, whose business offices are located at No. 49 South Pennsylvania street, in the Majestic building. The Company is an outgrowth of the Indianapolis Gas Light and Coke and Indianapolis Natural Gas Companies, chartered in 1876, to which this concern succeeded in 1890, and its career throughout has been a very prosperous one, and highly creditable to the judgment and ability of its management. The artificial plant of the company is situate at the junction of Pennsylvania and Louisiana streets, and covers an entire city square, the company likewise owning and operating one hundred and eighty gas wells at Hamilton, Madison and Tipton counties, Indiana, with an output capacity of 3,500,000 feet per day. The gas produced by this, the only artificial gas company here, is unrivaled for brilliancy, and is considered by able gas engineers and experts equal to any in the country, while the prices charged for it are as low as those of any other company. The following gentlemen, who are widely and favorably known in business circles for their ability, energy and integrity, constitute the personnel of the present executive management, viz.: Chas. E. Dieterich, president, resident of New York city, where the company has an office at No. 45 Broadway; E. C. Benedict, of New York, vice-president; John R. Pearson, general manager; A. B. Proal, assistant secretary and treasurer; S. D. Pray, secretary, resident here since 1867; James Somerville, superintendent artificial department, here since 1876, and engaged with this company for twenty years.

FAHNLEY & M'CREA.

Daggett & Company, manufacturing confectioners, 20 West Georgia street, were among the very first to engage in the jobbing trade in this city. The firm was established in 1856, and has enjoyed a prosperous and growing business throughout its busy existence. The firm was incorporated in 1892, and is now the largest of its kind in the state. The trade extends principally throughout Indiana, Ohio and Illinois. The offices and plant are located in the large brick building at 20 West Georgia street, consisting of six floors and basement. One hundred persons are employed in the house and six travelers visit the trade. The officers of the company are William Daggett, president; J. F. Messick, treasurer, and J. H. Wilson, secretary.

LEVEY BROTHERS COMPANY.

Levey Brothers Company, printers, stationers, lithographers and blank book manufacturers, 19 West Maryland street, were established in 1848, and have enjoyed nearly fifty years of uninterrupted business success. Their plant is among the largest in the state, and is equipped throughout with the very latest and most modern machinery and appliances of every description. They were the first to introduce typesetting machinery in a mercantile printing establishment. Over 100 persons are employed in the different departments, and the trade of the firm extends throughout every state and territory in the United States, their principal specialties being the execution of high grade mercantile printing and the manufacture of blank books and bankers' supplies. They also have the contract for publishing the law for the state of Indiana.

Hollweg & Reese, direct importers of china, glass and queensware, 84 to 98 South Meridian street, is the largest, best stocked, and most elegantly equipped china, glass and queensware jobbing house in the state of Indiana. Mr. Louis Hollweg, who established the business in 1868, the sole proprietor

HOLLWEG & REESE.

since the death of Mr. Charles E. Reese in 1888. The firm occupies a handsome five-story and basement building, 75x130 feet in dimensions, as salesroom and office, and the two adjoining buildings, each four stories high and 40x120 feet in dimensions, are used for the storage of heavy stock, the packing and shipment of goods, etc. They handle very heavy stocks, chiefly the products of the most famous European potteries, of which they are direct importers; also carry full lines of the choicest American manufacture of white and decorated wares, American glassware, lamps of every description in glass, porcelain, pottery, plain and decorated, lamp goods, supplies, novelties, ornaments, bric-a-brac, etc., of the finest quality, the firm who operates a plant at Greenfield, Indiana, for the manufacture of fruit jars, being the leading distributers of these goods in Indiana. They employ fourteen travelers and about sixty-five persons in the house, and their trade extends throughout the west and south.

McKee Shoe Company, successors to R. S. McKee & Son, and McKee & Company, 136 and 138 South Meridian street, wholesale dealers in boots,

M'KEE SHOE COMPANY.

shoes and rubbers. This concern has had a continuous existence since 1845, having been established at that time by John W. Ray & Company. Latterly the firm became known as Ray, Mayhew & Company, McKee & Branham, R. S. McKee & Son, and on November 13, 1896, incorporated under the title of the McKee Shoe Company. This is now the only boot and shoe jobbing house in the city and the largest one in the state. Eight travelers are employed, and the trade extends throughout Indiana, Illinois and Kentucky. The officers of the company are: Robert S. McKee, president; Edward L. McKee, vice-president; William J. McKee, secretary and treasurer.

DAGGETT & COMPANY.

J. A. Everitt, Seedsman, 121 and 123 West Washington street.—This business was established in 1886. In 1890 the concern was incorporated and in 1892 the large brick building now occupied, 195 feet in length, consisting of six floors, was built for the exclusive use of the business. It is now one of the largest and most completely equipped seed houses in the country. The trade extends throughout this and foreign countries, and half a million catalogues are printed and distributed annually to the patrons of the house. About 75 persons are employed by the concern. The stock embraces a full line of seeds of every description, grown to special order, chiefly in the North and

J. A. EVERITT.

East, including the standard varieties, such as bean, beet, cabbage, carrot, celery, sweet-corn, cucumber, lettuce, melons, onion, parsnip, pea, raddish, spinach, tomato, turnip, etc., of the choicest character, with novelties and specialties in the same lines; the plants from which show superior growth, producing qualities and better average results than those obtained from any other source. Their floral department is equally select and desirable. The list contains every seed known to the lexicon of florists, put up in handsome packages, each package containing the firm's trade-mark and full directions for sowing and cultivating. Their small fruit and plant departments, their departments of farm seeds, of lawn and other grass and clover seeds, of esculents, including the great early potato "The Everitt," are likewise unsurpassed in variety and completeness. The celebrated "Man Weight" farm and garden tools are also manufactured by this corporation, and have an extensive sale. The officers of the company are: J. A. Everitt, president; L. J. Everitt, secretary and treasurer.

CARLON & HOLLENBECK.

Carlon & Hollenbeck, printers, binders and blank book manufacturers, southeast corner of Meridian street and Monument Place, conduct the largest book binding and general job printing concern in this city. The business has had a continuous existence since 1864. For the past seventeen years it has been conducted under the present firm name, the members being John Carlon and Charles E. Hollenbeck. The character of the work produced by this house in not surpassed by any other printing establishment in the country. Many of the well-known illustrated periodicals published in this city are issued from its press and are fine examples of first-class printing. About one hundred persons are employed in the different departments.

The Pembroke Arcade was erected by Dickson & Talbott in 1895. It is one of the most strikingly beautiful structures, and next to the Monument Place as a center of attraction to all who visit this city. The architecture strongly resembles some of the beautiful work which marked the buildings at the World's Fair. It is located east of the Indiana Trust Building and connects Washington street with Virginia avenue.

JOHN RAUCH.

John Rauch, manufacturer of cigars, 82 West Washington street, began business in 1872. Many of the brands of cigars manufactured by him have attained a popularity and extensive sale beyond the borders of the state. Among some of his best-known and most popular brands are "Capital City," "Chess Club" and "Hoosier Poet," of which he manufactures over three million annually. In his factory he employs over fifty expert cigar makers. His retail establishment is recognized as one of the most popular smokers emporiums in the city.

J. P. KAVANAGH.

J. P. Kavanagh, importer and packer of Leaf Tobacco, 54 South Pennsylvania street.—In the establishment of a leaf tobacco house in this city by this well-known and old established packer of New York, Indianapolis comes in for strong recognition as an important market for leaf tobacco purchasers, and the trade that has heretofore been diverted to other centers will find special advantages in turning their attention to this point. The packing warehouse opened by Mr. Kavanagh in this city is located in the large three-story and basement brick building located in the "Haas Block" at 54 South Pennsylvania street in which is carried a heavy stock of all grades of imported and domestic leaf tobacco. The advantages this house offers to the trade in dealing direct with first hands are not to be overestimated. The territory to be supplied from this point embraces Indiana, Illinois, Ohio Michigan and Missouri. Several travelers will be employed to visit the trade in this field.

Krag-Reynolds Company, 31–33 East Maryland street, Wholesale Grocers.—This corporation is the successor by purchase in 1894, of the business formerly conducted by A. B. Gates & Company, who were engaged in the wholesale fancy grocery trade at this point for many years. The jobbing trade in groceries has always been one of the most vigorous and vital elements in the wholesale business of this city and this addition has added greatly to its strength. The concern carries one of the largest and as complete a stock as can be found in this or any other market. The trade extends throughout Indiana, Ohio, and Illinois, and twelve travelers are employed. The business is conducted at 31–33 East Maryland street in the large brick building consisting of four floors and a warehouse of three floors The company is also proprietor of the Champion Coffee and Spice Mills, located on Chesapeake street. The mills are among the largest in the West, completely equipped with the latest and most improved machinery for grinding spices; also five large roasters. The mills are situated in the rear of the wholesale department in a three-story brick edifice. The output embraces the well-known brands of coffee, "Blended Java," in packages, and "Mayflower" in cases; also the "Mayflower" brand of spices. The officers of the company are: Charles M. Reynolds, president and treasurer; Wm. A. Krag, vice-president and general manager, and William Wallace Krag, secretary.

KRAG-REYNOLDS COMPANY.

The When Clothing Company was established in this city in 1875 and from its foundation has been recognized as the leading establishment of its character in this city. It is magnificent in its appointments, and the "When Building," in which it is located, at 30 to 40 North Pennsylvania street, ranks as one of the handsomest and most attractive structures in this city. John T. Brush is the resident partner and manager of the business.

The Kahn Tailoring Company, 22 and 24 East Washington street, is one of the most important retail establishments in the city. The business was established by Henry Kahn in 1886, and incorporated in 1889. It differs from other institutions of a like character in this city, in that its trade is not confined to this locality, but extends throughout every state and territory in the Union. The advertisements of this concern have became familiar to the reader of all the great magazines whose pages have been liberally used for years past by this company. Through these mediums the name of the house has been brought prominently before the public, and the high grade and exceptionally good workmanship and style of the garments manufactured, together with moderate prices, have built up a trade not surpassed by any similar establishment in the west. The company make a specialty of dress suits. Over 150 persons are employed in the manufacturing department. The officers of the company are Henry Kahn, president, and Berry Self, secretary.

THE KAHN TAILORING COMPANY.

George J. Marott, who has been engaged in the retail shoe trade in this city on his own account since 1885, now conducts one of the largest and handsomest shoe emporiums in the United States at 26 and 28 East Washington street. This establishment is not only the pride of our citizens, but is a point of attraction to thousands who visit our city annually. The ground

EXCELSIOR LAUNDRY.

ORIGINAL EAGLE CLOTHING STORE.

GEORGE J. MAROTT.

floor and basement are utilized for business purposes and the splendid appearance of the former with its twenty-foot ceiling, and magnificent appointments, impress the visitor with the spirit of enterprise everywhere apparent. Nearly three hundred incandescent electric lamps, operated by an independent light plant in the basement, furnish a flood of light. The furniture is of the richest and most comfortable character, and everything that can add to the attractiveness of the establishment and facilitate business has been installed.

McCormick Harvesting Machine Company began business in this city over thirty years ago. Mr. J. B. Heywood, the present manager, has had charge of the company's business in this city for the past eighteen years. The premises occupied by him as offices and warehouses comprise the whole of the spacious and handsome McCormick building in South Pennsylvania street, embracing six floors and basement. The building is built of pressed brick and Bedford blue stone and is imposing in appearance.

Excelsior Laundry is located in the Masonic building, Nos. 2 to 6 Capitol avenue, South, and was founded by Major Taylor in 1878 at the present place. Commodious premises are utilized, being 80 x 100 feet and outfitted with the latest and most improved machinery known to the laundry business. It is the first and oldest steam laundry in the city or state. From forty-five

M'CORMICK HARVESTING MACHINE COMPANY.

to fifty people are employed, and three wagons are run daily in delivering and receiving orders. It has agents in Indiana, Illinois, Kentucky and Ohio. The work embraces all kinds of men's wear, as collars, cuffs, shirts, shirt waists, all underwear, lace curtains and ladies' shirts, shirt waists, and all work that is done in a first-class laundry. It has a capacity of 1,000 to 1,500 shirts, and 5,000 to 10,000 pieces daily, and the "Excelsior" has never failed to render satisfaction. Major Taylor is president of the Indiana Laundrymen's Association, and is also president of the Indianapolis May Musical Festival Association, and was president of the Country Club in 1895.

Original Eagle Clothing Company, Nos. 5 and 7 West Washington street, was founded in 1853, by Messrs. Griesheimer & Co., who were succeeded, in 1879, by Messrs. Strauss & Gundelfinger, and eventually, in 1887, Mr. L. Strauss became sole proprietor. Mr. Strauss brings great practical experience to bear on the business, and under his management has always been recognized as one of the most important and among the foremost in this line in the city. The premises occupied comprise a spacious store, 33x100 feet in dimensions, with a wing 17x55 feet in area, extending to South Meridian street, fifteen clerks and assistants being employed. This house has only one price, every article handled is fresh and choice, the stock being thoroughly overhauled and renewed at necessary intervals, and Mr. Strauss numbers among his permanent customers many of our influential and wealthy citizens. He can always obtain the newest fashions in hats and furnishing goods, and the varied nature of the stock gives a choice not to be duplicated elsewhere.

GEORGE MERRITT & COMPANY.

George Merritt & Company, manufacturers of woolens, 411 West Washington street, is one of the oldest industrial establishments in this city. The business was founded over forty years ago by George Merritt and William

Coughlen, under the firm name of Merritt & Coughlen. It was thus conducted for twenty-five years, when, on the retirement of Mr. Coughlen in 1881, Mr. Worth Merritt (son of George Merritt) was admitted to the firm, and the present firm name adopted. The works cover a ground area of 95x300 feet, in three main buildings having frontage on Washington street of 300 feet. This factory is equipped with the latest improved machinery known to this branch of industry. From sixty-five to one hundred skilled and experienced hands are provided with constant employment. Flannels, flannel skirts and lustre skirts are the specialties manufactured. The magnitude of their trade may be gleaned from the statement that they consume from 350,000 to 400,000 pounds of wool per annum in their manufactures.

Indianapolis Electrotype Foundry, Nos. 17 to 25 West Georgia street, was established in 1875. In 1888 it was incorporated under the laws of Indiana with a paid capital of $15,000, Mr. George F. Reeves being the president; Mr. George L. Davis, vice-president; Mr. D. W. Wiley, secretary, and Mr. A. W. Marshall, treasurer. The officers are thoroughly practical and able business men, fully conversant with every detail of this industry. The premises occupied are 35 x 120 feet in area, being three floors, fully equipped with the latest improved apparatus, appliances and machinery. They conduct a general electrotyping, stereotyping and engraving business, also deal in pattern letters and printers' supplies, and employ constantly fifteen first-class workmen. Superior plates for all printing purposes are made on wood or metal bases, half-tone being a specialty, while stamps are likewise furnished for bookbinders for embossing. The productions of this reliable concern always reach the highest standard of excellence and finish, the prices quoted for the same are exceedingly moderate, and its trade, which is steadily increasing, now extends throughout Indiana, western Ohio and Illinois.

INDIANAPOLIS ELECTROTYPE FOUNDRY.

INGALLS BLOCK.

The Railway Officials' and Employes' Accident Association of Indianapolis was established in 1886, by William K. Bellis. During the first two years of its existence the business of the company was confined exclusively to the insurance of men in the railroad business, but later extended its policies to other lines. From its organization its growth has been unchecked and it is now recognized as one of the strongest and most reliable of the mutual accident companies in this country. It has issued over 125,000 policies, and has disbursed nearly $2,000,000. The claims have been paid with a promptness and liberality unequaled by any other company, and among railroad men especially, is so thoroughly established, that its name has become a synonym for fair dealing and integrity. The officers of the company are Chalmers Brown, president; William K. Bellis, secretary and general manager, and Samuel Bellis, assistant secretary and treasurer. The offices of the company are located at 25 to 32 Ingalls Block.

The National Starch Manufacturing Company.—To W. F. Piel, Sr., one of our oldest and best-known pioneer citizens, is due the establishment of the business out of which has grown the National Starch Manufacturing Company of this city. In company with others he began the production of starch, in 1867, and built a plant which was known as the Union Starch Factory, which was located in the eastern part of the city. On the night of October 8, 1868, this plant was destroyed by fire, and was immediately rebuilt. In 1872 Mr. Piel purchased the interest held by his partners, and, in 1873, the business of the Union Starch Factory was dissolved, and the firm of Wm. F. Piel & Company was organized, and the removal made to the present site. On September 24, 1886, the firm was incorporated under the title of The Wm. F. Piel Company, with Wm. F. Piel, Sr., president; Wm. F. Piel, Jr., vice-president and treasurer, and Henry W. Piel, secretary. In April, 1890, the National Starch Manufacturing Company was formed, and the plant was purchased, and the old concern became a member of the new organization. Wm. F. Piel, Jr., is the president; Wm. F. Piel, Sr., manager; Henry W. Piel, assistant manager, the latter also being directors of the company, and Chas. F. Piel superintendent of the plant. The works are among the largest in the west, covering thirty-seven acres, five of which are under buildings. The plant is a model one in every detail, and rec-

THE NATIONAL STARCH MANUFACTURING COMPANY.

ognized as the finest and most complete in the country for the production of starch. Over 200 persons are employed and nearly 2,000,000 bushels of corn are consumed annually in the production of the goods. Enormous quantities of the product are shipped to countries throughout the world, and brands made by this concern have an established reputation for excellence of quality in every state and territory of the Union.

Hetherington & Berner Company, 19 to 27 West South street, is one of the oldest industrial establishments in this city. The business was founded by Benjamin F. Hetherington in 1861; and in 1863 Frederick Berner, Sr., became associated with him. The business has had an even and steady growth and is now recognized as one of the most important manufacturing plants here. The business was incorporated in 1893. The company manufactures architectural iron work, refrigerating machines, special machinery of every description, and it is the largest builder of asphalt plants in the country. The product is shipped to all parts of the world. The plant is a large one, covering nearly three acres, and admirably fitted with the latest and best improved machinery. Over 125 men are employed. The officers of the company are: Benjamin F. Hetherington, president; Fred. Berner, Sr., vice-president; Fred. A. Hetherington, secretary, and Fred. Berner, Jr., treasurer.

HETHERINGTON & BERNER COMPANY.

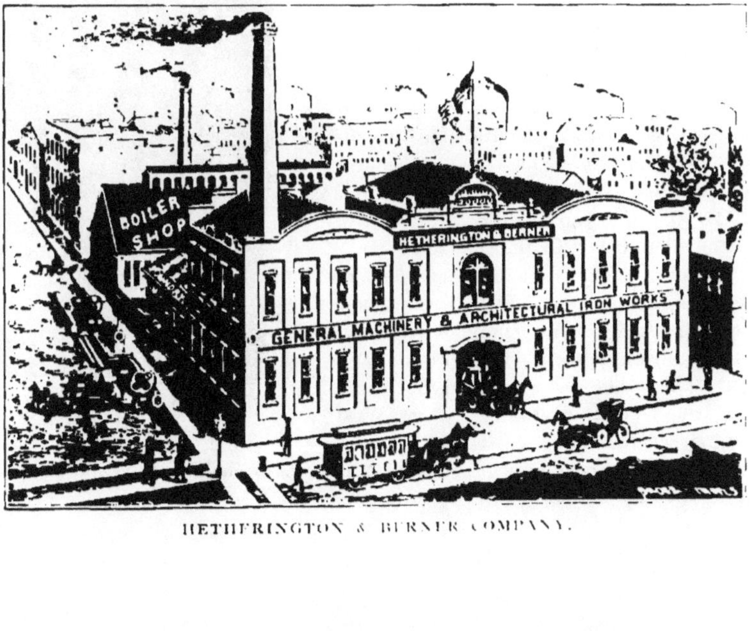

HETHERINGTON & BERNER COMPANY.

Carl Moller, 161 East Washington street, began business here in 1876, and has always been recognized as one of the heaviest dealers in wall paper and interior decorations in the State. During the decorating season he gives employment to a force of skilled assistants ranging from twenty-five to thirty. His stock embraces all the very latest American and European productions, and his house enjoys a wide-spread and entirely deserved reputation for elegance of supplies and superiority of workmanship.

CARL MOLLER.

Indiana Electrotype Company, No. 23 West Pearl street.—There is no branch of mercantile activity in this thriving mid-continental metropolis in which more distinguished enterprise has been manifested than in that comprising the arts of electrotyping, stereotyping, etc. Prominent among the representative concerns thus referred to ranks the Indiana Electrotype Company, conducted under the proprietorship of Messrs. William Wands, Jos. E., M. A., and Jno. B. Fleck, the active management being in the hands of Mr. J. H. Hutton. They founded their present establishment in 1893, and their patronage now radiates, apart from immediately local business, throughout Indiana, Ohio and Illinois. The premises comprise the entire ground floor of the building, No. 23 West Pearl street, the equipment being of the latest improved pattern, operated by an eighty-five horse power gas engine. All classes of electrotyping and stereotyping are economically and perfectly done.

INDIANA ELECTROTYPE CO.

INDIANAPOLIS BOOK AND STATIONERY COMPANY.

Indianapolis Book and Stationery Company, 75 South Meridian street, wholesale jobbers and importers of books, stationery, and fancy goods, etc., are successors to the business formerly conducted by the Burris-Herzsch Company and the Bowen-Merrill Company. The concern was incorporated in June, 1896, and is the largest one of its kind west of New York city engaged exclusively in the jobbing trade The company is located in commodious quarters consisting of four floors 22x195. Five travelers are employed, who cover the territory of Indiana, Ohio, and Illinois. The officers and directors of the company are: R. H. Barnes, president; A. F. Herzsch, vice-president; W. M. Cronyn, treasurer; J. H. Wilson, secretary; Thos. Dunn and Marshall Moore.

Progress Clothing Company, Bliss, Swain & Company, proprietors, 6 and 8 West Washington street, is one of the largest retail establisments in the city. The business was established in September, 1891, and from the opening of its doors took a prominent and foremost position in the retail trade. The firm is liberal in its use of printer's ink, and no concern is more deservedly popular. The members of the firm are George W. Bliss and Thomas A. Swain.

PROGRESS CLOTHING COMPANY.

W. J. HOLLIDAY & CO.

W. J. Holliday & Company, 59 and 61 South Meridian street, are the largest and most extensive dealers in steel and heavy hardware and carriage and wagonmakers' supplies in the state. The house was established in 1856 by the senior member of the firm, and is one of the oldest wholesale concerns in the city. The trade of the firm extends over Indiana, Illinois, Ohio and Iowa. The members of the firm are William J. and Jacquelin S. Holliday and Walter J. Goodall.

The Gordon-Kurtz Company, 141 and 143 South Meridian street, manufacturers and jobbers of saddlery hardware, enjoys the distinction of being the largest exclusively saddlery hardware house in America. The trade in this concern embraces Ohio, Indiana, Illinois, Kentucky, Michigan, Iowa, Missouri, Kansas and Colorado, and it is the largest handler of robes and blankets in the country. The business was established in 1872 and has enjoyed even and uniform prosperity from its beginning. The members of the company are I. S. Gordon, president; E. A. Wert, vice-president, and W. E. Kurtz, secretary and treasurer.

Hide, Leather and Belting Company, 125 South Meridian street, had its beginning in the war period. Its present proprietor, George W. Snider, assumed control of the business in 1870, and its growth has been uniformly prosperous. It now has in operation the largest plant in the state for the production of oak leather belting, besides carrying a large stock of rubber belting, hose and steam packing, also leather and shoe findings. The trade of the house covers all the central, southern and western states. Mr. John W. Elstun is the business manager.

GORDON-KURTZ CO.

HIDE, LEATHER AND BELTING COMPANY.

Tanner & Sullivan, wholesale tin-plate, sheet iron and metals, tinners' supplies, and manufacturers of tinware. Among the representative wholesale houses of this city is that of Tanner & Sullivan, which was established in 1878 and since which time the business has steadily increased until this firm is now conceded to be one of the largest operators in its line of business throughout the west. Their four-story and basement buildings, located at 116 and 118 South Meridian street, are admirably fitted for carrying on their extensive business, consisting of tin-plate, sheet iron, metals, tinners' supplies, tools and machines, all kinds of tinware and a general line of kitchen furnishing goods. This house has unequaled facilities for handling the business in their line, being well represented by a number of traveling salesmen who are thoroughly posted in the requirements of the trade, and it is a well-known fact that all business entrusted to the care of Tanner & Sullivan is attended to with promptness and in a most satisfactory manner. Both Messrs. Tanner and Sullivan are active workers in the Commercial Club and Board of Trade, Mr. Tanner having been president of the last named organization for two terms, and is the present U. S. surveyor of customs at this port.

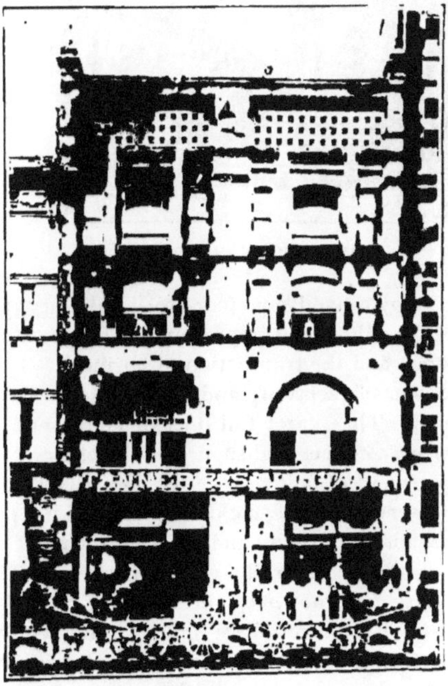

TANNER & SULLIVAN.

Home Stove Company, No. 79 South Meridian street, manufacturers of stoves, ranges and hollow ware, was incorporated in July, 1893. The manufact-

HOME STOVE COMPANY.

uring plant of the concern is located at Greenfield, Ind., embracing an area of nearly three acres, equipped with all the latest improved machinery, and furnishes employment to 120 operators. The celebrated "Home" and "Model" stoves, ranges and heaters and "Favorite" stove, hollow ware and stove trimmings are manufactured by this company. These goods are fully described in a handsomely illustrated catalogue which will be sent to any address on application. The stock carried in the store is the largest and most complete in the city. The officers of the company are Geo. Alig, president, and Louis Hitzelberger, secretary and treasurer.

Kothe, Wells & Bauer, wholesale grocers, 128 and 130 South Meridian street. An important member of the wholesale grocery trade of Indianapolis is the house of Kothe, Wells & Bauer, composed of George Kothe, William Kothe, Charles W. Wells and George Bauer, and was organized in January, 1889. The firm is located in the heart of the wholesale trade district where they occupy a handsome four-story building, 35 x 150 feet, and containing all modern facilities and improvements for the storage, display, sale and shipment of stock and the transaction of business. The firm's warehouse is located at the corner of Delaware and Merrill streets, where the large reserve stock is carried. They carry full lines of staple and fancy groceries, making specialties of teas, coffees and sugars of the choicest grades and varieties. In their department of fancy groceries they include canned and potted meats, fruits and preserves, sauces, pickles, spices, baking powders, etc., also handling the best brands of smoking and chewing tobaccos and cigars, with other articles appertaining generally to the business. The goods packed specially by this house and known by the brand of "Ko-We-Ba" are sold under a guarantee to give satisfaction or money refunded, and no goods sold in this market have a greater reputation for superior quality and absolute purity. The house has a large trade throughout Indiana, Ohio, Illinois, Michigan, Ken-

KOTHE, WELLS & BAUER.

tucky and Pennsylvania, which is visited regularly by 10 traveling men. The members of the firm are men of enterprise and business ability.

Louis G. Deschler, wholesale and retail dealer in cigars, tobaccos and smokers' articles, 51 North Pennsylvania street, and Bates House rotunda, has been engaged in the trade about fifteen years. His establishment on North Pennsylvania street, in the Lemcke building, is one of the handsomest and most attractive smokers' emporiums in the west. His establishments are noted as headquarters, both with the wholesale and retail trade, for strictly first-class high grade goods. He is a direct importer of fine Havana and Key West goods, and carries in stock the choicest and most popular brands of American manufacturers. He makes a specialty of box trade and hundreds of our leading citizens are among his regular patrons.

Judson & Hanna, 15 West Maryland street, are engaged in the wholesale jobbing trade. The business was established in 1893 and the trade extends throughout Indiana and parts of Illinois and Ohio, which territory is visited by several travelers. The members of the firm are Charles E. Judson and John A. Hanna.

Kruse & Dewenter, manufacturers of heating and ventilating apparatus, 223 and 225 East Washington street, began business in this city in 1884. Until recently they were established at 54 South Pennsylvania street, but having outgrown the facilities afforded in this location they purchased the present site and built the handsome three-story structure, 35 x 195, that is now used by them exclusively for offices, store-rooms and factory purposes. The building is a modern one in every respect, built of terra cotta, pressed brick with plate glass front, and furnished with the latest machinery and appliances. The firm is one of the largest in the country and the only one in the state making a specialty of heating and ventilating apparatus and the dry and flush closet system for schools, churches and public buildings. They are also extensive manufacturers of heating apparatus for dwellings and do a very large business throughout the country. Up to the present time they have employed about fifty men in the factory and three men on the road, but with their extended facilities will double their capacity. The members of the firm are Theo. Kruse and H. C. Dewenter.

KRUSE & DEWENTER.

The Bedford Indiana Stone Company, number 26 Baldwin Block. This company was organized and incorporated in 1894. The officers of the company are: Allen W. Conduitt, president; H. G. Coughlen, secretary and general manager, and Dr. O. S. Runnels, treasurer. The quarries of the concern are located in the celebrated Buff Ridge district at Bedford, Indiana, from which district over 95 per cent. of the best and finest grade of building stone is taken. These quarries cover over 400 acres, and are equipped with six steam powers and derricks, eight improved channeling machines, and four gang mills. Switches from competing railways run directly into the quarries, a facility that is not enjoyed by any other quarry in Indiana. Among the notable buildings in the United States which were built from the stone taken from the quarries of this concern may be mentioned the Majestic, Lemcke and Sayles buildings in Indianapolis, the Mail and Express, Y. M. C. A., San Remo Hotel, and School of Languages buildings in New York city.

The Vajen-Bader Company.—Of the many useful articles that are manufactured in Indianapolis, there are none that have attracted greater attention than the product of this concern. The Vajen-Bader Patent Firemen's Smoke Protector which is manufactured by this company has received the favorable comment of the press all over the world; it is the most perfect and practical device yet invented for the use of fire-fighters. It is built upon scientific principles and is considered of greater importance than the submarine diving apparatus which has in the past created so much interest. With the use of this helmet a person is enabled to enter rooms filled with smoke or noxious gases without the slightest discomfort to the wearer. It furnishes complete protection against fire, heat, smoke, steam, gas, electric wires and falling debris, and affords the only means for the saving of human life when all other efforts prove unavailable. This protector has been adopted by the fire departments of over one hundred of the largest cities, both in America and abroad. It is also used in the largest brewing establishments in the country, and by large miners and gas companies. It is estimated that during the first year over $3,000,000 worth of property was saved by the use of this new device. Great credit is due to Mr. Willis C. Vajen, who has brought this new protector to its present high state of perfection, and through whose energy it was brought to the notice of the fire-fighters and others who have made practical use of them. The helmet has been successfully tested before the many fire chiefs attending their annual conventions. First honors were taken at the meeting of the Pacific Coast Association of Fire Chiefs at Los Angeles, California, in May, 1895, and before the International Meetings of Fire Chiefs, at Augusta, Ga., in October, 1895, and at Salt Lake City, Utah, in August, 1896. The long list of testimonials received by the company would indicate that the helmet had done good service in many fire departments in saving much property both from fire and water as well as a life saving device. The materials used in the construction of this helmet undergo a chemical treatment. The cool pure air furnished to the occupant or wearer of the helmet comes from a compressed air reservoir having a pressure of 100 pounds, and enables him to breathe freely and comfortably for from one to two hours. The specially constructed diaphragm in the ear pieces offers the advantages of hearing which one would naturally have on the outside. The double plates of mica in the eye pieces give him the freedom of sight, overcoming the damaging results from different temperatures in which the helmet is frequently to be used. The helmet is most complete in all details, with handsome case, air-pump and other attachments. The factory covers considerable space on the second floor of the old library building at the corner of Ohio and Pennsylvania streets, where a number of men are employed constantly in the manufacture of these goods. Mr. Willis C. Vajen is president and manager of the company.

Theodore Stein, Abstracter of Titles, Notary Public and General Conveyancer, succeeded to the business of Wm. C. Anderson in 1887. Mr. Stein is a native of this city, having been born here November 7, 1858. After attending public schools he entered the service of H. Hermann's lumber mills as book-keeper, and afterward became manager of the business, which he continued until embarking for himself. In 1891 he became a director of the German Mutual Insurance Company, of Indiana, and president upon the reorganization of this company as the German Fire Insurance Company, of Indiana. He has at all times taken great interest in public affairs and served as city councilman two years, at which time he was a persistent advocate of the elevation of railroad tracks and the originator of the law regulating the use of bicycle lamps.

Gregory & Appel, Insurance, Real Estate, Rental and Loan Agents, 96 East Market street, have been engaged in business since 1884, and rank among the most important in their line in this city. The companies represented by this firm are the New York Underwriters Agency, Westchester of New York, Citizens' of St. Louis, Northwestern National of Milwaukee, Spring Garden of Philadelphia, American of Newark, N. J., and the German Fire Insurance Company of Indianapolis. The members of the firm are Fred A. Gregory and John J. Appel.

The American Plate Glass Company was incorporated in 1895. The officers are: C. T. Doxey, president; D. M. Ransdell, secretary and treasurer. The factory is located at Alexandria, Indiana, and furnishes employment to over 400 men.

HENRY COBURN'S PLANING MILL.

Henry Coburn, one of the largest and most extensive dealers in lumber in this city, was perhaps, the first person to engage in that line of trade exclusively at this point. He began business in 1859 at the southeast corner of Delaware and New York streets. The brick building that was used for office

HENRY COBURN'S OFFICE AND YARDS.

purposes at that time is still standing on the old location. The business was first conducted under the firm name of Coburn & Lingenfelter, and continued until 1862, when William H. Jones became a partner by purchasing the interest of Mr. Lingenfelter, and the firm became known as Coburn & Jones. In 1865 the yard was removed to the present location on the north side of Georgia street between Capitol and Senate avenues, then known as Tennessee and Mississippi streets respectively. In 1872 they erected the planing mill located at the intersection of the above mentioned streets. The mill has a capacity of more than 50,000 feet of dressed lumber daily and furnishes employment to 45 to 50 persons. The mill is devoted to the production of sash, doors and blinds, and interior wood finish of every description. Over 5,000,000 feet of lumber is embraced in the present stock in the yards. In 1885, upon the death of Mr. Jones, the sole control of the business was assumed by Mr. Coburn, who has conducted it ever since with his son William H. Coburn, who is associated with him in the firm. In addition to the above business Mr. Coburn is interested extensively in farming lands in this and Madison counties and in the Michigan Lumber Company of this city. Mr. Coburn is a native of this city, having been born in Indianapolis, September 17, 1834. His father, Henry P. Coburn, was clerk of the supreme court of Indiana, who came to this place from Corydon in 1824, when the capital was transferred from that place. Mr. Coburn has enjoyed a successful business career and has been closely identified with the progressive movements that have brought Indianapolis up from a struggling village to a thriving metropolis.

Indianapolis Manufacturers' and Carpenters' Union are the successor, by purchase, to the lumber business formerly owned and established by Warren Tate in 1863, and which was operated by him until the winter of 1871. Originally, the company was composed of some 60 or more individuals—carpenters and small contractors—who organized a stock company and purchased

INDIANAPOLIS MANUFACTURERS' AND CARPENTERS' UNION.

the plant. The severe panic of 1877 forced many of them to relinquish their holdings, and the majority of the stock was finally absorbed by the present management. Among the original stockholders were C. F. Resener, Fred Dickman, Val. Schaaf, Frederick Schmid, Henry Pauli and others. Mr. Resener was the first president and was succeeded by Mr. Pauli. In 1878 Mr. Schaaf was elected president and has served continuously since. With the exception of two years Mr. Schmid has been actively connected with the company since its organization, and has directed the business of the corporation in the capacity of secretary and treasurer. Under the management of these gentlemen, the business has been developed to one of the most important in its line, and is unquestionably the largest in the manufacture of finished lumber, fixtures of all kinds and interior wood finishing. In their mill they operate a force averaging from 50 to 75 men, according to the conditions of trade, not including the office force. They also operate extensive lumber yards in the vicinity of the mill. The main offices and factory are located at 38 to 42 South New Jersey street.

Mr. Frederick Schmid, the secretary of the company, as well as Mr. Schaaf, are pioneer citizens of Indianapolis, and have been instrumental in promoting the city's growth and welfare.

The Foster Lumber Company was founded in 1872, by C. C. Foster & Co., and was reorganized under its present title in 1895, with a capital of $50,000. The trade conducted in the different branches is widespread and commanding in proportions. The plant of the company is located at 402 and 420 North Mississippi street, covering a ground area of three acres, and with its splendid equipment of modern machinery and ingenious labor-saving devices and commodious dry kiln, is the most complete plant in the state. The planing mill, sash, door and blind factory include a two-story building, 140 x 180 feet in area, and two three-story frame buildings. A 100-horse-power engine drives the machinery; there is a 6 x 18 foot boiler, and the fur-

FOSTER LUMBER COMPANY.

naces are arranged either to burn natural gas or surplus shavings. The warehouse and offices occupy a three-story frame building, 40 x 160 feet in dimensions, from 75 to 100 men being steadily employed. There are numerous large sheds for the storage of dry and finished stock, while the spacious yards easily accommodate immense quantities of rough or dressed lumber. The ample switch connections with the "Big Four" railway afford splendid convenience for expeditious shipments. The product includes all kinds of planed and finished lumber, sash, doors, blinds, frames, mouldings, etc., their specialty being veneered door and fine interior finish. Their trade extends over the whole state and into Illinois and Kentucky. The hardwood finish in the City Library and Commercial Club Building and many of the handsome residences in this city are evidences of the superior character of their workmanship. The president, Mr. C. C. Foster, is one of the vice-presidents of the Commercial Club, a member of the Board of Trade, president of the Atlas Savings Association, vice-president of the Mutual Home Savings and Loan Association, a member of the Builders' Exchange. Mr. O. P. Ensley, secretary of the company, was chief clerk of the pension office at this point and is an energetic young business man.

Fraser Brothers & Van Hoff occupy a foremost position in the lumber trade, and rank among the heaviest dealers in this city. The business was established by Frazer Brothers & Colborn in 1880. The first partnership was composed of A. R. Colborn, who owns large interest in the lumber trade in Michigan City, Ind., and many other points throughout the state, and S. D. Fraser and S. P. Fraser, who came here in 1880. In 1883, J. G. Fraser came here, and was taken into the business, and in 1888 H. L. Van Hoff also purchased an interest. In 1892, Mr. Colborn retired, selling his interest to the remaining members, and the firm became known as Fraser Brothers & Van Hoff. Early in its existence this house made itself an important factor in the lumber trade of the city, and from the beginning has done a very large and successful business. The yards, which are located at the junction of East Washington street and Michigan avenue, are most favorably situated, covering area of nearly three acres, and supplied with private railroad switches running into the grounds, capable of accommodating twenty cars, connecting directly with the Pennsylvania Railroad. In addition to being extensive dealers in sash, door and blinds, the firm carries at all times in stock about three million feet of all kinds of building lumber.

WESTERN FURNITURE COMPANY.

The Western Furniture Company, Madison avenue and South Delaware street. W. L. Hagedorn, president; Chas. Fearnaught, secretary, and George Herman, superintendent, was established in 1873. The factory is one of the most extensive engaged in the manufacture of furniture in this market. The buildings cover five acres and are built substantially of brick, 170 feet long, by 100 feet deep, embracing four stories and basement. They are equipped throughout with the latest and most improved machinery. Over 100 men are employed in the factory, and the product which consists of beds and chamber sets find a market all over the United States and throughout foreign countries.

The Emrich Furniture Company are successors to the business established by Emrich, Paulini & Company in 1882. The company was incorporated March, 1895, and was one of the largest firms engaged in the manufacture of furniture in the city. The output consists of side-boards and bedroom sets. The trade of the concern extends throughout the entire United

States. The factory is located at 190 to 210 West Morris street, and covers over one and one-half acres of ground and furnishes employment to 125 men. The officers of the company are: Henry Emrich, president; George H. Drechsle, vice-president, and John H. Emrich, secretary and treasurer.

The Indiana Lumber and Veneer Company, Fifteenth street and L. E. & W. railroad. This company was organized in 1892. The business is devoted to the manufacture of sawed veneers and band sawed lumber. A specialty is made of quartered oak for fine interior finish, and the product includes band sawed lumber of every description. The market for the product of this concern extends throughout every state and territory in the Union, and throughout foreign countries. The officers of the company are: A. K. Hollowell, president; O. M. Pruitt, secretary; L. P. Hollowell, treasurer, and William Dickerson, superintendent. The plant covers over six acres, and is especially well equipped with modern machinery and has the most convenient railway shipping facilities, being located directly on the L. E. & W. railway, and in direct connection with all roads leading into the city.

The Union Embossing Machine Company, manufacturers of Drop-Carving machines, has acquired all the patents on Drop-Carving machines, and has now in operation over seven hundred machines in this and other countries. In truth, the "Union" Drop-Carving machine must be classed as one of the greatest of modern inventions, and is as startling an innovation in the field of wood-working as the typesetting machine has become to publishing. By its employment the most delicate and difficult hand-carving can be reproduced at a nominal cost, as compared to the hand process. In fact, the quality and beauty of finish of the work of this machine can not be equaled by hand work. The machines have been adopted by the large manufacturers of pianos and organs; also by the principal furniture and car decorators and builders. The offices of the company, as well as the manufacturing plant, are located in the Crist building, in West South street. The officers of the company are E. S. DeTamble, president, and W. M. Richards, secretary and treasurer.

Thomas E. Potter, 26 and 28 South Capitol avenue, established the business of manufacturing straw goods, such as hats and bonnets, in 1888. It is the only factory of the kind in this city, and the business extends throughout the entire central and western states. Employment is furnished to over 250 hands.

The Indiana Bermudez Asphalt Company and Paving Contractors was incorporated in 1894. The officers of the company are: John M. Cooper, president; Allen W. Conduitt, secretary and treasurer. This concern is one of the most important and largest of those now engaged in laying the asphalted streets in Indianapolis. Among the most important contracts filled by this concern were the paving of North New Jersey street, from Washington to Fort Wayne avenue, Liberty street, East Market street, Buchanan street, Palmer street, and many others. This concern operates an extensive plant at Brazil, Indiana, where it manufactures paving brick of superior quality on a very large scale.

The Parry Manufacturing Company, owing to its rapid growth, has attracted, perhaps, more and wider attention than any other industrial institution in the western country. The foundation of this magnificent and enormous business was laid fourteen years ago, at Rushville, Indiana, by David M. and Thomas H. Parry. At that point they began the manufacture of road carts and buck-boards. The road cart up to this time had not fully found favor with the agriculturists of America as a general utility vehicle, but the Parrys saw the "ear marks" of popularity in the "two-wheeler," and that the average man needed only a little persuasion to convince him that he could not be happy without one. Firmly convinced that the world could be converted and made happy by buying road carts and with "the faith that was in them" and with the aid of 40 employes, but limited facilities, they began the work.

PARRY BROS., 1886.

In 1884 their factory was destroyed by fire and they immediately sought new quarters and continued the work of "conversion." By 1886 the road cart had established a reputation as "a thing of beauty and a joy forever," and the

PARRY MANUFACTURING COMPANY, 1896.

Parrys were compelled to seek larger and better quarters for the production of their pet vehicle. In this year they moved to Indianapolis. From this time forth the business grew with leaps and bounds, and from an output of 100 carts a day in a short space of time the factory began to turn out 1,000 carts daily, sending them to all quarters of the globe. In 1890 the company began the manufacture of four-wheel vehicles on a large scale, such as surries, piano-box buggies, phaetons, road and spring wagons, etc. With the wide trade connections secured by this time in the sale of carts and the established reputation for making the very best goods for the smallest amount of money, they invaded the field occupied by the oldest and strongest carriage manufacturers for half a century. The plant was enlarged and equipped throughout with every modern appliance necessary to bring down the cost of production to the minimum. How well the Parry Manufacturing Company has succeeded in the manufacture of carriages is attested in the enormous plant, covering acres of ground—larger than the five largest carriage factories in the world put together—in which every portion of a buggy, with the exception of the cloth and leather, is manufactured from the raw material. In all there are 19 buildings, covering 20 acres, connected with railroad switches running into the factory grounds. Many special Parry "Jumbo" cars are used for the shipment of vehicles to all parts of the country. During the busy season of 1896 over 2,800 persons were employed. Two independent electric plants are used for lighting the factory, and all the machinery is operated by electricity. Over 350 four-wheel jobs are turned out daily, and 22 traveling men are constantly employed, visiting the trade in every state and territory in the Union. To pack the goods it requires 15,000 feet of lumber daily for crating, and 55 persons are employed in the book-keeping department. The trade in foreign countries is constantly increasing. The officers of the company are: David M. Parry, president; St. Clair Parry, secretary, and Thomas H. Parry, superintendent.

The W. B. Barry Saw and Supply Company was established by W. B. Barry in 1874, and for nearly a quarter of a century has maintained a foremost position as one of the leading industrial establishments of the city. The product consists of circular, band, and cross-cut saws, and has an established reputation for excellence of quality among the consumers throughout the United States. In 1895, at the Atlanta Exposition, the production of this concern was awarded a diploma and gold medal for superiority. The plant is located at 132 and 134 South Pennsylvania street, where a large force is constantly employed.

Parkhurst Brothers & Company, proprietors of the Indianapolis Bolt and Machine Works, is located at 122 to 128 Kentucky avenue. The business was established in 1875 and has always been recognized as one of the most important of the many institutions that add to the value of Indianapolis as a manufacturing center. The plant covers nearly two acres with substantial brick buildings, equipped throughout with the latest and most approved tools and modern machinery. About 50 operatives are employed, and the output of the plant consists of light and heavy castings, machine bolts, special machinery, and Olsen's Improved Freight Elevators. The members of the firm are: J. W., J. H., and J. M. Parkhurst, and M. E. McAlpin.

Nordyke & Marmon Company.—Manufacturing flour mill machinery, elevator machinery and special appliances used in milling is one of the great industries of Indianapolis; and is well represented by the Norkyke & Marmon Company, who own and have in successful operation one of the largest establishments of its kind in the world. The foundation of this now prosperous company dates from 1851, when the business was established by Messrs. Ellis and Addison H. Nordyke, as Nordyke & Son, and four years later Mr. Daniel W. Marmon became a partner.

Mr. Ellis Nordyke died in 1871, and Mr. Amos K. Hollowell was admitted to the firm. In 1874, the present company was organized and incorporated under the laws of the state, with Mr. Addison H. Nordyke, president; Mr. Amos K. Hollowell, treasurer, and Mr. Daniel W. Marmon, secretary, since when the manufacturing facilities have been increased and the trade extended. The plant of the company covers fifteen acres of ground on the line of a railroad in West Indianapolis, with which it is connected by side-tracks. The buildings are one and two-story structures, substantially built of brick, the group comprising foundries, machine shops, iron and wood-working shops, finishing shop, store and warehouses and handsome offices. There is also a spacious yard for the storing of material. A two-hundred-and-fifty-horse-power steam engine drives the machinery, and the services of five hundred skilled machinists are brought into requisition. Throughout all departments the works are perfectly equipped with the latest improved machinery and tools, and are among the best and most complete in the country. The various milling machinery and appliances turned out have a world-wide reputation, and are not only shipped to all parts of the United States, but also to Canada, European countries, Australia, Mexico, South and Central America, Africa, New Zealand and Japan, and the business is steadily growing in volume and importance each succeeding year. The company manufactures all kinds of flour mill and elevator machinery, corn mills and rice mills, also machinery for handling grain, the latest improved roller mills, portable mills, centrifugal bolts, pulleys, hangers, shafting, etc., and also deal in buhr mill stones, silk bolting cloth of all grades, and woven wire cloth, leather and rubber belting and flour mill supplies. The special features of the various machines and appliances manufactured by the Nordyke & Marmon Company are simplicity in construction, rapid adjustment convenience of operation and accurate workmanship. They are fully up to all that is claimed for them, and are in every point of actual value superior to any others in the market. All the officers are well and prominently known in this city in business and financial circles, and active members of the Board of Trade and Commercial Club.

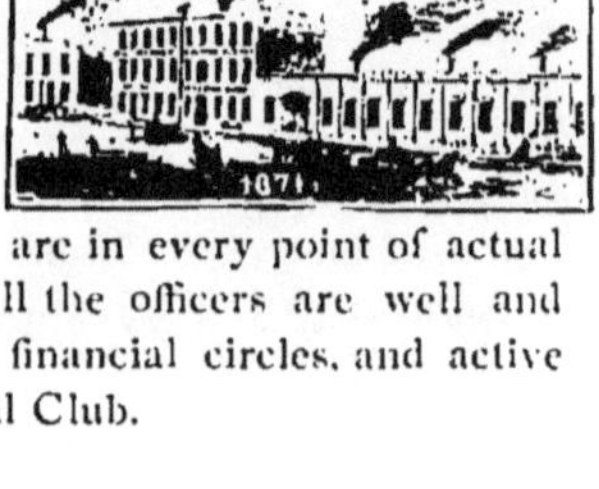

NORDYKE & MARMON COMPANY.

The National Electric Headlight Company was organized in 1890, by R. B. F. Peirce, H. H. Fulton and D. L. Whittier. For a number of years experiments were made by different parties, to produce an electric headlight for locomotives, and after the expenditure of vast sums of money in an unsuccessful attempt to produce a working machine, the idea was abandoned. It was at this time that Mr. Peirce, who was then the general manager of the I., D. & S. Railroad Company, became impressed with the importance of the electric headlight. His practical experience as a railroad man undoubtedly gave him a better knowledge of the importance and utility of the machine than was possessed by the original promoters; and recognizing this he undertook to bring the headlight to perfection. How well his plans materialized is evidenced in the broad use to which it has been applied on some of the most important railroads in the country. He spent over $100,000 to bring about the result, after facing many embarrassments that would have driven most men to abandon the project. The electric headlight stands out prominently as one of the great inventions that has been produced to minify the dangers of modern railroading. The first road to adopt the electric headlight was the Vandalia, where it gave uniform satisfaction. It is now in use on the locomotives of the C. H. & D. R. R., I. D. & W. R. R., T. H. & I. R. R., T. St. L. & K. C. Ry., C. & E. I. R. R., Gov. Railways of New South Wales, W. & N. R. R., C. & G. T. R. R., E. & T. H. R. R., P. D. & E. Ry., Texas Midland, G. S. & F. R. R., K. C. F. S. & M. Ry., C. N. O. & T. P. Ry., N. O. & N. E. R. R., C. & O. R. R., Gov. Railways of Brazil, etc., etc., B. R. & P. R. R., L. E. & St. L. Ry., Ala. Great Southern, Southern Pacific, Florida Southern, C. R. I. & P. R. R., St. L. & A. Ry., D. & H. Ry., Central Vermont, G. La. P. & H. Ry., H. & T. C. Ry., and other railroad companies, and in a number of foreign countries. The factory is located in West South street where the company employs a large number of skilled workmen. The present officers are R. B. F. Peirce, president, and E. B Peirce, general manager.

CRIST NATIONAL ELECTRIC HEADLIGHT.

The McElwaine-Richards Company, incorporated in 1890, succeeded to the busines of J. B. McElwaine & Company and George A. Richards. The company is engaged in the manufacture of gas and water supplies, and conduct the most extensive wholesale business in plumbers' and gas-fitters' tools and supplies in the West. The company operate a large manufacturing plant at Noblesville, Ind., employing about 135 hands. The offices and store rooms are located in the company's handsome building, at 62, 64 and 66 West Maryland street in this city; and the pipe yards and warehouses are situated at the corner of Delaware and Merrill streets where direct railroad connections with all lines leading into the city facilitate the handling of the heavy stock. Besides the above, the company manufactures the celebrated J. & R. changeable bicycle gear. The officers of the company are: M. M. McElwaine, president; Geo. A. Richards, treasurer, and M. O. Halderman, secretary and vice-president.

OFFICES AND STORE ROOM,
THE M'ELWAINE-RICHARDS CO.

FACTORY M'ELWAINE-RICHARDS CO.

The Rockwood Manufacturing Company, 176 to 190 South Pennsylvania street, is the outgrowth of the American Paper Pulley Company, established in 1883. Until 1891 the firm was conducted by Messrs. W. E. Rockwood and H. C. Newcomb, under this title, when Mr. Rockwood succeeded to the

DEAN BROS. STEAM PUMP WORKS.

ROCKWOOD MANUFACTURING COMPANY.

sole control, and changed the name to the present style. From the inception of the business it took a front rank among the most important manufacturing interests of this city, and has enjoyed uniform prosperity. The products consist of paper pulleys, paper frictions, machine castings, saw-mills, Rathsam patent flower pot machinery, Pyle automatic engines, from 2 to 250 horse-power, and all kinds of special machinery. The plant covers an area of 125x175 feet, the machine shop and office occupy a building 75x150 feet, the foundry, one 50x75 feet, and the blacksmith shop, one 25x40 feet in dimensions. These various departments are all finely equipped with the latest improved machinery. The output is one of great magnitude and importance, and the trade extends all over the United States, Canada, Mexico, South America, Australia and Europe.

Dean Brothers Steam Pump Works, established in 1870, one of the best planned industrial establishments in the country engaged in the manufacture of steam pumps for all purposes, is now located on First near Mississippi street. The shops are fitted with new and modern designed tools and machinery for manufacturing pumping machinery with accuracy and economy. The buildings have a width on the ground of 60 feet, by 1,000 feet in length. The different departments are, pattern shop, blacksmith shop, iron foundry, brass foundry, and machine shop. Every part of the pumps are made by the company. The list of pumps comprise over 300 different styles and kinds. In addition to Dean's patent single pumps, a full line of duplex pumps are manufactured. More than 50 sizes and combinations of cylinders in this style of pump are made. The officers of the company are: Edward H. Dean, president; Wilfred R. Dean, vice-president; John C. Dean, secretary and treasurer, and Ward H. Dean, superintendent.

HOLLIDAY & WYON.

Holliday & Wyon, manufacturers of harness and collars, and wholesesale dealers in horse goods, saddlery, hardware, leather, and shoe findings, began business in 1879. It was the first house in the State to engage in this line of manufacture on an extensive scale, and has maintained a foremost position since its organization. The trade of the firm is very heavy, and extends throughout the United States. Travelers, representatives of the house, visit the trade in Indiana, Ohio, Michigan, Pennsylvania, New York, Illinois, Kansas and Iowa. In the manufacturing department over 70 persons are employed, and the firm is commodiously housed in the large brick edifice at the northwest corner of Pennsylvania and Georgia streets, covering 65x110 feet, consisting of five floors. The members of the firm are John D. Holliday and Albert F. Wyon.

KNIGHT & JILLSON PIPE YARDS.

Knight & Jillson, manufacturers of natural gas, oil well, steam and water supplies, 75 South Pennsylvania street, is the oldest firm engaged in the line in this city, and ranks among the heaviest operators in the west. The firm was established in 1872. The business has been a very prosperous one from its inception, growing from a trade aggregating $60,000 for the first year until 1887 it had reached $175,000. With the discovery of natural gas in this section the growth became more rapid and substantial and the firm's business now approximates a million dollars annually. The offices and manufacturing

KNIGHT & JILLSON OFFICE AND FACTORY.

plant is located in the two-story brick building, 40x200 feet, at 75 South Pennsylvania street, in which from 40 to 50 persons are employed. The firm also operate an extensive pipe yard at the east end of the Union railway station, having a capacity of 75 car loads of pipe, in which they carry in stock about 50 car loads of black and galvanized iron tubing and oil well casing. The trade of the house extends throughout Indiana, Ohio and Illinois and is constantly growing. The members of the firm are E. J. Knight and Wm. M. Jillson. The vast proportions to which their business has grown is a significant testimonial as to their standing and the confidence accorded them by the trade.

Clemens Vonnegut, one of the most prominent and influential of our pioneer citizens, laid the foundation of the business which still bears his name, in 1851, and in which he is still interested with his four sons, Clemens, Jr., Bernard, Franklin and George Vonnegut. The business at that time was conducted under the firm name of Volmer & Vonnegut. In 1857 Mr. Vonne-

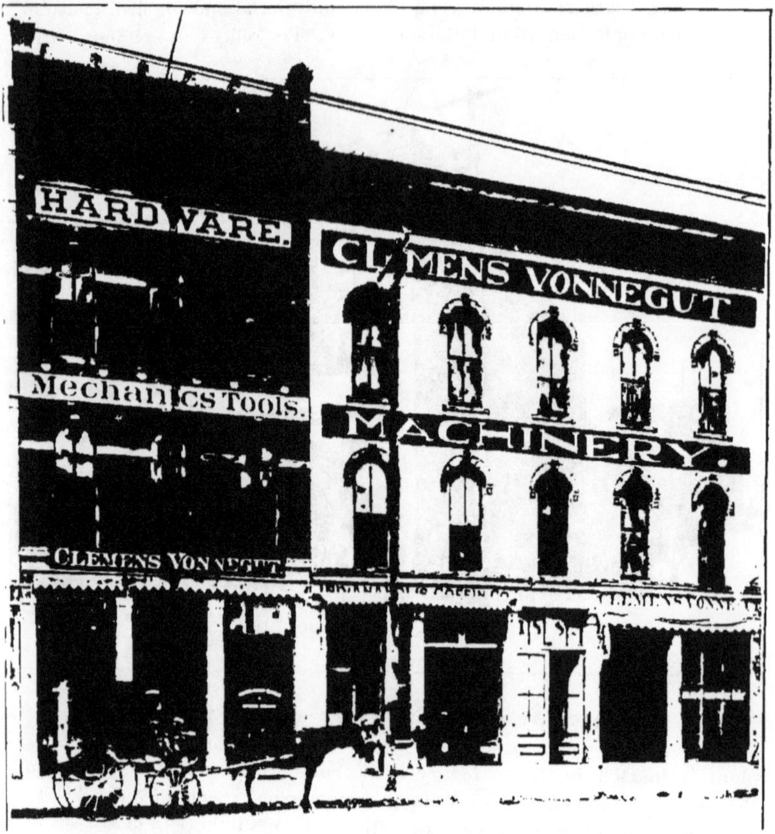

CLEMENS VONNEGUT.

gut succeeded to the business, and since that time has continued at its head. It is recognized to-day as one of the leading and oldest retail and wholesale hardware establishments in Indiana. The premises occupied are located at 184 to 192 East Washington street, and the stock embraces one of the most complete assortments of hardware of all kinds to be found in the State. This includes everything in the line of shelf and heavy hardware, mechanics' tools of all kinds, and mechanics' supplies. In the early part of this year, to meet the pressing demands of the trade of this market, they opened a machinery department, in which they carry a complete line of light machinery of every description for iron and wood working, embracing lathes, shapers, milling machinery, shears, punches, power drills, emery grinding machines, pulleys, shafting, hangers, etc. A special catalogue is issued for this department. The trade of this house extends throughout this State, and a number of traveling salesmen represent the firm on the road. Nearly thirty persons are employed in the house.

Clemens Vonnegut, during his long career, has been an active promoter of the city's welfare. For more than a quarter of a century he held a position on the school board, and during that period was recognized as one of its most useful members. He was largely instrumental in securing the establishment of industrial training school. His sons are all actively identified with public affairs, and their names are connected with many associations of local importance. Franklin Vonnegut succeeded his father as a member of the school board, and was recently re-elected to that position. Clemens Vonnegut, Jr., was elected a member of the Indiana Legislature of 1894.

H. LIEBER COMPANY.

H. Lieber Company, was originally established in 1854 by H. Lieber and Charles Koehne, and is one of the oldest mercantile concerns in the city. The company as at present conducted was incorporated in 1891, and is one of the largest concerns in the West engaged in the manufacture of picture frames and moldings. Over 150 workmen are employed in the factory located at 600 Madison avenue, and the trade of the company extends throughout this and foreign countries. The jobbing department is located at 33 South Meridian street, and 27 to 33 East Pearl street. Here over 30 people are employed. The Art Emporium conducted by the concern is one of the finest in the country, and it is also recognized as headquarters for artists' and photographers' supplies. The officers of the company are H. Lieber, president; Otto Lieber, vice-president, and William Williams, secretary.

E. C. Atkins & Company, incorporated, manufacturers of saws and saw makers' tools and supplies, is one of the very oldest industrial establishments of this city. The beginning of this important business was laid by Elias C. Atkins in 1856, when he began it single-handed in a little wooden building about 16x20 feet in dimensions, adjoining the old Hill Planing Mill on South East street. There are very few as great examples of thrift and industry in the United States. In 1860–61, Mr. Atkins moved to the present site on South Illinois street, and year after year has seen extensive additions and substantial growth. To-day it is recognized as the largest and foremost concern engaged in the manufacture of band and crosscut saws in the country. The superiority of its products has been evidenced by medals awarded at all the great and important industrial expositions held in this country during the last quarter of

E. C. ATKINS' SAW WORKS IN 1856.

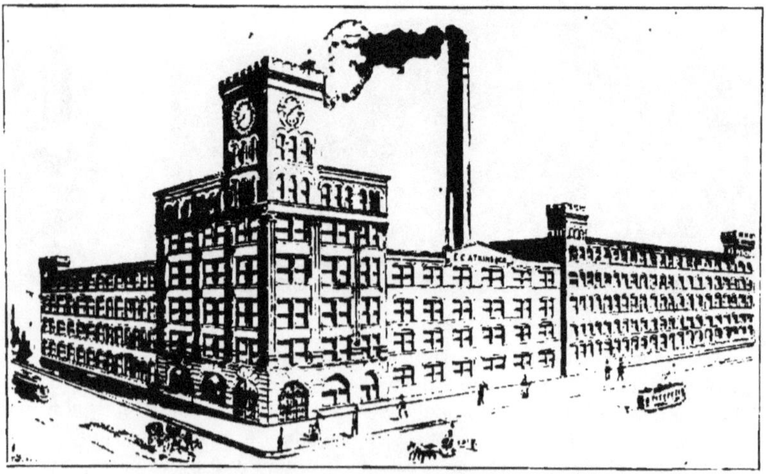

E. C. ATKINS & CO. SAW WORKS UNDER CONSTRUCTION.

a century. The works cover over three acres, with substantial and compactly built buildings ranging from two to five stories in height, and equipped throughout with the latest and most improved special machinery, much of which is of Mr. E. C. Atkins' invention and covered by patents. Trade extends throughout every State and Territory in the United States and in foreign countries. Nearly 500 hands are employed in the different departments

Extensive branches are operated at Memphis and Chattanooga, Tennessee, and Minneapolis, Minnesota. The business was incorporated in 1885, and the officers of the company are: E. C. Atkins, president; H. C. Atkins, vice-president and superintendent; W. H. Perkins, secretary, and M. A. Potter, treasurer.

Chandler & Taylor Company, boiler and engine manufacturers, 370 West Washington street, is one of the oldest industrial institutions of this city, as well as one of the most important in the State, and its operations extends throughout the United States, having also extensive trade connections in Mexico and South America, in which countries it enjoys a substantial business. The company dates its foundation back to 1858. In 1863 the firm of Chandler & Taylor was organized, and in 1888 the Chandler & Taylor Company was incorporated. The works comprise an immense plant, covering an area of three acres in extent, perfectly equipped in every respect with all the latest improved machinery and appliances, and employment is furnished to upward of 150 skilled and experienced workmen. A specialty is made of stationary engines of from 12 to 250 horse-power, the range of products also comprising both upright and circular saw-mills, and the necessary accompanying machinery. The company, in addition to a complete representation throughout the United States, has foreign representatives in Mexico, Central America, Spain, Germany, Russia and Australia. The manufacturing departments include a one-story boiler shop, 48x175 feet in dimensions; a sheet iron shop, 75x150 feet; a foundry, 80 x 80 feet; a two-story wood-working shop, and a two-story and basement warehouse, 46x165 in area. The office and works are located at 370 West Washington street, the facilities of the place for handling and shipping goods being unsurpassed. The officers of the company are: Thomas E. Chandler, president; Wm. M. Taylor, vice-president and treasurer, and George M Chandler, secretary and purchasing agent.

CHANDLER & TAYLOR COMPANY.

Indianapolis Harness Company, 10 to 16 McCrea street, wholesale manufacturers of harness and saddlery, and dealers in robes, blankets, whips, etc., was established in 1890. The firm operates one of the largest factories in the State for the manufacture of harness, saddlery and collars. The principal factory, salesrooms, and offices are located in the five story and basement

INDIANAPOLIS HARNESS COMPANY.

building on McCrea street, and the collar factory is located at 38 East South street. In all over 75 hands are employed. The trade of the house extends throughout the Middle, Western, and Southern States, and orders are filled all over the country. The members of the firm are J. M. Dalrymple and E. A. Hendrickson.

E. H. Eldridge & Company, dealers in lumber and manufacturers of sash, doors and blinds, have been engaged in the trade since 1879. They are the successors of Goss & Phillips, who originated the business in 1874. The firm is composed of E. H. and George O. Eldridge. Their factory, which is located at 166 to 174 South New Jersey street, is one of the best equipped in the city and furnishes employment to 50 men. The yards of the firm are located a block east of the mill and carry an average stock of about 1,000,000 feet of lumber.

Allison Coupon Company, manufacturers of mercantile, ice and restaurant coupons exclusively, was established in 1888 by N. S. Allison. He died December 5, 1890, and in August 1, 1893, the business was incorporated, with John S. Berryhill, president; W. S. Allison, secretary; and M. J. J. A. and D. C. Allison, associated with the above as directors. The trade of the concern is very large, extending all over this country, Canada, Cuba, Central America, and other foreign countries. It was among the first to engage in this business, and is the largest of its kind. The factory, which is located at 69 West Georgia street, occupies four floors, covering an area of 14,000 square feet. It is fitted throughout with modern machinery, is lighted by the company's own independent electric light plant, and furnishes employment to thirty hands.

ALLISON COUPON COMPANY.

INDIANAPOLIS COFFIN COMPANY.

Indianapolis Coffin Company, manufacturers of wood and cloth-covered coffins and caskets, and dealers in metalic cases, shrouds, lining and funeral supplies, whose office and ware-rooms are located at 188 East Washington street, was founded nineteen years ago. In 1890 the company was incorporated under the laws of Indiana, with ample capital, and its trade now extends thoughout Ohio, Indiana, Michigan, Illinois, etc. The officers are

Carl Von Hake, president; C. Vonnegut, jr., secretary and treasurer; Franklin Vonnegut, vice-president. The works are at the corner of Sixth and West streets, and comprise a three-story brick building, 45x140 feet, with a two-story addition, 45x120 feet, with ample storage sheds and lumber yards adjoining, the whole covering two acres of ground. The manufacturing departments are fully equipped with modern appliances and machinery, operated by a fifty-horse-power steam engine. Here forty skilled operatives are employed, who turn out 200 caskets and coffins weekly. Everything in the line of undertakers' supplies is also carried in stock, and orders are filled at lowest prices. Mr. Carl Von Hake, the president, is a large real estate owner of this city. The Messrs. Vonnegut are members of the hardware firm of Clemens Vonnegut, one of the oldest and most prominent houses in this city.

Van Camp Hardware and Iron Company, incorporated in 1884 is the outgrowth of a partnership formed in 1876. The concern conducts the largest and most important general hardware business in the State, and among the largest in the West. The trade of the house extend throughout Indiana, Illinois, Michigan, Kentucky, Iowa, and Missouri. Twenty-one travelers represent the company on the road, and about 80 persons are employed in the house. The stock embraces a complete line of light and heavy hard-

VAN CAMP HARDWARE AND IRON COMPANY.

ware, carriage and wagon makers' materials of every description, tinners' stock and roofers' materials. The bicycle and gun department is second to no other in the West. A complete tinware manufacturing plant is operated by the company, where 15 to 20 hands are employed. This extensive establishment is located in the substantial four-story and basement brick building, 65x200 feet, at 78 to 82 South Illinois street, and the six-story building 100 x 100 feet, at 64 to 74 West Chesapeake street, and 63 to 73 West Maryland street. The officers of the company are Cortland Van Camp, president, and David C. Bergundthal, secretary and treasurer.

The Sinker-Davis Company, successors to Sinker, Davis & Company and **The Eagle Machine Works Company,** is the outgrowth of the first two important industrial institutions established in this city. The present business was incorporated in 1888, as the Sinker-Davis Company, and in July, 1896, acquired the business of the Eagle Machine Works Company by purchase, moving to the plant occupied by the latter concern, on Missouri street and the Union Railroad, from the site occupied for more than thirty years. The Sinker-Davis Company is looked upon as one of the landmarks in the city's industrial development, growing steadily with the city in its forward movement. The business embraces the building of engines, boilers, saw-mills, etc., on an extensive scale, and the output finds a steady market throughout the United States and in Mexico and South American countries. Over 200 men are employed in the various departments, and since the establishment of the business, it has been in operation more continuous days than any other factory in the city. The new plant covers over three acres, and is fitted with all the best and latest improved machinery. The officers of the company are: J. H. Hooker, president; H. R. Bliss, secretary and treasurer, and A. J. Malone, superintendent.

THE SINKER-DAVIS COMPANY OLD SITE.

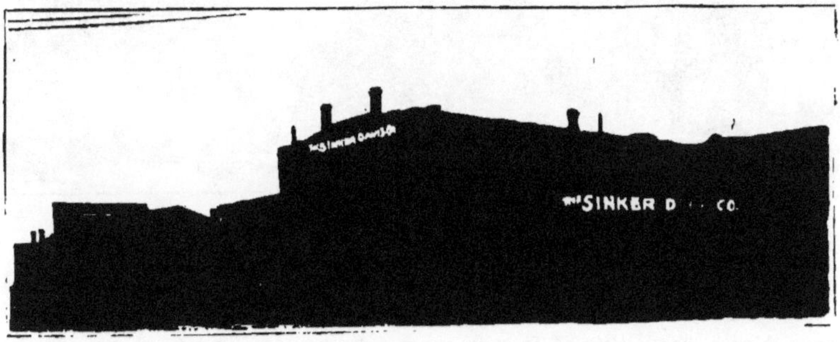

THE SINKER-DAVIS COMPANY.

H. T. Conde Implement Company, incorporated February 6, 1888, was established by H. T. Conde nearly a quarter of a century ago. The concern is principally devoted to the wholesale implement and vehicle business, and is the largest and most important one of the kind in the State. In the item of binding twine the company is the recognized leader in the West, carrying a larger stock than any other firm. In the bicycle trade it also occupies an important position, being the general selling agents for the "Arrow" bicycle beside handling many other well-known makes. The company are also

H. T. CONDE IMPLEMENT COMPANY.

the State agents of the Caligraph writing machine. The offices and storerooms are located in the imposing brown stone building, 27 to 33 Capitol avenue, North, consisting of four floors and basement 68x204 feet, aggregating in all 70,000 square feet of floor space, having exceptional facilities for the display and handling of goods. The carriage repository is the finest one in the United States outside of New York, and Chicago. The trade extends over Indiana, Ohio, Illinois, Michigan, Kentucky, and Tennessee, and eight travelers are employed. The officers of the company are H. T. Conde, president; Wm. A. Moore, vice-president; Will Cumback, jr., secretary, and S. C. Conde, treasurer.

Andrew Steffen, Manufacturer of Cigars, 220 East Washington street, began business in 1875. At present he employs over sixty men and manufactures over two million cigars annually, which find a market as far west as Utah. The Tish-I-Mingo cigar, manufactured by Mr. Steffen, has acquired great local popularity and has met with a greater sale than any other cigar.

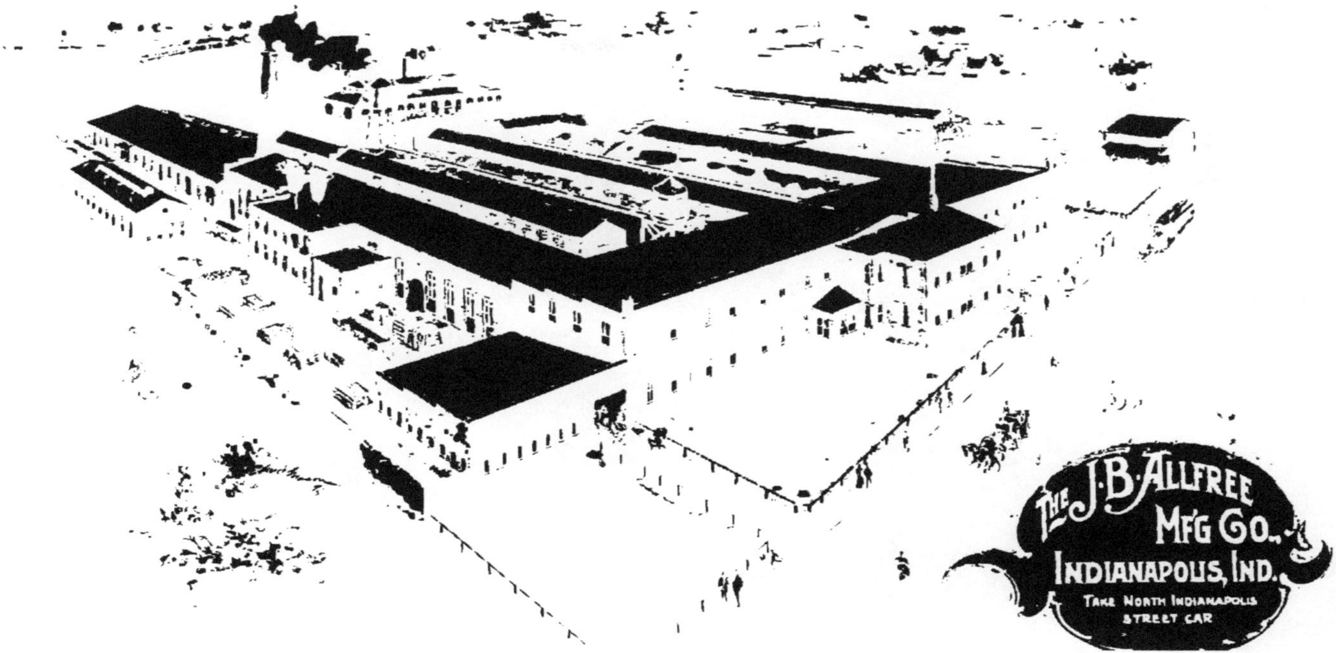
THE J.B. ALLFREE
MFG CO.,
INDIANAPOUS, IND.
TAKE NORTH INDIANAPOLIS
STREET CAR

Indianapolis Drop Forging Company, which was established January 1, 1896, is the first concern of the character to engage in the manufacture of drop forgings in this city. The rapid growth of the bicycle trade in the territory contiguous to Indianapolis, afforded a fine field for the establishment of a business of the kind, and since its beginning the demand in the large manufacturing centers has equaled the capacity of the plant. Over half a million forgings are

INDIANAPOLIS DROP FORGING COMPANY.

turned out annually, and from 35 to 40 men are employed. The plant is located at the corner of Hanway street and Madison avenue. Otto Stechhan, who for many years has been prominently identified with the manufacturing interests of the city, is secretary and treasurer of the corporation. F. P. Bates, the president and general superintendent, has had a long and successful connection in this line in the East prior to coming to Indianapolis.

The J. B. Allfree Manufacturing Company, manufacturers of the Allfree "High Mill" and "Economic" Automatic Engines, is one of the most important manufacturing establishments in the city. This company became known a few years ago as exponents of that type of flour mill construction known as the "High Mill," and since its introduction this concern has erected over thirty mills ranging in capacity from 50 to 3,500 barrels daily, demonstrating the merits of this system in the production of a better quality of flour, increase of yield, saving in power, space and labor. As mill builders this company ranks among the largest in the United States. No less important is the department devoted to the building of automatic engines. Three types of engines are built, simple, compound and condensing, specially designed for electrical and condensing work. The plant, which is one of the most conveniently arranged and modern equipped manufacturing plants in this city, covers over six acres with substantial buildings, and is located at the corner of Twenty-first street and Michigan Road. Over 250 persons are employed. The product is sold throughout this and foreign countries. The officers of the company are: Robert Schriver, president; J. B. Allfree, vice-president and general manager, and Charles E. Nordyke, secretary and treasurer.

JENNEY ELECTRIC MOTOR COMPANY.

Jenney Electric Motor Company was established by C. D. Jenney, in June' 1889. His brother, E. W. Jenney, was associated with him at the time of its organization. A year later the company was incorporated with J. F. Pratt and Addison Bybee, as additional stockholders. Afterward, A. A. Barnes, of the Udell Woodware Works, became interested. Before coming to this city, Mr. Jenney organized the Ft. Wayne Jenney Electric Light Company, in 1880, to manufacture electric lighting apparatus, and in the spring of 1885 organized the Jenney Electric Co. The manufacturing plant of this concern was located in West Indianapolis, on the premises of the Nordyke Marmon Company, the stockholders of which held stock of the Jenney Electric Company. Early in 1889, the Jenney Electric Company sold the plant to the Thomson-Houston Company, of Boston, Mass. Soon afterward Mr. Jenney organized the present company, and proceeded to manufacture a full line of motors and dynamos. The company, ever since its organization, has continued to extend its line of manufactured products and are now building, in addition to their full line of bi-polar motors and dynamos, a complete line of multi-polar dynamos for direct connection with engines. They are also building a line of multi-polar dynamos and motors for lighting and power service, and are making a specialty of electrical power distribution in manufacturing establishments. They also build a full line of dynamos for electro-plating, electrotyping and the refining of metals, and have recently perfected a new type of

dynamos having many advantages for this class of work. Last summer they moved into their new factory which was built on the Belt railroad, east of the city, in which they employ a large number of hands. It is their purpose to increase the plant soon, keeping step to the requirements of a modern institution. The product of this factory is shipped all over the world. The present officers of the company are—A. K. Hollowell, president; Chas. D. Jenney, vice-president and superintendent.

Mr. Hollowell, for many years past, was the treasurer of the Nordyke-Marmon Company, and recently sold his interest in that institution to become the executive head of the Jenney Electric Motor Company. He brings to his new enterprise the mature judgment of an experienced man of affairs and will undoubtedly keep the Jenney Electric Motor Company in the front rank of similar institutions of this country. Mr. Chas. D. Jenney is well known to the electrical world as an inventor. Among his more important recent inventions are the Conduit Railway System, on which he holds American and European patents and an electric locomotive headlight which he is now exploiting.

Atlas Engine Works, manufacturers of engines and boilers, corner of Martindale avenue and Nineteenth street.—Indianapolis is celebrated for many things; nothing, however, has given it a greater reputation, nor has been more potent in making it noted, than its large industrial enterprises. Its splendid location, and ample railroad facilities, its contiguity to the hardwood belt and coal fields, and with natural gas at the doors of its factories, all have wielded a powerful influence in its upbuilding. This city is specially noted for having several of the largest factories of their kind in America, prominent among these being the Atlas Engine Works, which was incorporated in 1878. It is devoted exclusively to the manufacture of engines and boilers. One of the important features of its engines is that the parts are all made interchangeable, which not only enables repairs to be made with great economy, but they can be sent to the remotest parts of the country in less time than they could be made in local shops. The types of engines manufactured embrace plain and automatic self-contained, side crank, heavy duty, double expansion automatic slide valve, and single and double expansion cycloidal heavy duty engines; also horizontal tubular and locomotive boilers, high pressure horizontal tubular, internal fired horizontal tubular and vertical boilers and horizontal and vertical water tube boilers. Over 14,000 Atlas engines and a greater number of boilers are now in use throughout this and foreign countries. The plant is located at the corner of Martindale avenue and Nineteenth street, embracing about twenty acres, over half of which are covered with substantial buildings. At times as many as nine hundred men are employed in the various departments. The officers of the company are H. H. Hanna, president; J. F. Pratt, vice-president and treasurer; R. M. Coffin, secretary; M. R. Moore, superintendent, and E. K. Marquis, assistant treasurer.

Hay & Willits Manufacturing Company. Some twelve years ago, the agent of one of the large eastern concerns came here from Columbus, Ind., and operated a riding school in the top floor of the old Zoo theater, now Cones' overall factory. Finding a gradual increase in his business, he removed to the old Meridian Rink on North Pennsylvania street. Afterward engaging in the manufacture of bicycles, he sold his retail business to two young men, Thomas Hay and V. B. Willits, who associated themselves together under the firm name of Hay & Willits, and located at 113 W. Washington street, opposite the state-house.

As they soon outgrew their small quarters, they removed to 70 N. Pennsylvania street, and were the first bicycle store to locate on Pennsylvania street, between Ohio and Washington. In 1895, believing that their customers could be served to a better advantage by making their own bicycles, they organized the Hay & Willits Manufacturing Company to make the Outing bicycle, and to-day the small concern of 113 West Washington street has on its pay roll 275 employes, and its product is known from the Atlantic to the Pacific ocean.

During the first year of the firm's existence as actual cycle manufacturers but 1,200 wheels were built, all of which were sold; last year their former output was nearly tripled, and notwithstanding the general dull and depressing condition of trade throughout the country, no trouble whatsoever was experienced in placing them all. So great has become the demand for the Outing bicycle in two years time that in the neighborhood of 5,000 of them will be built during the present season of '97.

The factory of this youthful and energetic concern is located on the edge of the city, at Vorster avenue and the Belt R. R. tracks. It is a model plant in every respect, fitted thoroughly with modern and improved machinery. V. B. Willits supervises every branch of construction, and, being a mechanical genius of undoubted ability, is everlastingly creating improved special tools, drilling machines, and so forth. When the present firm was organized, in '95, George H. Evans, treasurer, and Edward D. Evans, vice-president, were added to the list of officers. The Outing bicycles in '97 list at $100, $75 and $50. They are sold everywhere throughout the world, and in every city where Outing agencies are established, and in Indianapolis as well as elsewhere, have elicited the greatest praise for their excellence and superior finish.

"BELLIS" M'KINLEY RELAY RIDERS.

CENTRAL CYCLE MFG. CO. PLANT.

Central Cycle Manufacturing Company, makers of the famous "Ben Hur" Bicycles, was organized in 1891, and the business was established in

a very modest way in a small structure employing about fifty hands. To-day the plant is one of the most important of the many industrial institutions of our city. The plant is situated at Nos. 16 to 22 Garden street, which include a series of fine factory buildings in which are employed more than two hundred and fifty skilled mechanics. The sale of the "Ben Hur" Bicycles is increasing with their growing popularity and these famous wheels find a market all over the world. The officers of the company are Lucius M. Wainwright, president; Drikus Snitjer, vice-president; Albert D. Johnson, secretary and treasurer, and Louis J. Keck, second vice-president.

Indianapolis Veneer Works, Adams & Williamson proprietors, manufacturers of and dealers in veneers, burls and fancy woods, terminus of Massachusetts avenue. The central position of Indianapolis with reference to the most important regions of production in domestic hardwoods has led to the establishing here of several important industrial enterprises which utilize this prolific hardwood supply as their raw material. One of the most important establishments of this character is that conducted by the firm of Adams & Williamson, under the style of the Indianapolis Veneer Works, which was founded in 1879. Mr. M. D. Williamson died August 2, 1896, and Mr. G. F. Adams, the surviving member, is conducting the business under the firm name. The works now occupied cover three acres of ground, including a lofty, well-lighted brick workshop, 80 x 125 feet in dimensions, and a three-story and basement brick building, 70 x 150 feet, of which the ground floor is used as a stock room and the two upper floors as drying rooms. The equipment of the works includes every convenience and accessory calculated to aid or expedite the operations of the business, embracing a 100-horse power Corliss engine, fed by three tubular boilers 4½ x 16 feet, and all the most modern

INDIANAPOLIS VENEER WORKS.

and improved machinery for the manufacture of veneers. The veneer cutting is done by machines of the latest improved make, which cut from the log solid sheets seven feet wide, and these are sent to the sizing power knife machines, by which the veneers are cut into the desired sizes, including all thicknesses up to one-fourth of an inch, the latter being used for drawer bottoms. The drying is effectively done with the aid of two Sturvesant blowers, and eight large steaming vats provide the facilities for steaming logs before passing to the veneer cutting machines. Much of the machinery used is of a special character, invented for these works, and used by no other establishment. Ample light is provided by incandescent lamps supplied by the firm's own electric lighting plant. Railroad switches at the front and side of the works afford the most superior facilities for the receipt of materials and shipment of the manufactured product. Logs are received from the north, and veneers are manufactured from walnut, oak, ash, cherry and all kinds of hardwood. A force of one hundred workmen is employed, and an extensive trade is done, principally with furniture manufacturers in the east and in supplying manufacturers of sewing machines and other large consumers of veneers. The trade of the works is so firmly established as to require no canvassing, and consequently no traveling salesmen are employed. The firm owes it success to the maintenance in its product of the highest standard of quality, to close supervision of every detail of manufacture, and to uniform reliability in all its dealings with the trade.

The H. C. Bauer Engraving Company, 23 West Washington street, designers, engravers, electrotypers and printing plate manufacturers, established in 1889, is the most extensive concern of its kind in the state, where printing plates by every known process are manufactured with rare skill and excellence. Nearly all of the engravings used in *Hyman's Handbook of Indianapolis* and the *Indianapolis Index* are the products of this institution. A large force of skilled and experienced artists are employed in the various departments. Designs are furnished for catalogues and all kinds of book illustrations requiring wood, zinc or half-tone engraving, which is a leading specialty of this house, and the ample facilities which it commands enables it to handle the largest contracts with promptness and at prices as low as is consistent with high grade workmanship. The wax process is employed in the production of map work, charts, diagrams, etc., which produce results not attainable in any other method. The trade of this firm extends throughout this state and adjoining territory, where it enjoys an established reputation for first-class workmanship.

H. C. BAUER
ENGRAVING COMPANY.

Indiana School Book Company, of Indianapolis, was incorporated in 1889, by Josephus Collett, William Heilman, D. J. Mackey, E. P. Huston, James Murdock, William Fleming, R. C. Bell and Edward Hawkins. The company manufactures and supplies text-books for the common schools of Indiana, as authorized by the school-book law passed by the Indiana legislature of 1889. The entire list of books furnished under state adoption consists of twenty-three different text-books. This company furnishes nineteen of the adopted series and they are now used in all the common schools of Indiana. The officers of the company are James Murdock, president; Edward Hawkins, general manager and treasurer, and E. P. Huston, secretary.

Eli Lilly & Company, Pharmaceutical Chemists, whose laboratory is located in East McCarty street, is one of the most important concerns in this city and one of the largest of its class in the country. The buildings occupied, and which were especially designed for the purposes for which they are employed, are models of convenience, and for beauty of architecture, completeness of detail and finish, are not approached by any similar institution in the world.

LILLY'S LABORATORY, 1875.

The history of this house began in 1876, in which year Mr. Eli Lilly, the present head of the concern, began the manufacture of pharmaceutical preparations in a very unpretentious way in a small building in Pearl street on the sight now occupied by the rear of the Commercial Club building. The business developed early and in 1879 Mr. Lilly moved to 36 South Meridian street, and in 1879, more space being demanded by the growing business, the adjoining room, 38 South Meridian street, was added. The business was conducted in these rooms until 1881

ELI LILLY & COMPANY'S LABORATORY.

INTERIOR OF SENATE.

when the business was incorporated, the present site on East McCarty street purchased and the laboratory moved to its present location Since that time the advancement has been rapid, followed by many improvements and additions, that has resulted in the establishment of this great laboratory.

The preparations of Eli Lilly & Company are recognized throughout the medical and pharmaceutical world for their high standard of quality and purity, and its reputation is jealously guarded by the firm. The productions of the laboratory embrace Fluid Extracts, Powdered Extracts, Solid Extracts, Concentrations, Gelatine-coated Pills, Sugar-coated Pills, Elixirs, Lozenges, Syrups, Wines, Tablets, Hypodermic Tablets, Tablet Triturates and all Pharmaceuticals demanded by the medical profession.

Their famous blood remedy Succus Alterans, for over 12 years used and endorsed by the foremost physicians of America and England, heads their lists of specialties and together with Pil. Aphrodisiaca, Elixir Purgans and Glycones, completes their line of preparations which are accessible to the retail drug trade and physicians through the wholesale druggists of every jobbing center of the United States and Canada. Their agent for England and the Colonies is John M. Richards, 46 Holburn Viaduct, London, E. C. The company consists of Eli Lilly, president; James E. Lilly, vice-president, Evan F. Lilly, secretary and treasurer; Josiah K. Lilly, superintendent.

John U. Frietzsche Homeopathic Pharmacy, located at 62 East Ohio street, was established in 1875 by John U. Frietzsche who came here from Philadelphia, in that year. He was a physician of 58 years active practice, having graduated in Paris, France. This is the only pharmacy of its class in the state and does a business throughout the country. Occasional foreign shipments are made, a notable instance being an order recently received from Korea, Japan. Dr. J. U. Frietzsche died in 1892. The business is under the management of Ernest F. Frietzsche, who controls it for the estate. The firm manufactures homeopathic tinctures, dilutions and other homeopathic preparations, and carry a complete stock of homeopathic remedies.

BACK WATER BROAD RIPPLE.

Sloan Drug Company, organized January 1, 1896, is the outgrowth of the firm of George W. Sloan, originally established in 1887. Mr. Sloan has had a longer continued identification with the drug business in Indianapolis than any other person now living in the city. In 1850 he entered the service of his uncle, David Craighead, who was then operating a drug store in the same room that is now occupied by the present company, also with Craighead & Browning, and after the death of Mr. Craighead, with Mr. Browning, who became the successor. In 1862 he took an interest in the business and the firm became known as Browning & Sloan, and were recognized as the leading pharmacists of Indianapolis. The business having outgrown the capacity of the room then occupied, they moved to 7 and 9 East Washington street, where the business was conducted under this firm name until 1887, when Mr. Sloan retired and embarked for himself in the present location—the place occupied by the old house in 1850.

SLOAN DRUG COMPANY.

Through the long term of years that Mr. Sloan has been identified with the business interests of the city—longer than that of any business man now engaged in Washington street,—he has at all times been held in the highest esteem by his fellow citizens. He has been honored with the degree of "Doctor in Medicine" by the Medical College of Indiana, and with the degree of "Doctor of Pharmacy," Purdue University. He is ex-president of the American Pharmaceutical Association and is also a charter member of the Board of Trade, being a member of its governing committee; he is also a member of the Commercial Club, and a member of the Board of School Commissioners, being its treasurer.

The Sloan Drug Company are extensive manufacturers of various Pharmaceuticals, also Sloan's Carbolated Dentifrice, that has a large sale throughout the country, and many other preparations that bear their well known brand. Associated in the business with Mr. Sloan is his son Geo. B. Sloan, a graduate of Purdue University Pharmacy School, who has been reared in business under his father,

McCoy-Howe Company, manufacturing chemists, began business February 3, 1892. Their first establishment was located at 92 South Illinois street, where they began business with four employes. In January, 1893, the laboratory was moved to McCrea street near the Union Station, and in 1894 the

FEMALE REFORMATORY.

company purchased the present site and erected the laboratory now occupied. While it is not the largest in the country, it is equal in the character of equipment and facilities to any other laboratory in the United States. It is furnished with machinery especially designed for the purposes to which it is used, and all departments are arranged with a view to facilitate the business. The building is a solid red brick structure, consisting of three floors and basement, covering an area 44x200 feet. It is supplied with a cold storage department for the care of green drugs and essential oils, etc. Power is furnished from a 50-horse power engine. A deep driven well supplies the tank at the top of the building, from which pure water is supplied to all parts of the laboratory. The product of the laboratory consists of a large line of

M'COY-HOWE COMPANY.

pharmaceutical specialties, fluid extracts, elixirs, medicinal wines and syrups, tinctures, triturates and tablets, hypodermic table's and their well known specialties, Boro-Salicylicum, Chloro-Ferrine, Golden Liquid Hydrastis and Succus Solani, which are dispensed by the medical profession everywhere. They also manufacture a full line of strictly pure powdered drugs and handle a large line of chemicals made by the standard manufacturers throughout the country, also physicians' and surgeons' supplies.

The laboratory now furnishes employment to twenty-six persons. The trade extends throughout all the central and western states.

The members of the firm are J. B. McCoy, A. B. Howe, James M. Mowrer and W. A. Walker. Messrs. McCoy and Howe, prior to establishing this business represented a large chemical company of Cincinnati and Messrs. Mowrer and Walker were engaged in the drug business in New Castle, Ind.

Daniel Stewart Company, wholesale dealers and importers of drugs, widely known as the "Old Gibraltar Drug House" can trace a continuous business existence as far back as 1832, when it was originally established by Scudder & Hanneman. During 1850-8 the firm was known as Hanneman & Duzan; from 1858-63 it was conducted by William Hanneman, who was succeded by Stewart & Morgan. From 1878 until 1883 the business was conducted by Stewart & Barry, and from the latter period until January 1, 1896,

DANIEL STEWART COMPANY.

under the title of Daniel Stewart, when it was changed to the Daniel Stewart Company. Mr. Stewart's death occurred February 25, 1892.

The present members of the firm are John N. Carey, William Scott, Mary S. Carey and Martha S. Scott.

The Daniel Stewart Company are extensive manufacturers of pharmaceutical preparations, handkerchief extracts, etc., known to the trade under the "Old Gibraltar" brands. They carry the largest and most complete stock of plate glass in the state and are the only ones who carry plate glass in stock sheets which enables them to fill orders for irregular or odd sizes at all times. They are also extensive dealers in beveled plate, leaded art and window glass.

Their cigar department is an important branch of their business and many brands have reached an enormous sale and acquired great popularity through the "push" of this concern. The firm employs ten traveling salesmen who cover the territory of Indiana, Illinois and Ohio, and sixty-five persons are employed in the house. The firm occupies the large building, four stories and basement, at the corner of Meridian and Maryland streets and the large building in the rear on Maryland street that is employed to carry the large stock of glass and reserve stock.

Indianapolis Drug Company was established in December, 1890, and began business January 1, 1891. The firm deals extensively in crude, pressed and powdered botanical drugs, chemicals, essential oils, imported and domestic wines and whiskies, paints, oils and window glass; also have a large and growing cigar trade.

Not the least important branch of the business is the manufacture of pharmaceutical preparations, fluid extracts, wines, tinctures and syrups and several specialties that have found an extensive sale and great popularity throughout the country among which are the following—"Melol," a tasteless preparation of castor oil; "Caffaccin," a new anti-pyretic; "Mullein Balsam," cough and consumption cure; "Brunker's Carminative Balsam," cure for dysentery and bowel troubles; and "R. I. D.," Magnetic Roach Exterminator. They are the manufacturers of the well known "Japanese" brand of handkerchief odors, toilet waters and hair tonic, among which are the celebrated "Chrysanthemum Bouquet." The trade of this concern extends throughout Indiana, Illinois and Ohio, and is regularly visited by seven travelers. In the house over thirty employes are engaged. The firm occupies the large building consisting of three floors and basement, 63x100 feet, at Nos. 21, 23, 25 East Maryland street.

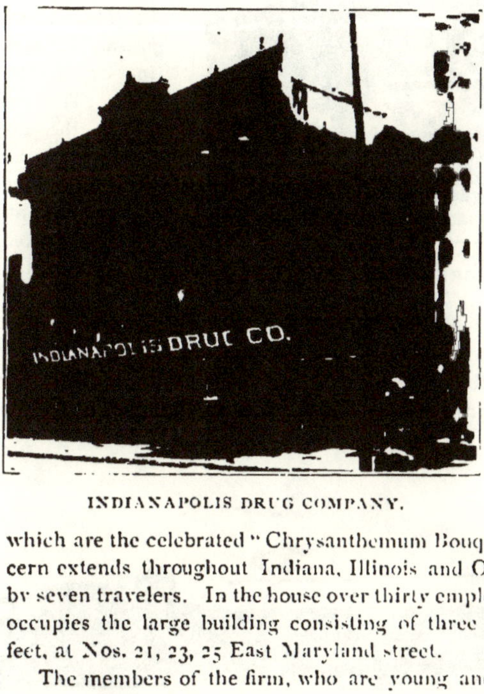

INDIANAPOLIS DRUG COMPANY.

The members of the firm, who are young and active business men, are J. George Mueller, Dr. Herman Pink and John R. Miller. Mr. J. George Mueller has been identified with the drug trade of this city for twenty-three years and is a graduate of the Cincinnati School of Pharmacy. Dr. Pink has for twenty years, and still enjoys an extensive and lucrative practice as physician and Mr. John R. Miller has been engaged in the drug trade for the past twenty years; a large part of that period with the wholesale drug business in this city.

From its beginning the business has been a prosperous one and enjoyed a vigorous growth, and now ranks as one of the largest in the state.

The Lilly Varnish Company is the oldest and most extensive business of its kind in the State. It was established in 1865, by H. B. Mears. In 1867 J. O. D. Lilly bought an interest in the firm and it was conducted under the title of Mears & Lilly for some time, when Mr. Lilly purchased the interest then represented by H. B. Mears and the firm became known as J. O. D. Lilly & Sons, and in 1888 incorporated as the Lilly Varnish Company, with Charles Lilly, president and Jno. M. Lilly, secretary and treasurer. The business was started in a small building by Dr. Mears, who conceived the idea that gum and turpentine could be fused. The result of the experiment was the burning of the primitive plant. He then erected a factory at the intersection of Kentucky avenue and Mississippi streets. The business was conducted at this point, through the different changes in the firm until 1875, when a new factory plant was built on the east bank of White river—the present site. None of the old buildings now remain, having given place to the modern structures built especially for the business. During 1895, new warerooms and offices have been built, equipped with the latest improvements. The buildings are as nearly fire proof as it was possible to make them. The factory has a capacity of 40 to 50 barrels of varnish per day. The product consists of the finer grades of carriage, wagon, agricultural implement, furniture and house painters' varnishes, embracing in all over 140 different grades. The product is sold all over the United States and the company has begun the introduction of its goods in foreign markets. The present officers of the company are Charles Lilly, president, and Jno. M. Lilly, secretary and treasurer.

LILLY VARNISH WORKS—OFFICES.

LILLY VARNISH WORKS—REAR VIEW.

The A. Burdsal Company, manufacturers and jobbers of paints and painters' materials, was incorporated in 1892. The business was originally established by Alfred Burdsal in January, 1875, at 32 South Meridian street. In the spring of 1876 the business was moved to 34 South Meridian street, and in 1885 the room south, No. 36, was added. Mr. Burdsal began to manufacture in a very small way in 1877, on the third floor of the present location. In 1879 he began building the present large factory, located at 241 to 249 South Pennsylvania street. Besides the factory he built the large warehouses on the adjoining property, one of which, 50 x 140, for the accommodation of surplus stock, at 251 and 253 South Pennsylvania street, and another, 25 x 140, at 239 South Pennsylvania, for the storage of glass, of which this firm are the largest dealers in this territory. The factory is equipped with the very latest and improved machinery, with special railroad switches leading to the factory and warehouse, facilitating the handling of the products, which are shipped throughout the central western states.

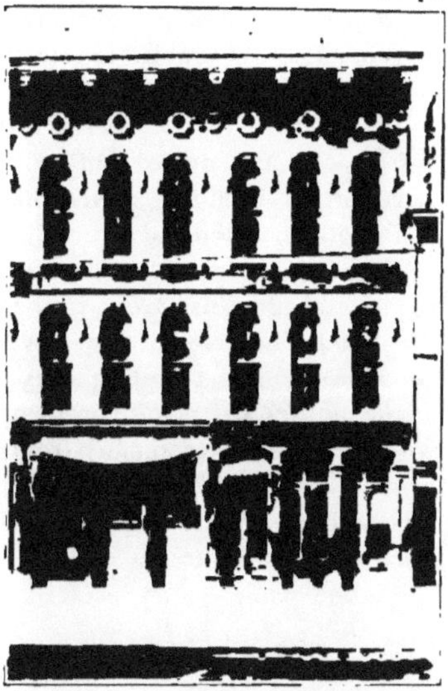

THE A. BURDSAL COMPANY.

The company manufacture all kinds of white lead, colored and mixed

BURDSAL'S PAINT WORKS.

paints, wood stains, coach and car colors, japans, varnishes and a full line of prepared paints for house, sign, carriage and decorative painters' uses. They are the manufacturers of the celebrated "Steamboat" brand of paste colors, the same as white lead, but so tinted that the consumer is enabled to select any desired shade, saving the painter the labor and expense of selecting and mixing.

At the time the firm was incorporated the business was owned and controlled by Mr. Burdsal, who took into the company William H. Meier, his bookkeeper; Sydney T. Jordan, chief clerk; Russell G. Allen and Granville G. Allen, traveling salesmen, and Frederick Poehler, foreman of the factory.

Mr. Burdsal was born in Cincinnati in 1839, and began his career in the paint business in 1858 with the Eagle White Lead Company of that city. He served the company in the capacity of bookkeeper and traveling salesman until 1863. He entered the army in the spring of 1864. On his return in 1865 he again re-entered the firm, and was secretary of the company from 1867 to 1870. Owing to ill health he retired from business, and was not again actively engaged until 1875, when he sold his interest in the Eagle White Lead Company and came to Indianapolis, since which time he has built the prosperous and extensive business of which he is the head.

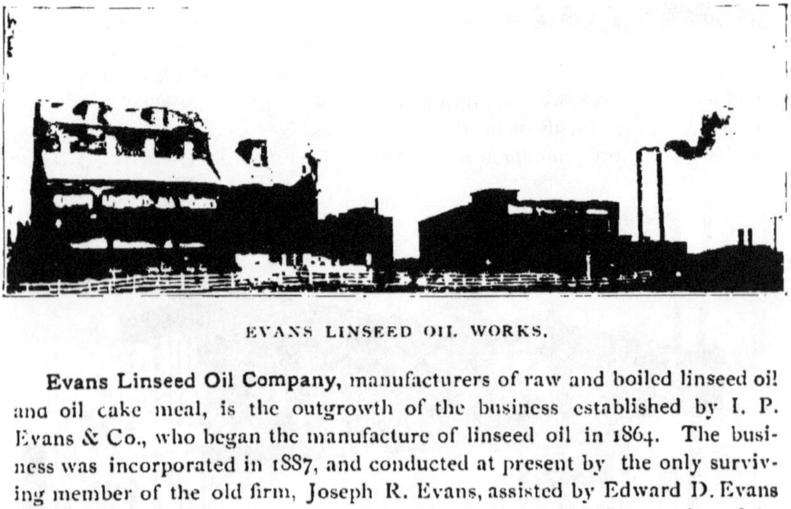

EVANS LINSEED OIL WORKS.

Evans Linseed Oil Company, manufacturers of raw and boiled linseed oil and oil cake meal, is the outgrowth of the business established by I. P. Evans & Co., who began the manufacture of linseed oil in 1864. The business was incorporated in 1887, and conducted at present by the only surviving member of the old firm, Joseph R. Evans, assisted by Edward D. Evans and Joseph J. Brown. The old mill, which was located at the crossing of the Union railway tracks and South Delaware street, was destroyed by fire December 8, 1885. The present plant, located on the west side of the river near the Michigan street bridge, was built in 1881.

J. E. Bodine & Company, manufacturers and dealers of dental supplies, were established in this city in 1883. They are located at Nos. 27 and 29 Monument place, where they carry the largest and most complete stock of dental supplies of every character in the state. Before becoming established in this city the firm was located at Toledo, Ohio, and Mr. J. E. Bodine traveled throughout this territory for six years prior to locating his firm in this city. J. E. Bodine & Company are recognized as one of the foremost firms in its special line in the west, and the trade extends throughout Indiana, Ohio, Illinois, Kentucky and Tennessee. Beside the line of dental goods the firm are extensive dealers in and manufacturers of barbers' supplies, and do a thriving business in this branch of trade.

Joseph Haas, V. S., now one of the foremost manufacturers of live stock remedies in the country, began business in Dayton, Ohio, in the fall of 1876. He started in a very small way, and personally sold his entire product in Butler county, Ohio, and vicinity. Finding his field limited, and desiring a location upon which he could more readily extend his operations, he came to Indianapolis in 1877. His first office was located in the Abbott block, in Virginia avenue. His business grew rapidly, and in 1881 he purchased the building at the corner of Pennsylvania and Maryland streets, embracing

JOSEPH HAAS'S BLOCK.

rooms from No. 52 to 60 South Pennsylvania street, moving his laboratory to the rear half of 52 South Pennsylvania. The present offices and laboratory are located in No. 56 of the same building, and occupy three floors and basement. The product consists of the celebrated and widely advertised Haas' Hog and Poultry Remedy, Haas' Alterative (condition powder), Haas' Epizootic Remedy and Haas' Cattle Remedy, which have a large and constantly increasing sale in every state and territory, and in Canada and Hawaiian Islands. From the European agency, located in Birmingham, England, British possessions throughout the world are supplied. A special feature in connection with the sale of the hog remedy is the indemnity contract by which, for a small fee in addition to the price of the remedy, Dr. Haas guarantees to pay for every hog that dies out of 500 that are treated with it.

In addition to his laboratory, Dr. Haas is proprietor of the Indiana poultry farm, located at Fiftieth street and Central avenue, which is noted for its fine breeds of poultry and pet stock. It is recognized as one of the finest and best equipped poultry farms in the country.

W. M. Williams & Bros., manufacturers of the celebrated Nine O'clock Washing Tea, are located at Nos. 214, 216, 218, 220 and 222 South Meridian street. The firm was originally established by Mr. W. M. Williams in 1891. Since the beginning of the business, owing to its rapid and phenomenal growth it has been necessary to move five times to secure sufficient space to meet its requirements. The present laboratory and offices occupy five floors and the same number of basements. The product of the laboratory is confined exclusively to Nine O'clock Washing Tea, a compound for general house cleaning. Over 1,000 of the largest wholesale grocery houses throughout the country now handle these goods. To illustrate the rapidity with which the trade has grown is shown in the following record of sales: In 1891 the sales for the year amounted to 4,100 boxes; 1892, 10,475 boxes; 1893, 18,360 boxes; 1894, 31,000 boxes; 1895, 44,175 boxes; and at the present rate sales this year will reach nearly 100,000 boxes or one million packages. About 100 people are employed in the laboratory. Associated in the business with Mr. Williams are his brothers, Dr. J. L. Williams and L. G. Williams. Before engaging in this business, for a number of years, Mr. Williams represented Moore Bros., of Lima, Ohio and Schrader Bros., wholesale grocers of this city as traveling salesman.

W. M. WILLIAMS & BROS.

The Indiana Dental Depot was established in 1867 by Strong, Smith & Pierson. In 1874 Moore, Herriott & Co., of Ohio, succeeded them, conducting the business in the same place, the Vinton block, until 1877, when Dr. Herriott purchased his partner's interest and continued in charge until his death, Nov. 4, 1884, and since then by his widow, Mrs. W. M. Herriott.

Bellis Cycle Company, 27 Ingalls block, is one of the largest cycle manufacturing concerns in this city. The officers are Chalmers Brown, president, Wm. H. Schmidt, vice-president; W. K. Bellis, secretary, and Benj. L. Webb, treasurer. An important enterprise undertaken by this concern was the organization of a relay of "Bellis" cycle riders, who carried the congratulations of the firm from this city to Canton, Ohio, to Wm. McKinley, when his election was assured on the night of November 2, 1896.

John M. Todd & Company, established in 1861, is one of the oldest firms in this city now engaged in the real estate business. Todd's first subdivision, at the corner of Gregg and East streets, one of the original subdivisions to the city, was made in 1864. This property at that time was in the suburbs. Mr. Todd has been identified with many other subdivisions during the growth of the city, and has also been prominently identified with the promotion and building of our railroads and manufacturing enterprises. Mr. Todd and his son, Newton Todd, occupy rooms in the Ingalls block, the site where he engaged in business in 1861.

Newton Todd, investment broker, fire insurance and rental agent, whose offices are in the Ingalls block, is the leading broker and dealer in local securities in the city, buying and selling Bank, Trust Company, Belt railroad and other stocks, Barrett law, Water Company and other bonds. Mr. Todd does a very large real estate, mortgage loan business for local individuals and eastern corporations. He is the sole Indianapolis representative of the Fire Association of Philadelphia and the Sun Insurance Office, of London, England, two of the largest and oldest fire insurance companies in the world. Mr. Todd also does a rental business, having charge of some of the largest buildings in the city.

W. D. Allison Company, manufacturers of physicians' tables, chairs, cabinets, and invalid rolling and reclining chairs, is the outgrowth of the business established by J. N. Clark & Company in 1881. Mr. W. D. Allison, the present head of the firm, became associated with the business in 1884. In 1886, Mr. R. B. Roberts, purchased an interest in the business, and the firm became known as Roberts & Allison, and continued in this manner until 1891 when Mr. Allison became sole owner.

The product of this firm maintains a high reputation among physicians and surgeons throughout the world, and the export trade is constantly increasing. Several traveling salesmen visit physicians personally and all the leading physician and surgeons' supply houses in this and foreign countries handle their product. The factory is located at 85 East South street. Branch offices are located in Chicago, New York, St. Louis and San Francisco. F. L. Furbish & Co., are the selling agents in Mexico City.

Wm. H. Armstrong & Company, manufacturers and dealers in surgical instruments, began business in 1885, in Terre Haute, Indiana, and moved to Indianapolis, January 1, 1889, at which time Mr. Emil Wilbrandt was

WM. H. ARMSTRONG & COMPANY.

admitted to the firm. The business was established by Wm. H. Armstrong. This house has one of the most complete plants in the country for the production of physicians' and surgeons' instruments and appliances. Their business has grown to such an extent that they on the first of this year secured additional manufacturing room and enlarged facilities, and are now operating a separate plant at No. 57 West Georgia street, where they employ from twenty to thirty hands. The trade of the firm extends all over this country and Mexico, and their traveling men cover the entire territory. They carry in stock, as well as manufacture to order, anything needed by physicians or surgeons for the successful practice of their art. The sales department is located at 77 South Illinois street, within easy walking distance from the Union Station.

George William Hoffman, manufacturing chemist, whose laboratory and offices are located in his building at 255 East Washington street, began business in 1882. The productions of his laboratory are more extensively sold and are better known than any similar preparations. Notably among them are Hoffman's U. S. metal polishes, cream cosmetic lotion, hog and poultry remedies, horse and cattle powders and insect powders. These goods can be found in almost every town and hamlet in the country. Mr. Hoffman is an extensive advertiser, and has branch establishments at Nos. 1-3 Park Row, New York City; corner of Madison and Clark streets, Chicago; No. 503 Montgomery avenue, San Francisco and 318 Royal street, New Orleans.

GEORGE WILLIAM HOFFMAN.

INDEX.

Black figures (**178**) *indicate illustrations.*

C

G

K

L

Y

Z